OXFORD MONOGRAPHS ON CLASSICAL ARCHAEOLOGY

Edited by

JOHN BENNET

JOHN BOARDMAN

JIM COULTON

DONNA KURTZ

R. R. R. SMITH

MARGARETA STEINBY

APPROACHES TO THE STUDY OF ATTIC VASES

Beazley and Pottier

PHILIPPE ROUET

TRANSLATED BY
LIZ NASH

OXFORD
UNIVERSITY PRESS

OXFORD
UNIVERSITY PRESS

Great Clarendon Street, Oxford OX2 6DP

Oxford University Press is a department of the University of Oxford.
It furthers the University's objective of excellence in research, scholarship,
and education by publishing worldwide in

Oxford New York

Athens Auckland Bangkok Bogotá Buenos Aires Cape Town
Chennai Dar es Salaam Delhi Florence Hong Kong Istanbul Karachi
Kolkata Kuala Lumpur Madrid Melbourne Mexico City Mumbai Nairobi
Paris São Paulo Shanghai Singapore Taipei Tokyo Toronto Warsaw

with associated companies in Berlin Ibadan

Oxford is a registered trade mark of Oxford University Press
in the UK and certain other countries

Published in the United States
by Oxford University Press Inc., New York

British Library Cataloguing in Publication Data

Data available

Library of Congress Cataloging in Publication Data
Rouet, Philippe.
Approaches to the study of Attic vases: Beazley and Pottier / Philippe Rouet;
translated by Liz Nash.
p. cm.—(Oxford monographs on classical archaeology)
Includes bibliographical references and index.
1. Vases, Black-figured—Greece—Athens. 2. Vases, Red-figured—Greece—Athens.
3. Vase-painting, Greek—Greece—Athens—Research—Methodology. 4. Beazley, J. D.
(John Davidson), 1885–1970—Criticism and interpretation. 5. Pottier, Edmond, 1885–1934.
Corpus vasorum antiquorum. I. Title. II. Series.
NK4648 .R68 2001 738.3′82′0938—dc21 2001036410

ISBN 0–19–815272–8 (alk. paper)

1 3 5 7 9 10 8 6 4 2

Typeset by Best-set Typesetter Ltd., Hong Kong
Printed in Great Britain
on acid-free paper by
T. J. International, Padstow, Cornwall

For Howison

Acknowledgements

This work has been completed with the help of a number of people and institutions, to all of whom I am deeply grateful. First I would like to thank Liz Nash for the quality of her translation, Hilary O'Shea and Jenny Wagstaffe for seeing the project safely through to its conclusion, and Véronique Davis for her collaboration on the production of the book. My especial thanks go to Donna Kurtz, who was the mainstay of the editorial enterprise. She read the typescript, and her comments, along with those of Sir John Boardman, helped me to correct certain errors. For any that remain, I am of course fully responsible.

The book could not have been produced without the assistance of the Jowett Copyright Trust (Balliol College, Oxford), the Ceramica-Stiftung in Basle, the Centre Louis-Gernet in Paris, and the British Academy. My thanks are also due to I. Aghion, J. Anderson, J. Andreau, D. von Bothmer, N. Boulouch, A. Brown, H. A. Cahn, M. Collinet, C. Colvin, H. Damisch, M. Denoyelle, J.-L. Durand, S. François, F. Frontisi, R. French, D. W. J. Gill, P. Griener, J. Griffin, R. Guy, F. Haskell, B. Holtzmann, A. Jacques, L. Langlade, M. Lanthoinette, J. Leclant, M. Lévy, F. Lissarrague, N. Lubtchansky, H. Metzger, N. Momigliano, O. Murray, J.-L. de Paepe, P. Parsons, P. Petitmengin, D. Plantzos, E. Pommier, D. Reid, M. Robertson, S. Sarti, A. Schnapp, T. J. Smith, T. Staehelin, J. Stallworthy, E. Steiner, G. Tiberghien, G. Tsetskhladze, M. Vickers, P. Vidal-Naquet, F. Villard, N. Wilson, and P. Wilson.

Contents

List of Plates

PHOTOGRAPHIC CREDITS

Abbreviations

ABV	J. D. Beazley, *Attic Black-figure Vase-painters* (1956)
AK	*Antike Kunst*
AIA	Association Internationale des Académies
AJA	*American Journal of Archaeology*
ARV¹	J. D. Beazley, *Attic Red-figure Vase-painters* (1942)
ARV²	J. D. Beazley, *Attic Red-figure Vase-painters²* (1963)
AVS	J. D. Beazley, *Attische Vasenmaler des rotfigurigen Stils* (1925)
BCH	*Bulletin de correspondance hellénique*
BSA	*Annual of the British School at Athens*
CVA	*Corpus Vasorum Antiquorum*
FR (i–iii)	A. Furtwängler, K. Reichhold, *et al.*, *Griechische Vasenmalerei*, i (1904); ii (1909); iii (1932)
GBA	*Gazette des Beaux-Arts*
JHS	*Journal of Hellenic Studies*
MDAI(R)	*Mitteilungen des Deutschen archäologischen Instituts,* römische Abteilung
MMAI	*Monuments et mémoires publiés par l'Académie des Inscriptions et Belles-Lettres* (Fondation Piot)
RA	*Revue Archéologique*
TLS	*Times Literary Supplement*
UAI	Union Académique Internationale
VA	J. D. Beazley, *Attic Red-figured Vases in American Museums* (1918)

Introduction

We classify, as best we can, but we classify.

C. Lévi-Strauss quoted in
a painting by Ben

Taking as its position the point at which archaeology, art history, and historiography coincide, this work sets out to trace the development of the study of Greek pottery in the late nineteenth and early twentieth centuries, with particular emphasis on the works of Sir John Beazley on Attic vase-painting, and Edmond Pottier's *Corpus Vasorum Antiquorum*.

Beazley, who was Professor of Classical Archaeology and Art at Oxford University from 1925 to 1954, ranks as one of the great figures of twentieth-century archaeology. His major achievement lay in the classification of the painted vases produced in Athens between the sixth and fourth centuries BC. The distinctive feature of his work was the methodical attribution of vases to painters; by carrying out a close study of the style of painting on black- and red-figured vases, he was able to classify the pottery with precision.[1] Approximately 25,000 vases and fragments were listed in *Attic Black-figure Vase-painters* and *Attic Red-figure Vase-painters*[2] (5,000 in the first, 20,000 in the second), and at the same time he identified a remarkable total of more than a thousand craftsmen. Furthermore, his stylistic approach was highly influential in the development of trends in the study of pottery, since other researchers went on to apply it successfully to vases produced in various other regions of Greece and southern Italy.[2] It is partly due to this influence—which in the field of pottery has led the twentieth century to be thought of first and foremost as the century of attributionism—that Beazley is regarded today as a somewhat controversial figure.[3]

It should be noted, however, that some of the criticisms levelled at him today were already being voiced in Pottier's time. Indeed, although the meticulous classification of a body of pottery as prestigious as that of Athens could undoubtedly be seen as representing real progress in both the archaeological and art historical knowledge of that period, some of the initial reaction to it

---

[1] Beazley (1956; 1963; 1971).   [2] See Sparkes (1991: 42–55).
[3] Hoffmann (1979); Vickers (1985); Vickers and Gill (1994).

was hostile. This was largely due to differences of opinion concerning the stylistic criteria whereby a given corpus (the whole collection of pieces that can be ascribed to a painter) was attributed, and also to the fact that as time went on Beazley devoted less and less of his work to reflections on methodology, producing articles and then books in which he often did no more than catalogue vases and attribute them to their respective artists. This was a departure from the basic rule (of practice) which enables specialists in a discipline to exchange their knowledge and experience. Even so, it was primarily Beazley's theoretical stance, his notion of style, that initially conflicted with the accepted ideas of the time until his work gained the lasting recognition which it enjoyed from the 1920s on.

In this respect, the reception given to Beazley's work in France was an excellent example of the way in which the cultural transmission of a theory can be affected in its early stages by a view of archaeology inherited from specific intellectual traditions (in this case, French). Pottier was one of the most eminent representatives of this view at the turn of the century. He was a professor at the École du Louvre and the École des Beaux-Arts, and a member of the Académie des Inscriptions et Belles-Lettres (1899), but, most important, he was Curator of the Département des Antiquités orientales et de la Céramique antique at the Louvre, and the author of the museum's series of catalogues of ancient terracotta vases.[4] He entered the Louvre in 1884, and was head of the department from 1910 to 1924. One very specific feature of his time there was the integration of vases into the Oriental Antiquities collection, which needless to say had some influence on his conception of the study of pottery. It should also be said that he was a man of science and of institutions who at over 78 years old (six months before he died), was still a member of thirty-four scientific committees, in fields as varied as the excavations in Persia, Albania, and Afghanistan, the examinations at the École d'Athènes, the work at Delphi and Delos, the École du Caire (Cairo), etc.[5] Thus he was certainly a highly influential figure, even if he did not conform exactly to the stereotype of an ambitious career scientist.

One fact which is crucial to the theme of this book is that Pottier never concealed his disagreement with Beazley. Indeed, he spoke out several times against Beazley's methods, claiming that they were over-ambitious and unscientific. The distance between the two men was mainly due to their differing conceptions both of style and of the study of vases. What did, however, give Pottier a particular claim to be regarded as the leader of that body of opinion which accused Beazley of being too quick to attribute vases that had not

---

[4] Pottier (1896–1906; 1897–1928).

[5] Letter from Pottier to the administration (Paris, 2 Jan. 1934); Paris, Archives Nationales, F^{17} 17283.

even been published, was that he himself was at that very time proposing to remedy what had hitherto been one of the major hindrances to coherent progress in the study of pottery: the lack of easy access to pictures of vases and the factual data concerning them.

To overcome this problem, Pottier devised a vast project on an international scale, the aim of which was to publish and catalogue every vase kept in a public museum or private collection: the *Corpus Vasorum Antiquorum*. The first fascicle, devoted to a series of vases at the Louvre and written by Pottier himself, was published in 1922. The *CVA* is still being published today, although its aims are now significantly different, in terms of both form and content, from those of the original project. In imitation of the numerous lists and collections that already existed in other areas of research, the *Corpus* project set out in principle to publish all ancient clay vases, in other words not only Eastern, Greek, and Italian pottery, but common pottery as well.[6] In a subject area as vast as this, considerations of method were of the utmost importance; Pottier proposed that the vases should be listed by museum, using an extremely meticulous system of classification. This was based on a preliminary division of the various types of vases into groups according to what were first termed their 'regions of production', but which he quickly amended to 'stylistic groups'. Indeed, the question of the origin of some centres of production was still a real problem for archaeologists, who could not agree beyond the establishment of broad geographical divisions.[7] It seemed therefore that style was the only common denominator capable of winning the support of archaeologists involved in the grouping and classification of pottery.

This meant that, paradoxically, in the conflict that arose before and after the First World War between two approaches to vases and two scientific projects which may appear today to be complementary, but which nonetheless originally corresponded to two more or less conflicting conceptions of the study of pottery, both sides of the argument had as their central focus the notion of style. The paradox is no more than apparent, however, since the notion of style is open to such a wide range of interpretations that its definition depends primarily on the field of research to which it is applied. In fact the two approaches adopted by Pottier and Beazley were truly emblematic of the different directions that archaeological research took at the end of the nineteenth century.

In the latter half of the nineteenth century the growth of collections of antiquities in museums brought with it both archaeological forgeries and an ever-increasing number of objects for which it was impossible to rely on written documentation (this was especially true in the case of vases) or on

---

[6] Pottier (1937: 575–87).   [7] Pottier ([1922]: p. iv).

inscriptions whereby they could be more easily identified. These and other factors led directly to the emergence of a new school of scientific thought which rapidly grew to dominate archaeological research. This school, which began in the seminars of German universities, abandoned the study of the religious, poetic, and historical content of ancient art (the approach associated with *Altertumswissenschaft*) to concentrate first and foremost on the development of artistic forms.[8]

As early as 1879 Adolf Michaelis had detected the beginnings of a split in archaeological studies between two approaches: one global, in keeping with the German tradition of 'the science of antiquity', and aiming to reconstruct a unified picture of reality by using the tools of different disciplines (textual criticism, ancient history, epigraphy, religious history, iconography . . .), and the other much more specialized, with a greater emphasis on natural history and *Wortphilologie*.[9] Michaelis still believed in 1879 that these two schools could reconcile their objectives; twenty-five years later, however, at the time when Beazley was about to begin his research, he had reached the conclusion that the hegemony of the stylistic school marked the end of an era in which archaeologists had put their vast erudition to the service of research into the content of works of art, and the beginning of a new age of specialization and concentration on formal and stylistic detail.[10]

The emergence of the stylistic school of archaeological research in the late nineteenth and early twentieth centuries is an historiographical phenomenon of vital importance. We restrict ourselves here to examining its effects on the study of pottery. In the first chapter we concern ourselves with Beazley's predecessors, archaeologists such as Wilhelm Klein, Paul Hartwig, and Adolf Furtwängler, who were the first to win renown by carrying out a formal analysis of vases with a view to identifying individual Attic vase-painters.[11] Strictly speaking, Pottier was of the same generation as these men, and it is therefore not surprising that his writings show clear evidence of his interest in the stylistic analysis of painted vases. When we come to the question of his relations with German archaeology, however, we shall see that one of his main concerns was to find a path of his own, and that this was inclined to veer towards anthropology, which derived its explanatory models from the sciences of nature, evolutionism, and diffusionism. This must be seen in the particular context of France's position with regard to Germany after the defeat of 1870, when it was felt that there was an urgent need to take up the challenge of German science.[12] We can see evidence of this in Pottier's

[8] This paragraph, and the next, based on Marchand (1994: 317–29; 1996: 104–15).
[9] Michaelis (1879: 150).   [10] Michaelis (1906: 261).
[11] Klein (1886); Hartwig (1893); A. Furtwängler, Reichhold, *et al.* (1904–32).
[12] See the essential book by Digeon (1959).

unpublished account, written in 1888, of a scientific mission to Germany and Austria that he had undertaken the previous year in order to study the main collections of vases there, in preparation for writing his own catalogue of the ancient vases in the Louvre.[13]

Another point to consider is that the method used by archaeologists in their stylistic research had close links with art history. It is not surprising that this should have been so, since in German universities archaeology and art history were taught jointly until the beginning of the twentieth century. It is this area somewhere between the two disciplines that is usually referred to today as connoisseurship, a field of art criticism which is somewhat on the fringe of official art history, and is not exactly synonymous with the idea of attribution.[14] In the second half of the nineteenth century the methods used by connoisseurs underwent a profound change, as attempts were made to systematize the empirical approach whereby works were attributed according to external or stylistic evidence, and to use it as the basis for a scientific history of art; the names of Morelli and Berenson are emblematic of these attempts.[15]

We deal specifically with Beazley in two separate chapters. The first examines his intellectual background as a philologist who trained himself in the connoisseurship of vases. The most notable point to emerge from this research is the importance of poetry in his life; it is in fact in my view the key to an understanding of the essence of his relationship with vase-painters. Beazley himself had a vocation as a poet, as can be seen from an unpublished notebook containing twenty-five of his poems which we have had the good fortune to discover in the Bodleian archives.[16] He rapidly gave up this ambition however, possibly owing to his own doubts about the intrinsic quality of his poems.

'The Attic vase-painters are Beazley's discovery; not, I am sure, his invention, but he did invent the field.' Martin Robertson, himself a poet and one of the most knowledgeable experts on Beazley, has given an excellent account of his work, both in its broad outlines and in its specific detail.[17] Not only did Beazley identify the main individual artists in the workshops of the Kerameikos (the potters' district to the north-west of Athens, near the city's cemetery), he also established very subtle distinctions between the master's works and those of the pupil, between the painter's workshop and his school, between vases in the manner of the painter and those of the circle, and so on. In a second chapter, we show how this approach was put into practice, by

[13] Pottier's report on an archaeological mission (1887) to study museums in Germany and Austria (Munich, Vienna, Dresden, and Berlin); Louvre: Department of Etruscan, Greek, and Roman Antiquities.

[14] See Gibson-Wood (1988).

[15] Lermolieff (pseud. of Morelli) (1890–3); Berenson (1901–16).

[16] 'Twenty-five poems by John Beazley' (Oxford, Bodleian Library, MS Eng. poet. f. 32).

[17] Robertson (1992: 6).

taking as examples the works of two great vase-painters, the Kleophrades
Painter and the Berlin Painter, both of whom appear regularly in Beazley's
work, and thus enable us to put the logic of his thinking and the coherence of
his attributions to the test. It should be noted that Beazley's language was not
neutral, and largely determined the nature of his subject matter, as in any historical discourse; thus we have been able to show that his interpretative
schema was probably drawn originally from the model of Italian Renaissance
painting. In 'Citharoedus', however, a didactic article in which he explained
in detail his conception of connoisseurship, it became clear that his main concern was to react against an opinion which was widespread in his time,
according to which the majority of painters were mere nonentities, scattered
around a sort of industrial empire in which the only figures of significance
were a few master painters who took the trouble to sign their vases.[18]

Our interest in the reaction to Beazley's work in France is justified by
the fact that this re-assessment of the status of painters was specifically
aimed at Pottier, whose critical stance was based on a conception of Greek
art which was radically opposed to research into individual artists. This was
fundamental to his way of thinking, which was also clearly influenced by
his interest in the origins of Greek civilization further to the East. In fact,
Beazley and Pottier are almost perfect embodiments of two models, the one
centripetal and turned towards Athens, the other centrifugal and turned
towards Asia.

Pottier's interest in the Eastern origins of Greek civilization found a
natural outlet in the *CVA*, since it was at his suggestion that the *Corpus* set
out in principle to include all ancient vases from the Near and Middle East
with those of the Mediterranean basin. This project reflected a global vision of
the history of peoples' influences on one another, and was also intended
to resolve some fundamental questions of general anthropology. It has since
been abandoned, but the history of these nineteenth-century conceptions
sheds light on certain original aspects of the scientistic aims of a type of archaeology with anthropological leanings that has been carried on closer to our
time by researchers such as Vere Gordon Childe and André Leroi-Gourhan;
it is quite significant that when Leroi-Gourhan began his research into wall
painting, one of his fundamental concerns was to construct a relative chronology based on the preliminary identification of four stylistic phases.[19]

To touch briefly on our conception of historiography, the word itself
denotes the viewpoint of the historian who studies a field of research and the
way in which it has developed. This can largely be regarded as a social history
of knowledge; in other words, we examine specialist works and the methods

---

[18] Beazley (1922).   [19] Leroi-Gourhan (1964–5: ii. 219–31).

and problems described by their authors, but at the same time attempt as far as possible to define the links between these and society as a whole.

If the reader wishes to pass without further delay to the heart of the matter, he may move straight on to the first chapter. In the second part of this introduction we shall give some idea of how the study of pottery began in the eighteenth century, because although scientific considerations were not of primary importance at that time, some knowledge of the period will give a better understanding of later developments in the discipline, in particular those concerning the attribution of vases: 'To understand a phenomenon we have to know not only what it is, but also how it came into being.'[20]

The rediscovery of Greek vases goes back no further than the beginning of the eighteenth century, and was connected with the rise at that time of 'Etruscomania', according to which the vases were of Etruscan origin. This myth was to have a lasting influence; equally if not more important, however, was the adoption of the vases by the neo-classical movement, the 'Greek revival' of the last decades of the Enlightenment. In its early days the archaeology of vases was first and foremost a matter of aesthetics. This was largely due to the publication of the first Hamilton catalogue, *Etruscan, Greek and Roman Antiquities* (1767–76), which formed the epicentre of a vast historiographical phenomenon. As Aubin Millin, the Curator of the Cabinet des Médailles, remarked: 'It has done more than anything else to spread the taste for painted vases, and has introduced into all the arts the fashion for ornament known as Etruscan.'[21] At the end of this aesthetic phase, which also witnessed the emergence of art history as an autonomous discipline and of the museum in its modern form, the second Marquis of Northampton summed up the situation at the beginning of the nineteenth century perfectly when he declared that the aims of a public collection of vases ought to be 'archaeological, artistic and commercial'.[22]

GREEK VASES AND THE ETRUSCAN MYTH

The earliest reports of large collections of vases pertain not to the area of central Italy formerly known as Etruria, where several thousand vases were to be discovered at the beginning of the nineteenth century, but to southern Italy, and in particular to Naples, one of the most important European capitals, and still regarded by Stendhal in 1826 as 'the only capital of Italy'.[23] Another distinguished visitor to the bay of Naples, Winckelmann, claimed that the first

---

[20] Boas cited by Finley (1975: 188).   [21] Millin (1808–10: vol. i, p. iv, n. 18).

[22] 'Original Papers' XIV (19 Apr. 1836); Arch. British Museum; cited by Jenkins (1992: 277).

[23] Stendhal (1826; ed. V. del Litto 1973: 516).

major collection of vases had been made as early as the end of the seventeenth
century by the Neapolitan lawyer Giuseppe Valletta.[24] Francis Haskell
emphasizes, however, that although we know of collections developing here
and there, the fashion for objects of this kind seems to have been slow to
spread in the first half of the eighteenth century, and that references to it are
rare in the accounts of travellers passing through Naples in the course of their
'Grand Tour'.[25] One of the richest collections was that of Marquese Felice
Mastrilli in his Palazzo di San Nicandro; this boasted almost four hundred
vases, mainly from the ancient site of Nola.[26]

Most scholars in southern Italy were of course inclined to regard the
western Greek world as the original home of these objects, as is shown by
the common use of the terms 'Graeco-Campanian' and 'Graeco-Sicilian' to
describe vases. The pre-eminence of southern Italy over the rest of the country in terms of discoveries and of interest in ancient vases (a pre-eminence
which it should be added was entirely relative, since vases of this type had
been unearthed on Italian soil since time immemorial, and occasionally been
put together in collections since the Renaissance) demonstrates with hind-
sight the tremendous impact that the theory of Etruscan origin must have
had when it started to gain ground. Thus any debate as to where the modern
history of vases began will focus as much on archaeological discoveries as
on theories advanced by scholars. Fresh discoveries of vases in southern Italy
did not fundamentally call into question the theory of Etruscan origin, not at
least initially, because the Etruscan enthusiasts explained them by arguing
that the Etruscans had been dominant over the populations of ancient Italy.
Nevertheless the matter may be considered to have been settled in principle
at least as early as 1764, when Winckelmann asserted that the inscriptions and
style of the figures on the vases testified without doubt to their Greek origin,
and certainly in 1806, when Abbé Lanzi used recent discoveries of painted
vases in Greece itself, and in particular in Athens, as evidence on which to
base the same opinion.[27]

According to Krzysztof Pomian, the parochial attitude that led the Tuscan
scholars to claim all the painted pottery found in Italy for Etruria was linked
to a general trend in Europe, fuelled by ideologies in search of new cultural
identities, towards interest in cultures other than the classical civilizations of
Greece, Rome, and Italy.[28] The great landmarks in this movement were the
publication, more than a century after it was written, of *De Etruria Regali*[29] by
the Scot Thomas Dempster, the foundation in 1726 of the Etruscan Academy
in Cortone, and the publication ten years later of Anton Francesco Gori's

---

[24] Winckelmann (1789: i. 193).   [25] Haskell (1980: 32).   [26] Lyons (1992).
[27] Winckelmann (1789: i. 187 ff.): Lanzi (1806: 42 ff.).   [28] Pomian (1992: 60).
[29] Dempster (1723–4 [1726]); see Leighton and Castelino (1990).

book, *Museum Etruscum*.[30] It is important to note that the claim for Etruscan art of a status comparable with that of Graeco-Roman art is an example of the Etruscan enthusiasts' desire to place Etruscan civilization on an equal footing with the great models of antiquity.

Filippo Buonarroti, the Florentine antiquarian who published *De Etruria Regali* in collaboration with Giovanni Bottari, the friend and future chaplain of Pope Benedict XIV, took the opportunity to add reproductions of vases to the book, even though Dempster devoted only one short chapter to them, the purpose of which was to compile quotations from Latin authors.[31] The engravings of vases, forming a total of about thirty plates, came from two main sources, the Medici Museum belonging to the Grand Duke of Tuscany, and Cardinal Gualtieri's collection in Rome. The illustrations in the works by Dempster and Gori showed a mixture of Attic and southern Italian vases, with Etruscan vases, as it turned out, being the least well represented. After Dempster's book it became more and more common to include reproductions of vases in works on Etruscan antiquity, while at the same time the circle of contributors grew wider. From the list given by Gori of the owners of the objects shown in the engravings in his book, we can see that they came from all over Italy, including of course from Naples, which also indicates that in the second quarter of the eighteenth century the fashion for what were known as Etruscan vases was beginning to become quite widespread, and that they were fairly easy to come by.[32] As soon as people had learned to appreciate them, vases became a much more attractive proposition than statues, since they were a great deal less expensive, and it was also much easier to build up a collection rapidly that contained a good selection of the type of objects collected and was in keeping with the social distinction of the owner.[33]

We may wonder when all is said and done whether the popular theory of Etruscan origin did not have more impact on the artists of the time than Winckelmann's efforts to form his aesthetics of Greek art by studying Roman copies in the Vatican museums. The notion of 'Etruscan decoration' refers to a wildly eclectic ornamental style which borrows indiscriminately from various civilizations, and 'ends up incorporating and mingling all the ancient discoveries, whether they be figurative renderings on Greek ("Etruscan") vases, or the paintings and antiquities of Herculaneum and Pompeii'.[34] Clearly most artists and other decorators did not view these vestiges of the past in a historical way, but rather used them to create new compositions on the general theme of reference to the ancient world. This capacity for

[30] Gori (1737[–43]).   [31] Dempster (1723–4 [1726]: i. 424–8).

[32] Gori (1737: vol. i, pp. xxxi–xliiii).

[33] For an indication of prices, Reitlinger (1961–70: ii. 369).

[34] Govi (1992: 302).

inventing new forms of expression by combining elements of the past belonging to different civilizations is a common characteristic of the neo-classical style. We need only look at 'Egyptian' decoration, which often mixed strictly Egyptian motifs with ornament borrowed from the Graeco-Roman world, to realize that 'Etruscan' eclecticism was not unique; it was in fact quite possible for the same artists to work in both styles.[35] This tendency to syncretism does not make the work of archaeologists and art historians any easier, and Kerry Downes comes very close to throwing the baby out with the bathwater when he writes: 'There must be as many different definitions of Neo-Classicism as there are recipes for cooking rice.'[36]

THE COMTE DE CAYLUS AND THE
RECUEIL D'ANTIQUITÉS

The *Recueil d'antiquités égyptiennes, étrusques, grecques, romaines et gauloises* by the Comte de Caylus began to be published in the middle of the century. It seems an appropriate starting-point for our study, since it prefigures certain essential aspects of the Hamilton catalogue.[37] Caylus was one of France's earliest and most influential enthusiasts for the return to antiquity, and, not surprisingly, he too was a believer in the Etruscan origin of vases. Moreover, a rather despairing Padre Paciaudi pointed out to him: 'It seems to me that you are suffering from the same illness that poor Gori died of; everywhere you look you find things Etruscan.'[38]

Caylus was a member of the old aristocracy, a patron of the arts and man of letters who had come to antiquarian studies late in life, but with an enthusiasm which astonished Abbé Barthélemy. He was not the first Frenchman to include reproductions of vases in a book on antiquities, as he did in the *Recueil d'antiquités* to which he devoted the latter years of his life. However this work differs in two essential respects from the other great manual of antiquities which preceded it, *L'Antiquité expliquée et représentée en figures* (1719–24) by the Benedictine scholar Bernard de Montfaucon, who also provided illustrations of ancient vases. First, unlike Montfaucon, Caylus based all his descriptions, commentaries, and illustrations on the objects in his own collection, or on ones which he knew through having examined them personally.[39] It is clear from Caylus's correspondence with Paciaudi, the Duke of Parma's librarian and antiquarian, that Paciaudi made a vital contribution to the set-

---

[35] Dugourc, 'Projet de décoration: grotesque à l'égyptienne' (1787–1808); in Louvre (1994: 135–6, cat. 60); cf. Govi (1992: 304).

[36] Downes (1988).   [37] Caylus (1752–67).

[38] Letter from Paciaudi to Caylus (n.p., n.d.); Sérieys (ed.) (1802: 303 no. 77).

[39] Caylus (1752–67: i. 1); Schnapp (1985: 69).

ting up of his collection, and thus to the creation of the *Recueil*, by offering to procure the objects which were to appear in the work on his behalf (more than 800 plates of line-engravings).[40] While the last five volumes were being put together, he regularly supplied Caylus with his 'little purchases', although it must be said that Caylus also had a network of correspondents which extended as far as Syria.[41] But despite the fact that the correspondence between the two men abounds in information of every kind, notably concerning the traffic in antiquities at a time when a number of Italian cities were drawing up more and more legislation for the protection of ancient monuments,[42] there is little to be found in them on the subject of vases. This silence was due, paradoxically, to the fact that since Caylus's needs 'in the Etruscan department' were amply provided for, he was much more concerned about the Greek section of the collection, which was not as well supplied as he would have liked. To find out what he thought about vases, one can do no better than to leaf through the *Recueil*: 'Given that this is a people who have made the noble simplicity that uplifts the spirit shine out from vases intended for the most everyday use, what care will they not have taken when working with more precious materials!'[43] Although Caylus regarded the arts as the best means of gauging the ethics and spirit of a nation, he also saw the simplest objects, which were plentiful and a good indicator of taste, as an equally sure way of measuring 'the nature of its customs'.[44]

The Comte de Caylus had a great passion for vases, even though there were not many who shared it at the beginning of the 1760s: 'As regards broken pots,' he wrote, 'in a sense, no one is in the same market as I am.'[45] 'Broken pots' were in any case very much in keeping with Caylus's taste for 'bits and pieces'. 'Fine pieces', he said, were of less interest to him, since they fitted in less well with the didactic aim of his book: 'I am not holding an exhibition, I am giving a lesson in antiquities, and I am looking in the case of customs for what makes them possible, and in the case of practices for what demonstrates them.'[46] In addition, however, to the archaeological and hermeneutic importance of the collection, in other words the light that it could throw on the 'thousand singularities of the History, religion, customs & mores of these famous Peoples', it had another aspect which was equally in evidence from the outset: 'that of being useful to these young people, by making them engrave and draw objects which will serve them throughout their lives by giving them the benefits of the forms and taste of antiquity.'[47]

[40] Nisard (1877).   [41] Schnapp (1993: 238).   [42] Emiliani (1978).
[43] Caylus (1752–67: vol. i, p. xi).   [44] Haskell (1993: 181).
[45] Letter from Caylus to Paciaudi (Paris, 11 Feb. 1760); Nisard (1877: i. 141).
[46] Letter from Caylus to Paciaudi (Paris, 25 [Dec. 1759]; ibid. (i. 116).
[47] Letter from Caylus to Paciaudi (Paris, 18 June 1759); ibid. (i. 74).

The 'young people' here were the young Parisian artists who worked under Caylus's powerful patronage, and this was his system: 'The bits and pieces arrive; I examine them; I get young people whose taste is forming to draw them. What I give them prepares them for life and study. I throw the engravings into a corner with explanations of what they are, and when there are enough of them to make up a volume, I give them to someone in our Academy who is willing to correct the proofs and oversee the printing, which I would not be able to do.'[48] It is clear from this that the patronage of the Académie royale des Inscriptions was not limited to financial and moral support, but that Caylus also received a great deal of practical help with his project: a further example of Caylus's habitual practice of using the royal institutions to back his reforms of taste.[49]

The idea of imitation was now central to the notion of a return to antiquity; in Caylus's *Recueil* it was put into practice, and this is the second aspect of the work which was innovative compared to Montfaucon. The Benedictine monk belonged to an entirely different generation, to whom the idea of using a scholarly work as a laboratory for young artists was completely alien. The fact that Caylus viewed the *Recueil* as both demonstrates the links between art and archaeology, as well as the originality of his project compared to those of his predecessors.

The Comte de Caylus, who had been campaigning more or less officially since the 1730s for a return to 'the great, natural taste of the ancient world', as Président de Brosses called it, cannot but have been sensitive to the artistic aspects of the *Recueil*. It must be admitted, however, that at least as far as vases are concerned, the plates are not really up to the standard one might have expected from an artist and art-lover who had been actively involved in the *Recueil Crozat*, a work which not long before had made a decisive contribution to the birth of what would later become the art book (the first volume of the *Recueil Crozat* was published in 1729, the second in 1742).[50] The outlines of the figures are often very blurred, and on the red-figured vases the plain background is covered with hatching; the effect is not very successful when the process is reversed for black-figured vases, and this time the figures themselves are hatched.

The Comte de Caylus was himself a talented artist whose excellent engravings in particular were much admired by his peers. Joshua Reynolds heaped praise on him in the first of his *Discourses on Art*, for the rigour with which his engraving of a drawing attributed to Raphael adhered to the

---

[48] Letter from Caylus to Paciaudi (Paris, 21 Apr. 1760); ibid. (i. 178).

[49] Fumaroli (1993); as a member of the Academy of Painting in 1731, and of the Academy of Inscriptions in 1742, Caylus is 'le seul membre de ces deux académies qui appartienne à la haute noblesse' (p. 571).

[50] See Haskell (1987).

Italian master's original.[51] This was not entirely without ulterior motive, since it was aimed at the pupils of the Royal Academy, who were meant to be rekindling the flame of classical art by learning to imitate the ancient models as faithfully as possible. Not all his contemporaries received the message as he intended, however; on the contrary, we shall see that in the Hamilton catalogue the tendency to idealize the images on vases was if anything the general rule.

When he actually saw the first volume of the Hamilton catalogue, Reynolds too was struck by the beauty of the images, although he was not able to judge how faithful the illustrations were by comparing them to the originals. He also had some difficulty in concealing his surprise at the grace of these pictures, which reminded him more of Italian Mannerism than of the early Renaissance: 'The grace and genteelness of some of the figures are exquisite, particularly the Atalanta, and it is that kind of grace which I have never observed before in the antique, it is much in the Parmegiano style.'[52]

WILLIAM HAMILTON AND *ETRUSCAN, GREEK AND ROMAN ANTIQUITIES*

The joint venture set up by the English ambassador Sir William Hamilton and Pierre d'Hancarville to illustrate Hamilton's collection of ancient vases was to result in one of the most beautiful works of the eighteenth century.[53] It would be tempting to see it also as the first proper art book on ancient pottery, were it not for the fact that most of the text bears very little relation to the illustrations, and thus fails to conform to the definition of the art book given by Haskell.[54] D'Hancarville's splendid 'historical imagination' prompted Arnaldo Momigliano to say of him, a little severely perhaps, that he 'stupefied those more able than himself by his stubborn determination to understand nothing about vases'.[55]

The story of Sir William Hamilton and his dual passion for vulcanology and the relics of antiquity is well known.[56] For thirty-seven years, from 1764 to 1800, he represented his country as an envoy extraordinary to the court of King Ferdinand IV of the Two Sicilies. He took advantage of his time there to build up two large collections; the finest pieces in these were ancient vases, but they contained a highly diverse range of other objects besides. The first

---

[51] Reynolds (1988: 20). In the 2nd ed. (1737) of the *Temple du Goût*, Voltaire praised Caylus in these terms, cited by Rocheblave (1889: 50 n. 1): 'Cailus, tous les arts vous chérissent | Il [le dieu du Goût] conduit tes brillants desseins, | et les Raphaëls s'applaudissent | De se voir gravés par tes mains.'

[52] Letter from Reynolds to Hamilton (London, 28 Mar. 1769); Morrison (ed.) (1893: i. 11 no. 17).

[53] [d'Hancarville] (1766–7 [1767–76]); see Ramage (1991).

[54] Haskell (1987: 7).   [55] A. Momigliano (1983: 281).

[56] See Fothergill (1969); Jenkins and Sloan (1996); Burn (ed.) (1997).

collection was acquired in 1772 by the trustees of the British Museum, thanks to a special grant of £8,410 donated by Parliament. For the museum, which had been founded in 1759, this purchase was its first major publicly funded acquisition, and was to form the nucleus of its department of Greek and Roman antiquities. It was with a view to selling his collection to the British Museum that Hamilton brought out his luxurious four-volume catalogue.[57] He put together a second collection, this time with the main emphasis on vases, and financed a second catalogue, illustrated by the painter Tischbein who was director of the Academy of Fine Art in Naples.[58] This collection comprised a little over a thousand vases, but about a third of them were lost at sea on the way to England, near the Isles of Scilly, and the remainder were sold in 1801 to Thomas Hope, another great acolyte of neo-classical taste, for the sum of £4,000.

Although they belonged to different generations, it is not difficult to draw a parallel between Caylus (born in 1692) and Hamilton (born in 1730). Both came from the same high aristocratic background, began their careers on the field of battle, and had a major influence on the taste of their age: Caylus by flying the flag very early on for the return to Antiquity, Hamilton by truly launching the fashion for ancient vases. These similarities would seem to confirm the idea that under the *ancien régime*, changes in public taste were usually initiated by royal courts and influential members of the aristocracy. There was, however, an important difference between Caylus's *Recueil* and the Hamilton catalogue: the first relied on the Académie royale des Inscriptions, an institutional organ functioning on royal subsidies and serving as a prestigious cog in the wheel of monarchial power within the republic of letters, whereas the second stemmed from a private partnership, operating on a subscription system with the clear intention of making a profit.

From a very early stage Hamilton was concerned to produce a work which would advertise his collection of ancient vases to a wider public. Like Caylus, he was a patron and arbiter of taste, and was anxious to benefit antiquarians and artists by drawing attention to the historical interest and beauty of his objects.[59] As it turned out, however, the artistic repercussions of his catalogue were to prove immeasurably greater than anything Caylus could have imagined.

The role of d'Hancarville in this affair cannot be minimized, as his correspondence with Hamilton shows.[60] Although it was the ambassador who had the idea for the catalogue, probably laid down the guidelines for the project in discussions with d'Hancarville, and also provided the majority of the funds,

[57] See Griener (1992).   [58] Hamilton (1791–5).
[59] Fothergill (1969: 48).   [60] Published by Griener (1992: 118–44).

the two men were equal partners from the start.[61] Thus it was d'Hancarville who was left to take the initiative in writing and making up the catalogue. One of his happiest strokes of inspiration was to send specially to Venice for 100,000 printer's characters that had been 'cast expressly for the purpose'; this would add an extra degree of luxury to the typography of the work, which was printed on imperial paper.[62] D'Hancarville was a French adventurer, who in 1765 had made a name for himself as an entrepreneur with an illustrated book about the Gulf of Naples. He had developed a particular way of working, which again played an important part in the general organization of the catalogue. This involved surrounding himself with hand-picked collaborators, as if he were running a real family business. All the material, as well as the instruments needed for the manufacture of the catalogue (paper, coloured inks, prints, etchings, copperplates, presses, characters, etc.) were stored in d'Hancarville's home, where they took up half the house.[63] The artists worked on their drawings and engravings on the spot, under his direction, and most of them actually lived in his home, where they received free board and lodging. 'For five years I have fed fifteen people who are working on my book,' wrote d'Hancarville at a critical moment in the history of the catalogue.[64]

An adventurer of great talent

Eccentric figures were by no means uncommon in the eighteenth century, but Pierre François Hugues, known as Baron d'Hancarville, was without doubt one of the most eccentric of them all. He was not only a complete mythomaniac, an inveterate charmer, a blackmailer, crook, and pornographer, but also a true visionary.[65] Born in 1729 as the son of a Nancy draper, Pierre Hugues initially embarked on a career as a soldier, as Montfaucon and Caylus had done before him. He was almost the living embodiment of La Fleur, the French officer in Sterne's *Sentimental Journey*: 'La Fleur had set out early in life, as gallantly as most Frenchmen do, with *serving* for a few years; at the end of which, having satisfied the sentiment, and found moreover, That the honour of beating a drum was likely to be its own reward, as it open'd no further track of glory to him—he retired *a ses terres*, and lived *comme il plaisoit*

---

[61] 'Compte-rendu à Monsieur Hamilton sur l'état présent de l'ouvrage des Antiquités étrusques, et sur l'argent avancé à Mr d'Hancarville pour l'exécution dudit ouvrage', (n.p., n.d. [first half of 1766]); Griener (1992: 118–20); letter from d'Hancarville to Hamilton (Florence, 30 Jan. 1770); Griener (1992: 136). (Dates in square brackets given by Griener in his book.)

[62] Memoir from d'Hancarville to Hamilton (n.p., n.d. [end of 1766, beginning of 1767]); Griener (1992: 123–4); [d'Hancarville] (1766–7 [1767–76]: vol. i, p. xxii).

[63] Letter from d'Hancarville to Hamilton (Florence, 30 Jan. 1770); Griener (1992: 136–7).

[64] Letter from d'Hancarville to Hamilton (Florence, 30 Jan. 1770); Griener (1992: 136).

[65] See Haskell (1984).

a Dieu—that is to say, upon nothing.'⁶⁶ The difference was that Pierre Hugues
had no fortune but Mother Nature, and that he tried to make the best of a
bad job by travelling all over Europe and taking on such diverse identities as
the Marquis de Lenoncourt, the Comte de Saint Elme, the Baron du Han,
the Comte de Graffenegg, and finally Baron d'Hancarville, the *nom de plume*
which was to remain with him. Until 1765, when, having gone to live in
Naples the year before, he met Hamilton there, 'd'Hancarville's trajectory was
that of a runaway disguised as a gentleman on the Grand Tour'.⁶⁷ With his love
of salons and ideas and his interest in philosophy, d'Hancarville gave of his
talents to the full when he joined Hamilton to write his catalogue. His stroke
of genius was that he conceived of something completely new, more to do
with the form in fact than with the content, as Winckelmann was to acknowledge after receiving the first plates of the Hamilton catalogue: 'Ein Werk von
dieser Art ist noch niemals zum Vorschein gekommen' ('No work of this kind
has ever been produced before').⁶⁸

No doubt what aroused Winckelmann's admiration were the catalogue's
magnificent ochre and black watercoloured plates. They were the most
striking feature of these illustrations, and they stood out even more because
of the way in which they were arranged in the elegant folio. One important
detail concerning these 'plates' was that the scenes on the curved surfaces of the vases were painted flat here, and framed by richly decorated
borders which took up the ornamental motifs of the vases. These two ingre-
dients—the fact that the painted scenes unfolded on the flat plane of the
easel board, and that the images were framed by borders which gave them
an outline and formed a picture moulding—inevitably gave the reader
the impression that he was looking at reproductions of paintings, or even
cartoons for tapestries. The tapestry model should not be overlooked;
d'Hancarville claimed that the way in which the plates were printed was
due to Giuseppe Bracci, a draughtsman from Pisa who was the most note-
worthy artist to work on the Hamilton catalogue.⁶⁹ Until then he had been
employed by the royal tapestry-makers in Naples, where he had special
responsibility for the design of the works intended for the royal family, and
made an enviable reputation for himself when he worked on orders placed by
King Charles of Bourbon.⁷⁰ Another notable feature of the work was its geometrical plates; these were views of the vases in cross-section, giving the exact
measurements and proportions of the different parts. The aim of this last
innovation, which can also be put down to Bracci, was to make it easier for

---

⁶⁶ Sterne (1768); Jack (ed.) (1984: 31–2).   ⁶⁷ Griener (1992: 36).
⁶⁸ Letter from Winckelmann to Baron Stosch (Porto d'Anzio, 2 Apr. 1767); Rehm (ed.) (1952–7: iii. 246
no. 836).
⁶⁹ [d'Hancarville] (1766–7 [1767–76]: i. 170).   ⁷⁰ Ramage (1987: 447).

potters to model their work on ancient vases when attempting to create modern replicas.[71]

From the luxurious treatment given to the illustrations it is clear that the catalogue was intended primarily for collectors and artists:

Our end has certainly been to show a considerable collection of exquisite Models, but we likewise have proposed to ourselves to hasten the progress of the Arts by disclosing their true and first principles. And it is in this respect that the nature of our work may be considered as absolutely new, for no one, has yet undertaken to search out what system the Ancients followed to give their Vases, that elegance which all the world acknowledge to be in them, to discover rules the observation of which conduct infallibly to their imitation, and in short to assign exact measures for fixing their proportions, in order, that the Artist who would *invent* in the same stile, or only *copy* the Monuments which appeared to him worthy of being copied, may do so with as much truth and precision, as if he had the Originals themselves in his possession. It is by this means, that the present work may contribute to the advancement of the Arts, and make the master-pieces of Antiquity that are worthy [of] our imitation understood as they deserve to be.[72]

Michael Vickers has given a full account of how d'Hancarville set about presenting a theory of the value of painted vases in the ancient world which would fit in with his system of fine art.[73] D'Hancarville mainly sought to emphasize that 'these vases were become very precious and very rare, in ancient times', and to extol the elegance of line and the simplicity which are such a distinctive feature of these drawings, and 'above all, the genius, which must be supposed in the Artists, who invented them and that strange variety of contours'.[74] He did not hesitate to quote at length from Winckelmann, the greatest living authority on antiquities at that time, who stated in essence: 'The smallest and seemingly most lowly of insects are the masterpiece of Nature. Likewise painted earthenware vases are the marvel of the Art of the Ancients.'[75]

Winckelmann's enthusiasm as an antiquarian ought of course to be seen in its proper context of the return to Antiquity; d'Hancarville was primarily interested in art, however, and he was prepared to leap to conclusions about the importance that vases might have for artists, even if it meant inventing a new fable. What he really wanted to emphasize was that very great artists such as Raphael, Jules Romain, Jean de Oudine, and Poussin had studied these objects with care in order to draw inspiration from them: 'Where is then the Sculptor, the Painter, or the Artist, that will not have a pleasure in studying models which served as Masters to those of whom they esteem it an honour

---

[71] [d'Hancarville] (1766–7 [1767–76]: i. 172).   [72] Ibid. (vol. i, p. vi).
[73] Vickers and Gill (1994: 6–14).   [74] [d'Hancarville] (1766–7 [1767–76]: ii. 58; 104).
[75] Ibid. (i. 168 n. 46).

to be disciples?'[76] With that purpose in mind, he had included in the catalogue a model which owed more than a little to invention and was intended
to show artists how much benefit they could derive from painted vases.

Copying and inventing: beautiful but unfaithful

Generally speaking, reproductions of vases tended to move further and further away from the originals as the project went on, in particular through
the use of colour. This was particularly noticeable in the fourth volume,
which was certainly the most successful from the artistic point of view, but
also the one in which the illustrations were least faithful to the originals. One
plate to which we would like to refer briefly was engraved by Carmine
Pignatari, the catalogue's chief engraver, and is to be found in the second volume. It shows a series of four plates illustrating the same vase, the famous Meidias hydria. The vase dates from the end of the fifth century BC, and shows the
abduction of the Leucippides by the Dioscuri on the shoulder, and Heracles
and his companions resting in the Garden of the Hesperides on the lower
frieze.[77] D'Hancarville correctly identified the theme of the lower body; as
regards the main scene, he believed that it portrayed the race between
Atalanta and Hippomenes in the presence of Atlas and the Hesperides; we
owe the correct identification of the subject to Eduard Gerhard, who during
a visit to the British Museum in 1839 also recognized the signature of the
potter Meidias.[78]

Two different versions of the abduction scene appeared in the catalogue.
The first remained quite faithful to the original and gave a fairly accurate idea
of the reproductions shown in the first two volumes; the painted scene was on
a flat plane, there was a border taking up the ornamental motifs of the vase
(meanders, intertwining lotus leaves, a group of dotted squares alternating
between red and black), and polychromy was limited to the two shades of
baked clay without the addition of further colours. The second version
(reproduced as Pl. 2 at the end of this book) was considerably less faithful to
the original; most of the figures had been touched up with white gouache
laid on in fine brushstrokes so that the contours of their draperies stood out
in sharp relief, and satiny shades of blue had been added to give the light a
vibrant quality. The most obvious changes, however, were in the picture's
composition; the perspective had been altered by indicating the line of the
ground, the arrangement of some groups of figures had been freely adapted
from the original, shadows were marked on the ground, thus indicating a

[76] [d'Hancarville] (1766–7 [1767–76]: i, p. xviii).
[77] Ibid. (vol. i, pls. 127–30; vol. ii, pl. 22). London, British Museum E 224; *ARV*² (1313 no. 5).
[78] Gerhard (1840).

source of light, some details had been omitted (laurels), and a new figure had been added, sitting beside Zeus in the lower left corner of the picture.

D'Hancarville justified the presence of this *unicum* by repeating the terms of his preface, and by emphasizing the value of the figure as a model:

In order to make this book as useful as I possibly can, I have engaged Monsieur Pécheux [. . .]. At my request he has drawn the figures more correctly than they are drawn in the Ancient painting, & has arranged them in such a way as to show how a skilful man may turn these pieces to good account. He would have done a great deal more had I not asked him to adhere as closely as possible to the Original Composition. It is up to the Public, which can now look at both drawings, to see how much assistance artists can derive from the figures that are in this work, from the agreeable positions they display, & from that noble simplicity of which the greatest modern Painters have been the imitators.[79]

This is the only occasion on which Pécheux's signature appears, but his identity is of some importance. Born in Lyons, Laurent Pécheux worked throughout his career as an artist in Italy, first in Rome, then in Naples and Turin, where he was Director of the Academy of Painting and Drawing and the King of Piedmont's leading painter.[80] On his arrival in Rome in 1752 he became the pupil of Mengs and Pompeo Batoni. Interestingly, Batoni was the first artist to paint a well-known portrait of an aristocratic personage on the Grand Tour who chose to have vases appear in the background of the painting instead of the traditional sculpture.[81] This portrait (reproduced as Pl. 3 below), which has been studied by Adolf Greifenhagen, is of Prince Karl Wilhelm Ferdinand, later Duke of Brunswick and Lüneburg, and was painted while he was visiting Rome in 1766.[82] The prince was accompanied by Winckelmann, who, in the absence of his compatriot Mengs who was in Madrid at the time, probably selected the vases in the painter's collection to appear in the portrait.[83] Mengs had built up a large collection of 300 vases in 1759, almost all of which came from Nola, and he was one of the first artists to be enthused by the perfection of the drawings on the vases, and also one of the first to support the idea that they were of Greek origin. It is amusing to note, moreover, that Mengs's fortunate acquisition aroused covetous feelings among other enthusiasts, and even a certain envy on the part of the Comte de Caylus: 'We must console ourselves for Mengs's Etruscan vases; one cannot have everything. It is true, however, that they are painted with greater facility than his own works.'[84]

[79] [d'Hancarville] (1766–7 [1767–76]: ii. 168).   [80] Baldin (n.d. [1983]).

[81] *Prince Karl Wilhelm Ferdinand, later Duke of Brunswick and Lüneburg* (1767); Brunswick, Herzog Anton Ulrich Museum 676; A. M. Clark (1985: cat. no. 310 pl. 284).

[82] Greifenhagen (1939: 200–7; pls. i–iii).   [83] Jenkins (1988: 449–50).

[84] Letter from Caylus to Paciaudi (Paris, 2 Feb. 1761); Nisard (1877: i. 228).

No doubt the paradigmatic value attached to Pécheux's plate and the Meidias hydria came about because Hamilton intended it to; we know that he chose to have the vase feature prominently in the portrait of himself by Joshua Reynolds (now in the National Portrait Gallery in London) which he commissioned during one of his visits to England.[85] There are several allusions in d'Hancarville's letters to the 'great vase', in connection with the cost of the engraving, and we may reasonably assume that he is referring to the Meidias hydria. From a few scattered pieces of information we can even form an idea of the sum that was spent on its illustration, probably more than £100; the ambassador did not skimp when it came to showing his vase off to advantage.

Hamilton was not alone in appreciating the beauty of the Meidias vase, which may be regarded as representative of the taste of that period in ancient pottery. 'These Paintings are manifestly more beautiful than any others we know of on vases, & we are not afraid to affirm that the vase on which they are painted is the most precious of all those that have been conserved until the present day.'[86] Winckelmann also did not hesitate to judge them to be 'der schönsten und reizendsten Zeichnung von der Welt' ('among the most beautiful and charming drawings in the world').[87] Reynolds, as we have seen, particularly valued the Atalanta which appeared in the first volume of the Hamilton catalogue, for its 'grace and genteelness', even though he was a little surprised to discover stylistic features in it that were more readily identifiable with the Italian Mannerists ('it is much in the Parmegiano style'). No doubt the discovery of these similarities across the centuries was welcome to him, since it seems that one of the dominant features of the neo-classical aesthetics of the 1760s was a notion of ancient art seen through the prism of the Italian painters of the sixteenth century, in particular Raphael, Leonardo, Correggio, and Parmigianino, in other words the painters of grace.

In conclusion it should be said that interest in the Meidias Painter continued long after the fad for neo-classicism was over, and was further heightened for nineteenth-century archaeologists by the discovery of a signature on the vase in 1839. In the middle of the century it drew an enthusiastic response from Jean de Witte, who regarded it as 'one of the most beautiful of all signed vases'.[88] Lucilla Burn has noted that it continued to be held in high regard until the early years of the twentieth century, for archaeologists such as Adolf Furtwängler, and indeed for Pericle Ducati and Georges Nicole, both of whom wrote monographs on it.[89] The discordant voice came from Beazley,

---

[85] Workshop of Reynolds: *Sir William Hamilton, KB* (1777); London, National Portrait Gallery 680; Burn (1987: pl. 1b).

[86] [d'Hancarville] (1766–7 [1767–76]: ii. 168).   [87] Cited by Burn (1987: 1 n. 6).

[88] Witte (1848: 7).   [89] Nicole (1908); Ducati (1909).

who after the First World War criticized the sickly-sweet prettiness of the work in a style which managed to be both impeccable and cutting: 'Here also there is beauty; the gleam of gold, love and ladies with soft limbs, in soft raiment, and all that is shining, easeful and luxurious: perfume, honey and roses, till the heart longs for what is fresh, pungent and hard.'[90] Beazley tended to prefer the archaic art of the severe period, the works of Pindar and Aeschylus, the Berlin Painter and the early Italian Renaissance, and in this respect his views were a good indicator of the appreciable ways in which taste in Greek vases changed at the beginning of the twentieth century.

JOSIAH WEDGWOOD AND THE FORTUNES OF THE HAMILTON COLLECTION

Too much is known about the influence of the Hamilton catalogue on Wedgwood's decorated pottery for there to be any need to dwell on it here.[91] We would merely like to make a few remarks along the same lines as what has already been said; these will give a somewhat better understanding of what the second Marquis of Northampton meant when he wrote that a public collection of vases should also represent a commercial interest.

The first of these concerns the famous observation that Josiah Wedgwood made to Parliament in response to criticisms that had been voiced after the purchase of the Hamilton collection for the British Museum. 'Two years later,' wrote Hamilton, 'Mr Wedgwood proved before the Parliament of England that by imitating my vases in his pottery he had attracted more than three times as much money to our country as the collection cost the nation.'[92] It should be noted that this report of the declaration was made by Hamilton to the Countess of Lichtenau, the mistress of King Friedrich Wilhelm II of Prussia, at a time when the ambassador was trying to find a buyer for his collection in Germany who was willing to pay £7,000. Nonetheless there is no reason to question the veracity of Wedgwood's riposte, and we know of other examples of his concern for the good of the nation. A further reason why this link between public interest and private economy is significant is that it also suggests some striking points of contrast. As Wedgwood specialists have emphasized, there was an essential difference between an industrial empire such as Wedgwood's and the two other great pottery factories of the eighteenth century, Sèvres and Meissen. This was because the Staffordshire factory was a purely private and commercial enterprise whose growth depended entirely on the profits made from the sale of its products, whereas Meissen and

---

[90] Beazley (1918: 185).   [91] See Ramage (1989; 1990).

[92] Letter from Hamilton to the Countess of Lichtenau (Naples, 3 May 1796); Lichtenau (1809: ii. 132 no. 52).

Sèvres were not primarily engaged in the pursuit of profit in Wedgwood's sense of the word, since they both operated largely on royal subsidies and were owned by monarchs who viewed them more as sources of prestige than of revenue.[93]

Given these differences, it would appear that Wedgwood was a precursor of modern capitalism; it should be noted, however, that in the case of the Hamilton collection his interest in the good of the nation was based primarily on artistic considerations, notably on the hope that public taste would improve as a result of the introduction of ancient vases to England:

The whole nation, as well as I, have long spoken with gratitude of the patronage you have afforded, and the assistance you have given, to the arts of the country by the introduction of so many of the valuable relicts of antiquity. The collection of Etruscan vases in the British Museum will ever be resorted to for the finest models of elegant and simple forms, it is a source from which you will know how greatly I have profited.[94]

Wedgwood would have been nearer the truth had he said that on the whole he had modelled the decoration of his vases on the catalogue, since it was mainly from books on antiquity that he and his employees worked.[95] On the other hand, Hamilton reflected a widely held opinion when he wrote that Wedgwood and Bentley had done a great deal to spread the simple taste of the ancient world:

It is with infinite satisfaction that I reflect on having been in some measure instrumental in introducing a purer taste of forms & Ornaments by having placed my Collection of Antiquities in the British Museum, but a Wedgwood and a Bentley were necessary to diffuse that taste so universally, and it is thanks to their liberal way of thinking & [. . .] acting that so good a taste prevails at present in Great Britain.[96]

In a sketch by Benjamin West from the same period, we find the metaphorical expression of what neo-classicism saw as the role of antiquity, and notably of pottery, in the renaissance of the arts, the development of manufacturing industry, and the enrichment of the nation. The sketch (reproduced as Pl. 4 below), which dates from 1789–91 and is variously entitled *Etruria, Manufactory Giving Support to Industry* and *British Manufactory*, was one of a set of pictures intended to decorate the Queen's Lodge at Windsor Castle.[97] The dominant theme of this allegorical scene is the manufacture of vases inspired

[93]   Finer and Savage (eds.) (1965: 8); Reilly (1989: i. 18–19).
[94]   Letter from Wedgwood to Hamilton (16 June 1787); Finer and Savage (eds.) (1965: 307).
[95]   Johnson (1990).
[96]   Letter from Hamilton to Wedgwood (1786); Young (ed.) (1995: 59).
[97]   West, *British Manufactory (Manufactory Giving Support to Industry) (Etruria)* (1789–91), Cleveland Museum of Art; Erffa and Staley (1986: 411–12; cat. 437).

by Wedgwood's workshop; in the foreground, under the benevolent gaze of
an associate, a female figure of matronly appearance is putting the finishing
touches to the decoration on a vase, while one of the children sitting at the
very front of the picture is holding a replica of the famous Portland vase.
Hamilton had acquired this vase in Rome for £1,000, an enormous sum, and
in 1784 had sold it at a comfortable profit to the Duchess of Portland. Her son,
the Duke of Portland, lent the vase to Wedgwood in 1786 so that he could
make replicas of it.[98] Wedgwood did not find it easy to produce a satisfactory
copy, but the fact that a replica of the vase appears in West's sketch shows the
rapid rise to popularity of this type of copy inspired by antiquity.

The exceptional fame that ancient pottery enjoyed thanks to modern
adaptations of it was not restricted to the shores of Great Britain, although no
one else had as much success in spreading the taste for it as Wedgwood did. It
was very much part of the general context of a return to antiquity, and yet
it might have seemed that economic notions such as profit and investment,
on which so much emphasis was laid at the same time, were ill-matched to
a vision of the ancient world. It was this that prompted Abbé Sieyès, on the
eve of the Revolution when references to the ancient world were cropping
up everywhere, to say that the world he lived in was nothing like that of
antiquity, since all his age really cared about was manufacturing and con-
sumption: 'The modern European peoples bear very little resemblance
to the ancient peoples. All we are interested in is commerce, agriculture,
factories etc.';[99] by which he was merely making a barely veiled reference to
Rousseau's declaration to the citizens of Geneva in the ninth of his *Lettres
de la montagne*: 'You are neither Romans nor Spartans; you are not even
Athenians. [. . .] You are Merchants, Bourgeois, always taken up with your
own private interests, work, trade and gain.'[100]

We shall conclude by noting that these economic preoccupations continued to be of importance long after the period under consideration here, and
indeed throughout the nineteenth century, in the context of competition
between European countries in the field of the decorative arts. There are various ways of viewing this continuity; Ian Jenkins, for example, has shown that
taste and the centres of interest had sufficiently evolved by the beginning of
the nineteenth century for the British Museum to envisage the purchase of
the Durand collection in 1836, and that in fact this purchase represented a will
to go beyond mere artistic taste and embrace other forms of encyclopaedic
knowledge.[101] It is clear, however, that the effects of the aesthetic phase lasted
in other ways, and also that pottery continued to serve as a model for the

[98] Letter from Wedgwood to Hamilton (Etruria, 24 June 1786); Finer and Savage (eds.) (1965: 295–6).
[99] Cited by Saisselin (1992: 64–5).   [100] Cited by Vidal-Naquet (1985: 5).
[101] Jenkins (1992).

decorative arts. Indeed, the fame of artists who had modelled their works on Greek vases was such that archaeologists and the general public could hardly fail to remember them. So it was that when, at the end of the 1920s, the Keller publishing house in Berlin decided to respond favourably to Beazley's and Paul Jacobsthal's plan to devote a series of works to individual Attic vase-painters, the editor of the collection for Keller, a man called Fleischer, had the idea of promoting the editorial enterprise by referring to the great figures of neo-classicism who had done so much to establish the pedigree of Greek pottery. Shrewd though Fleischer's initiative may have been, it was to provoke a reaction of utter disapproval from Beazley, who let it be known to Jacobsthal that he found the idea intolerable. 'The references to Flaxman and Tischbein in Fleischer's general advertisement of our series sadden me. Flaxman is to me the Beast. He, Thorvaldsen and Wedgwood are the Bogus Classics, as the English Preraphaelites are the Bogus Gothic and early Renaissance. And nothing more.'[102]

---

[102] Letter from Beazley to Jacobsthal (Oxford, 15 June 1931); Oxford, Beazley Archive.

I

The Beginnings of Research into Greek Pottery

THE STUDY OF ATTIC VASES BEFORE BEAZLEY

> The modern Berlin school—Furtwängler, Kalkmann, Graef, Winter—
> go in for nothing but measurements. You must have a history of the way
> the eye was gradually developed, the neck, the shoulder, &c. Furtwängler's
> great test is the height of the head in lengths of the eye-ball.
>
> John Marshall to Edward Warren, 8 November 1893

The efforts of nineteenth-century archaeologists to put together a history of artists had a great deal in common with the way in which vases were received during the neo-classical aesthetic phase. As then, the necessary conditions for progress were in place, but not yet sufficiently developed; there was a need to push forward research into individual artists, the response to which would in the end, in the view of the art historian Lionello Venturi, prove to be the finest jewel in nineteenth-century art criticism.[1] The problem was, however, of a rather special nature in the case of vase-painting, since apart from a few names that were known through signatures, most of the painters remained anonymous. This explains why it was not possible for systematic research into vase-painters to begin until the last quarter of the nineteenth century.

In this chapter we shall give particular attention to three German-speaking archaeologists, Wilhelm Klein, Paul Hartwig, and Adolf Furtwängler. They may be regarded as Beazley's predecessors, and their works were all major landmarks in the process of identifying individual Attic vase-painters. All three belonged to the same generation; Klein was born in 1850, Furtwängler in 1853, and Hartwig in 1859.[2] They were interested in exploring the personalities of painters for a number of reasons; first, they saw pottery as the reflection of major Greek painting, all of which had been lost; second, they wanted to follow the example set by researchers into Greek

---

[1] Venturi (1936: 233).
[2] See Wolters (1925); Schiering (1988); A. E. Furtwängler (1990).

sculpture and Renaissance painting; and more generally, they were influenced by the classical aestheticism of the late nineteenth century.

THE BEGINNINGS OF RESEARCH BEFORE KLEIN

Following the massive discoveries of pottery in Italy, in particular during the Vulci excavations in 1828–9, archaeologists had methodically recorded the inscriptions they found on vases. In Eduard Gerhard's report on the Vulci Vases, for instance, he had carefully noted the signatures of their 'makers or designers'.[3] It was the discovery of Vulci, one of the largest archaic and classical necropolises in the ancient world, that provided most of the names of potters that were known in this early stage. Before that, hardly any were known apart from those of Alsimos, Taleides, and Asteas. As early as 1827, however, Julius Sillig, a modest teacher in Dresden, published a catalogue of the artists of antiquity in the form of an alphabetical dictionary, *Catalogus Artificum Graecorum et Romanorum*, which also included the names of potters that were known at that time. The book, which was translated into English in 1836, was dedicated to his master and friend Carl Böttiger, 'the prince of archaeologists', and author of *Griechische Vasengemälde*.[4] Sillig's use of Latin was rather anachronistic, considering that authors such as Böttiger and Winckelmann wrote in German, but it can be explained by the fact that the work has a philological slant, and that the author wanted to follow directly on from the first example of the genre, *De Pictura Veterum* by Franciscus Junius, the second edition of which was the first volume to contain a dictionary of this kind.[5]

Since Sillig's book was published just before the finds at Vulci, his list of artisan potters almost immediately became out-of-date. Subsequent lists by other archaeologists met the same inevitable fate; excavations regularly brought to light pieces bearing inscriptions, some by potters who were already known, others by new ones. A good example of these repeated updatings was the *Lettre à M. Schorn* from Raoul Rochette, the Curator of the Cabinet de Médailles et Antiques. This was first published in 1832 as an unofficial update of Sillig's book, and again in 1845, as part of a revised and expanded edition. What is interesting in Rochette's case is that during this time he was planning to write an 'Histoire générale de l'Art des anciens', in which the section on Greek pottery would have been 'one of the most important chapters'.[6]

In the end Rochette did not have time to see his project through, but Heinrich Brunn, a professor in Munich, took up the same idea in his monu-

---

[3] Gerhard (1831:67–83).   [4] Böttiger (1797–1800).
[5] Junius (1694); Sillig (1836: pp. x–xi).   [6] Rochette (1845:64).

mental *Geschichte der griechischen Künstler.*[7] Brunn's manual was notable for the fact that it was the first to deal extensively with painting and pottery as well as architecture and sculpture. The German archaeologist and philologist was, however, much more hesitant than Rochette over the status of vases. Indeed, he only included them in his book as documentary evidence of the evolution of taste: 'Taken as a whole and by virtue of their large numbers they are able to provide a fairly clear context for the evolution of artistic taste.'[8] He questioned the possibility of giving substance to every craftsman named in the inscriptions on vases, and also of carrying out a comprehensive classification of pottery according to external criteria. The problem in his view was that the signatures were too arbitrary, and that there were too many anonymous potters. Despite this, a number of archaeologists wrote monographs on vase-painters in the 1860s, notably Heinrich Heydemann and Ludwig Urlichs on 'Brygos', and Adolf Michaelis on Douris.[9]

WILHELM KLEIN AND THE SIGNATURES OF MASTERS

At this time it was hoped that the study of inscriptions, and especially signatures, would provide the basis for a satisfactory classification of pottery. The first stumbling-block was that signatures were rare, in addition to which it was hard to determine exactly what they meant. Klein summed up these problems in the introduction to his collection of signatures, *Die griechischen Vasen mit Meistersignaturen.*[10] He gave about a hundred names of painters and potters, taken from more than four hundred vases, and found that the different ways of signing came down to four types:

A master signs:

   (1) with ἐποίησεν only; ['made by Aristonophos']

   (2) with ἔγραψεν only; ['painted by Chares']

   (3) with one of the two forms, while a second signs with the other; that is to say:

      in (3*a*), when one signs with (1), and the other with (2): ['made by Nikosthenes and painted by Epiktetos']

      in (3*b*), the reverse;

      in (3*c*), when one signs with (1), and the other with (1) (there are no double signatures with (2)); ['made by Archikles and made by Glaukytes']

   (4) with both forms. ['painted and made by Exekias'][11]

Klein could not state with certainty why and in what conditions a vase was signed, but it must be said that his findings still hold more or less true today. A

---

[7] Brunn (1853–1859).   [8] Ibid. (i. 641); cited by Isler-Kerényi (1980: 11, n. 19).

[9] Heydemann (1866); Urlichs (1875); Michaelis (1874).

[10] Klein (1887: 1–26).   [11] Ibid. (11).

doubt remained as to how *epoiesen* should be interpreted. It was thought that this form on its own (1), which was the one used in the great majority of cases, had in fact taken on a double meaning in the archaic period, and that from then on it could denote both the painter and the potter. Two cases were known of signatures in which *epoiesen* was used twice (3c), the first stating 'made by Archikles and made by Glaukytes', and the second 'made by Nikosthenes and made by Anakles'. On the basis of this, Klein claimed that *epoiesen* could also denote the painter, but he then pursued a rather curious line of reasoning according to which these two examples showed that *epoiesen* in fact represented an abbreviated form of (4).[12] Since *epoiesen* was by far the most common form, appearing in 90 per cent of cases, Klein's interpretation of it was fraught with consequences. Clearly what underlay his thinking was a principle that for him was fundamental, the primacy of the painter's role over that of the potter ('der grösseren Wichtigkeit der Rolle des Malers gegenüber der des Töpfers').[13]

Klein's judgement was not entirely representative, however. Pottier, for example, took the opposite view of the meaning of *epoiesen*, which he regarded as nothing more than a stamp denoting a workshop.[14] Similarly, Furtwängler believed that there could be various painters hiding behind this general maker's trademark.[15] On another point Pottier and Furtwängler parted company; the German came closer to Klein when he claimed that the actual making of vases was of little significance and was entrusted to a lower-ranking workman.[16] As we can see from these differences of opinion, the problem was far from resolved. By the end of the century, however, the interpretation that tended to prevail was that *epoiesen* was the maker's trademark.

Camillo Praschniker, who succeeded Klein in the chair of archaeology at Prague University, noted that Klein was motivated in his research primarily by the desire to reveal the personalities of artists, 'to bring their individuality forth from the shadows'.[17] That in effect was the task he set himself from the time of his first book on *Euphronios*, which he had submitted as a thesis (Habilitationsschrift) in 1879 in Vienna, under the supervision of Otto Benndorf. In his book, Klein listed nine vases bearing the signature Euphronios. If we compare his list of these vases with Beazley's, we shall notice that only three of the nine are given by Beazley as named works. This is not to say that Beazley was necessarily right in all his attributions, but it should be noted that Klein included in his list a work by the Pistoxenos Painter, because it was signed Euphronios with the form *epoiesen*, even though there was an obvious

[12] Klein (1887: 14).   [13] Ibid. (6).   [14] Pottier (1902: 25–9).
[15] A. Furtwängler (1894: col. 144).   [16] Ibid. (col. 142); Pottier (1902: 28).
[17] Cited by Schiering (1988: 99).

difference in style between the two painters.[18] Perhaps because of this mechanical tendency to interpret the form *epoiesen* in every case as denoting the painter, Furtwängler considered that Klein's book succeeded only in defining the 'phantom of Euphronios'.[19] That was the opinion of a seasoned connoisseur, but nonetheless Klein's work represented a bold attempt to achieve an overall vision of the red-figured pottery of that period: 'Then Klein's "Euphronios" appeared,' wrote Michaelis. '[. . .] It was the first enlightened general view of the Pottery of Athens.'[20] And Percy Gardner considered that 'the scientific study of vases may be said to have begun with the publication of Klein's *Euphronios* in 1879, a book which for the first time gave an adequate criticism of style in red-figured vases'.[21]

The cast gallery

Klein was born into a middle-class family of German-Jewish businessmen, in Caransebes, a town in the Hungarian part of the Habsburg Empire (now Romania). He had particular feeling for art and artists, and had close ties throughout his career with the artists, musicians, and writers of his time. During his years as a *Privatdozent* in Vienna, he was friendly with musicians such as Anton Brückner and Hugo Wolf, and in Prague, where he moved in 1886, he was close to Max Brod, Kafka's friend and editor of his posthumous works. At one point his passionate interest in art led him to participate in the creation of a *Förderungsgesellschaft* (society for the promotion) of German art in Bohemia. He taught for thirty-seven years in Prague where, in several rooms in the Clementinum, he built one of the best collections of casts of the time; he even owned one for his own personal use. It was in this collection of casts that Klein's artistic nature was best able to find expression, 'when, with the help of sculptor friends, he strove to reconstruct the Greek original as it existed before it was spoiled by Roman copies'.[22]

Cast galleries such as Klein's played a crucial role in turning the interest of researchers towards the study of style. Andreas Furtwängler, the grandson of the great German archaeologist and son of the famous conductor, recalls that his grandfather's choice of career was determined not by his teachers or any scientific school of thought, but by the cast gallery at Leipzig University.[23] At that time it was not long since the need for cast galleries as aids to university teaching had been recognized, but they rapidly came to be regarded as indispensable, as the 'laboratories' of German archaeological science.[24] Friedrich Welcker and Otto Jahn were among the first to introduce the study of casts

---

[18] Klein (1886: no. 9 in his list); cf. Berlin 2282 in *ARV²* (859 no. 1).

[19] FR ii. 11. See Louvre cat. (1990).   [20] Cited by Schiering (1988: 98).

[21] Gardner (1926: 19).   [22] Schiering (1988: 99).

[23] A. E. Furtwängler (1990: 85).   [24] Michaelis (1908: 299).

into the degree course, as a means of teaching the subtle art of visual criticism. By the end of the century, cast galleries were to be found in all the main German cities, in the museums of Berlin and Dresden, and in the universities of Bonn, Munich, Strasbourg, and Leipzig.

Edmond Pottier became aware of the great educational value of these galleries when he went to Germany in 1887 to study the organization of collections of vases in public museums. In his report to Léon Heuzey on his visit to the Glyptothek in Munich, he said that 'in the cast museum we learned more in a few hours than we have learned from books in years. This is undoubtedly the great lacuna in our teaching of archaeology.'[25] He was therefore delighted when, in 1899, a cast museum was set up in Lyons by Maurice Holleaux. The following year a gold medal was awarded to the museum, and Pottier justified this by declaring that 'the jury wanted to present the museum to other universities as a model, and to set it decidedly apart from and above its competitors'.[26]

The cast gallery not only played a significant part in the way in which students were taught to perceive objects, but also testified to the stylistic bias of archaeological research in Germany.[27] Museums of this kind were created there very early in the nineteenth century (in some cases as early as the eighteenth), whereas most of those in England were set up in the last two decades of the nineteenth century. Oxford is an interesting example; it appears that at the end of the century the university's collection of casts was a great deal less well developed than those of other prestigious centres. In 1887, however, Percy Gardner took over the chair of Classical Archaeology and Art, and thanks to his efforts the situation improved considerably. Gardner stated at that time that the collection, comprising about 120 pieces, offered a good selection, but that it was 'too small to be really representative: it represents about a sixth of the Cambridge collection, a third of the South Kensington collection and a twentieth of the one in Berlin [which contained more than 2,000 objects]'.[28] By 1925, it had grown to the same size as the collection in Cambridge.

PAUL HARTWIG AND *DIE GRIECHISCHEN MEISTERSCHALEN*

We shall now return to vase-painters, and to an essential work on them, *Die griechischen Meisterschalen*, published in 1893 by Paul Hartwig. He originally intended to base his book on a personal collection of his own, consisting of a

---

[25] Letter to Heuzey (Vienna, 30 Oct. 1887); Paris, Institut de France, MS 5774.
[26] Cited by R. and F. Etienne (1990: 153).   [27] See Connor (1989).
[28] Cited by Boardman (1985: 47).

number of cups which he had procured in Rome during the winter of 1887–8. His research was then extended to other private collections, notably those of Alfred Bourguignon in Naples and Alphonse van Branteghem in Brussels, and eventually led to a global analysis of cups produced at the peak of the severe style in red-figured pottery. It was also Hartwig's aim to achieve the recognition of individual artists: 'Die Erkenntnis der Individualitäten der Vasenmaler war mein vornehmstes Bestreben' ('The recognition of individual vase-painters was my finest endeavour').[29] He also wanted, however, to give vase-painting a clearer identity of its own as opposed to major painting. And if these modest paintings were to be regarded as models, it was mainly in terms of what they could offer his contemporaries:

It is to the pure joy of beauty that the cups of the masters make their modest contribution. Every feature reproduced here comes from a Greek hand, and the artistic feeling of some of the Greek vase-painters deserves the gratitude of every age. Even if only a few artists draw benefit from my work I shall feel that I have been richly rewarded.[30]

His enthusiasm for vase-painting was unreserved, and he dismissed as fanciful the idea that major painting or sculpture had had any influence on vase-painting. This was not the only notable difference between his position and that of Klein, since Klein confined himself to analysing vases bearing signatures, whereas Hartwig's work resulted in a decisive step forward for the practice of attribution. Indeed, his judgements were based far more on stylistic analogy than on the study of inscriptions. He went further by creating anonymous personalities such as the 'der Meister mit dem Kahlkopfe' ('the Bald-headed Master') and 'der Meister mit der Ranke' ('the Tendril Master'). Hartwig justified this by using a paradox based on sound observation: 'Sometimes the most beautiful works by the masters of that time have come down to us without the names of their artists or any inscription, and the only painters who are clearly identifiable by the distinctive features of their style are ones who did not in fact sign their works.'[31]

The book thus moved away from the idea of a corpus of cup-painters in the 'Blütezeit' whose existence was attested with certainty by inscriptions, and looked instead at other artistic personalities who, although they did not sign their works, were still recognizable through close observation of their style. In view of this it is interesting to discover what became of 'der Meister mit der Ranke' and 'der Meister mit dem Kahlkopfe' in Beazley's lists. Hartwig named the first of these after one of the cups he procured in Rome in 1887. He saw the tendril motif on it as the mark of a distinct individual, and grouped eight cups around 'der Meister mit der Ranke', whom he took

---

[29] Hartwig (1893: p. viii).   [30] Ibid.   [31] Ibid. (p. v).

to be a pupil of Douris. Beazley preferred to regard these cups as late pieces by Douris himself, with the exception of one which he attributed to the Oedipus Painter, who was 'close to Douris' last period'. The stylistic definition of 'der Meister mit dem Kahlkopfe' was more unclear, judging at least by the standards of Beazley's analyses; the seven pieces that Hartwig attributed to his painter (six cups and one pelike) were divided in Beazley's lists between the Pistoxenos Painter, the Briseis Painter, an artist close to the Painter of Bologna 228, the Telephos Painter, Makron, and one of the early mannerists, unspecified.

These two examples clearly demonstrate the fundamentally empirical nature of connoisseurship. More important, however, was Hartwig's evident desire to show the particular style of the Attic cups of that period, in all the various stages of its development. To carry this out exhaustively he had no option but to create fictitious personalities, marked out solely by the stamp of style. Thus the project was launched to chart the evolution of Attic style, and to group around the principal painters others who had contributed to it in a secondary but nonetheless decisive way. This was the real importance of Hartwig's book, as Pottier noted in his review in the *Gazette des Beaux-Arts*.[32]

While saluting the innovative nature of Hartwig's work, Pottier expressed a number of reservations about his methods. He criticized him for being over-enthusiastic about vase-painting and for failing to give any analysis of the meaning of signatures. Hartwig, in the spirit of his time, spoke indiscriminately of the works of Brygos and Douris, without distinguishing between what was presumed to be the work of the potter or the painter. Where his predecessors normally felt it prudent to use the generic term 'workshop', Hartwig claimed to recognize the personal style of each painter, and for this he was reproached by Pottier.

One particularly important aspect of Hartwig's book where connoisseurs of vases were concerned was the care that was taken over the illustrations, and the fact that the reproductions were drawn on the scale of 1 : 1 with the original. 'There is one principle to which I have held firmly; it is that the plates of the vases should be life-size reproductions, since the relative size of the figures on the vases is a decisive factor in characterizing the personalities of the different painters.'[33]

Thus the size of the illustrations was ultimately dictated by the needs of connoisseurs. To keep to his plan, Hartwig had to employ several artists (the earliest of whom we know to have been the painter Ernst Eichler). This resulted in drawings of differing quality and appearance; some were simple

----

[32] Pottier (1902: 22–3).　　　　[33] Hartwig (1893: p. vii).

line-drawings, while others reproduced the black background on the cups. In the end Hartwig favoured the latter technique, and it was also the one which Furtwängler's collaborator, Karl Reichhold, used for their monumental joint publication of the masterpieces of Greek vase-painting.

Attribution and collecting

Before we discuss this publication, it is of some importance to note that unlike Klein, Hartwig was not a university academic. The son of a wealthy lawyer, he studied archaeology at the universities of Heidelberg, Munich, and Leipzig, then travelled throughout most of Europe, and in 1892 went to live in Rome as a *Privatgelehrter*.[34] He was very interested in contemporary art, and was responsible for the sumptuous publication of the mural decoration painted by Hans von Marées in the German Zoological Station in Naples.[35]

It was during his first visit to Rome in 1887 that Hartwig bought the little collection of Greek vases which gave rise to his *Meisterschalen*. He was later obliged for financial reasons to sell this collection to Johns Hopkins University in Baltimore. He then began to buy ancient works of art regularly, and to gain a foothold in the art trade, while at the same time continuing with work of a more scientific nature. His biographer, Paul Wolters, who was a professor in Munich and a colleague of Furtwängler's, noted certain striking features of his character: 'his interest in antiquity, as in culture generally, was mainly of an aesthetic, contemplative, almost sensual nature.'[36]

With his passion for collecting, Hartwig had formed a habit that is peculiar to those who suffer from 'collectionitis': the belief that he alone had the right to talk about a vase that he owned, even after he had parted with it. This sort of obsession might explain what is meant by the famous art historian Aby Warburg in a letter he wrote in 1903 to Adolf Goldschmidt, a medievalist specializing in ivories and manuscripts. Outlining the state of art history studies, Warburg condemns the enthusiasm of connoisseurs and 'attributionists':

they are professional admirers, desirous of protecting the peculiar characteristics of their hero either through delimitation or through extension in order to understand him as a logically coherent organism—Bayersdorfer, Bode, Morelli, Venturi, Berenson, and the whole nosey tribe . . .

These are hero-worshippers, but in their ultimate derivations they are only inspired by the temperament of a gourmand. The neutrally cool form of estimation happens to be the original form of enthusiasm peculiar to the propertied classes, the collector and his circle.[37]

---

[34] See Wolters (1925). [35] Hartwig (1909).
[36] Wolters (1925: p. iii). [37] Cited by Gombrich (1970: 142–3).

Clearly this letter bears the hallmark of Warburg's hostility towards connoisseurs of every kind; nonetheless it is of interest for the fact that he makes a link between attribution and collecting. This seems reasonable enough, since it is obvious that connoisseurs were almost bound to be collectors as well. What is not so certain is that this was also bound to lead to the intrusion of commerce into the world of scholarship. In Hartwig's case, the confusion stemmed from the fact that he himself never admitted to being a dealer. There are strong reasons to suspect that he compromised himself seriously at least once in the sale of an ancient object, the faked dish of Nephele. The episode is related in detail by Arvid Andrén (born in 1902), the former director of the Swedish Institute of Classical Studies in Rome, who mentions this transaction in a recent instructive study of the trade in ancient works of art.

One of Helbig's colleagues in Rome, the German archaeologist Paul Hartwig, expert in Greek vase painting, had certified the authenticity of the dish; but Furtwängler was able to establish the fact, on basis of a close examination, that the dish itself is certainly genuine, while the white ground, the four figures, their names and the 'signature' show every sign of being a clever forgery. This is also suggested by the fact that one side of the dish has been broken into small pieces, while the central part with the figures is almost intact.

The person who designed and named these figures must have been thoroughly acquainted with Greek mythology and vase painting, the one who executed them had a sure hand guided by a keen eye. There is no proof of who perpetrated this forgery; but the fact that Hartwig had commercial interests in common with Martinetti and, with his special expertness, vouched for the authenticity of the faked dish, suggests that he may have had a hand in this fraud.[38]

It should be pointed out that the German archaeologist Friedrich Hauser, a close friend of Hartwig's, was also a *Privatgelehrter* in Rome. But as in Hartwig's case, this label was a mask for a more lucrative professional occupation, that of connoisseur-dealer. Ludwig Pollak (1893–1943) mentions several times in his memoirs that Hauser was for several years the agent of Edward Warren, the wealthy American collector.[39] It is even known that Warren took the unusual step of paying Hauser an annual income for letting his sponsor know of interesting pieces that came onto the market, and for acting as his agent.[40] That Warren should have agreed to pay Hauser an annual income for a given period is an indication of the German archaeologist's exceptional gifts, to which Ludwig Curtius bore witness; he considered Hauser to be the best connoisseur of ancient art he had ever met.[41]

[38] Andrén (1986: 94–5).

[39] 'Hauser wurde Vertrauensmann von Warren, für den er einige Jahre hindurch Ankäufe vermittelte': Pollak (1994: 98).

[40] Burdett and Goddard (1941: 240–41).   [41] Cited by Fuchs (1988: 132).

Edward Warren and the Museum of Fine Arts in Boston

In many respects it is impossible to form an accurate picture of the relationships that existed at the turn of the century between the ancient art market, collectors, museums, and archaeologist-connoisseurs unless we fully understand the role played by Edward Warren at that time. Warren came from a family of wealthy industrialists, and had received, first at Harvard and then at Oxford, the education that befitted a distinguished young Bostonian. On his father's death in 1888, Warren inherited a colossal fortune, and this enabled him to acquire a large country residence in England, Lewes House in Sussex, where he lived in the tradition of the great English aristocracy.[42] He rapidly became an exceptional collector; his main interest was in ancient art, but he also owned works by Rodin, including a copy of *The Kiss* which is now in the Tate Gallery of Modern Art in London. In the first biography of Warren (to which Beazley contributed by writing the chapter on his activities as a collector and connoisseur), it became clear beyond doubt that it was he who had established the nucleus of the ancient section of the Museum of Fine Arts in Boston, founded in 1870.[43] Lacey Caskey's catalogue of the sculpture in the Boston museum (1925) did indeed show that of the 136 pieces in this section, all but twenty-six had come to the museum through Warren. The agreement between Warren and the museum stated that he would charge the cost price of his purchases, plus an additional 30 per cent to cover his expenses. Given the extensive network that Warren had set up in order to control the ancient art market, this agreement must certainly have left him out of pocket. Nevertheless the contract worked well during Warren's great collecting period, which stretches over roughly ten years, starting with the sale in Paris of the Branteghem collection in May 1892. Warren's method consisted of encouraging young men with degrees from the great universities, who in his view possessed the qualities of the true connoisseur, to act as 'scouts' on his behalf while they were travelling abroad to further their education.[44]

Warren's natural taste was for sculpture, and above all for ancient gems. He began by buying Count Tyszkiewicz's collection, and gradually developed a genuine passion for these objects; interestingly it was Beazley who compiled the catalogue of his collection.[45] As far as vases were concerned, it was John Marshall, an intimate friend of Warren's, who persuaded him to collect this other type of object. Born in Liverpool, Marshall studied at Oxford, where he was intending to enter the priesthood when he met Ned Warren, and developed a passion both for him and for antiquity. Not without much hesitation,

---

[42] See Sox (1991).   [43] Beazley, in Burdett and Goddard (1941: 331–63).

[44] Simpson (1987: 57).

[45] Beazley (1920); the Boston Museum bought the collection in 1928.

he abandoned a brilliant university career to enter Warren's service and assist
him in his activities as a connoisseur, archaeologist, and collector. When they
officially parted, Marshall worked on his own account for the Metropolitan
Museum in New York.[46]

At first the trustees of the Boston museum showed very little enthusiasm
for vases. This emerges clearly in a letter from Warren to his mother, written
a few months after the sale of the Branteghem collection, in which he
explains the importance of vases to her so that she can plead his cause to the
Bostonians. Painted pottery, says Warren, highlights the best phases of Greek
art, certain vases are true works of art in their own right, while the majority
provide information that adds to our knowledge of ancient Greece, and
in many cases are in fact the only sources of that information.[47] One of
the famous vases which ended up in the Boston museum was the krater
with Acteon on one side and Pan on the other; it was this piece that gave
his name to the Pan Painter created by Beazley.[48] Beazley's relationship with
the Boston museum was of considerable importance; starting in 1924 he,
along with Lacey Caskey, the Curator of the Department of Antiquities,
published the masterpieces of the Attic vases section of the museum.[49]
The luxurious presentation of this publication was very much in the spirit
of the work produced jointly by Furtwängler and Reichhold, to which we
must now return.

FURTWÄNGLER *EPOIESEN*, REICHHOLD *EGRAPHSEN*

At the turn of the century, the interest in masterpieces and detailed descriptions of them culminated in the monumental work (one large folio volume
for the plates, another in normal folio for the text) by Furtwängler and
Reichhold on Greek vase-painting, *Griechische Vasenmalerei*, which was published over a period of twenty-eight years. Originally it was only intended to
consist of a series of six fascicles, each accompanied by ten plates; these began
to come out in 1900 and made up a volume which was published four years
later. Unlike Hartwig's book, the project was aimed at a fairly wide public.
In view of its success, the authors decided to publish other fascicles, and
two more volumes appeared, one in 1909 and the other in 1932. After
Furtwängler's premature death in 1907, Hauser took over from him, but
the text relating to forty of the plates in the second series was by
Furtwängler; Ernst Buschor, Carl Watzinger, and Robert Zahn collaborated
on the third volume.[50] The work did follow Hartwig's example by devoting

[46] See Burdett and Goddard (1941: chap. 6); Sox (1991: pt. 4).
[47] Burdett and Goddard (1941: 151–2).   [48] Beazley (1912*a*).
[49] Beazley and Caskey (1931–63).   [50] A. Furtwängler, Reichhold *et al.* (1904–32).

a great deal of space to illustrations; these were printed in separate volumes, and the reproductions were life-size. Reichhold, who produced 180 of the plates, was a remarkable artist who had developed a special technique for copying the painted images on the vases. He reproduced the black background of the paintings (in the case of red-figured vases), so that in many cases they looked like real pictures.[51] After more than a century, the care that was taken over the illustrations was reminiscent of the monumental Hamilton catalogue; this time, however, the aims and methods of the work were very different. Unlike the 'beautiful and unfaithful' drawings of the Hamilton catalogue, Reichhold's sought to reproduce the originals as faithfully as possible. Edmond Pottier found them 'a little heavy and cold', but Beazley sometimes made great efforts to achieve the meticulous line of Reichhold's drawings. For normal use, however, he always preferred simple line-drawing. This was because the contours of the figures in vase-paintings are often indicated by means of a boundary line, sometimes broken, sometimes not, which appears in low relief if one examines the drawing closely. The disadvantage of showing the black background is that it masks this line, which is very important in the expert evaluation of vases. Thus Beazley's choice of technique was in response to the needs of the connoisseur rather than those of the artist.

Reichhold worked jointly on *Griechische Vasenmalerei* with Adolf Furtwängler, the initiator of the project. Furtwängler, who was the pupil and successor of Brunn at Munich University, had a remarkable visual memory and capacity for work which made him the natural leader of a new trend towards the study of style and significant detail. His book on vase-painting did not include an introduction explaining the ins and outs of the project, but in his catalogue of the vases in the Berlin museum, he had announced his intention of publishing in the near future a manual on Greek vase-painting, in which he could provide 'a scientific basis' for his stylistic observations, by means of individual descriptions.[52] The clearest statements of his ideas about art history can be found in his most famous book on sculpture, *Meisterwerke der griechischen Plastik*. This detour via sculpture may to some extent explain his theory of a science of pottery.[53]

Furtwängler had discovered a method whereby he believed he could relate anonymous works to ancient texts. He worked on the assumption that the more or less recent copies conserved in museums were intended to reproduce as faithfully as possible, for the Roman public, the classical masterpieces of Greek art, in other words those which were mentioned in ancient texts by authors such as Pausanias and Pliny. To reconstruct a history of artists

---

[51] See Reichhold (1919); Ohly (1975).   [52] A. Furtwängler (1885: vol. i, p. v).
[53] A. Furtwängler (1893).

on the basis of scattered fragments was a connoisseur's job if ever there was
one, and it was more than a little paradoxical; why study the work of these
artists when everyone knew that virtually none of it remained? Furtwängler
explained:

It is among these copies that we must look for the masterpieces mentioned by the
authors, the statues which made a mark on their time or were ahead of it. If we had
only copies of the noble creations of a Raphael, a Michelangelo or a Rembrandt, it
would still be preferable to study them rather than the multitude of other original
works of their time.[54]

His attitude was in the tradition of the philological and stylistic interpretation of art, for which Heinrich Brunn had prepared the ground, and the
method he used for his project was directly inspired by textual criticism.
Conscious that where Greek sculpture was concerned he was dealing for the
most part with copies from the Roman era, he took the works of Pliny and
Pausanias as a basis for establishing a lost archetype which would take account
of all the known variants. In many cases it may have seemed over-audacious
to take existing pieces in museums that were thought to be copies, and
attribute them to famous artists in the sense that they were supposed to be
more or less exact replicas of their original works. Furtwängler justified this
by a statement which underlies his whole conception of the development of
art history:

No doubt some will object that it is too soon to enquire into the different individual
artists, when we still know so little about the main issue of the development of
particular forms. However, the study of these forms [. . .] is inseparable from, in fact
identical to, the investigation of the individuals to whom we owe precisely this or
that particular development of form.[55]

The Lemnia's *ear*

We shall now look briefly at an attribution that was famous in its time,
the Athena Lemnia by Phidias; this was made by Furtwängler in his book
on sculpture. It divided archaeologists into two camps, and at the same time
brought the issue of connoisseurship to the fore, since there was no previously
known instance of sculpture in the round by this famous sculptor.[56] Our intention is not, however, to examine the validity of the attribution, but to show
that Furtwängler resorted here to the type of argumentation that had been
popularized by the Morellian method, one which involved elements of
both pathological anatomy and graphology, as we shall see in Chapter 3.

---

[54] A. Furtwängler (1893: p. ix).   [55] Ibid. (p. xi).
[56] See Hartswick (1983); Protzmann (1984); Palagia (1987).

Furtwängler claimed that it was possible to identify the marble copy of Phidias' bronze statue, the Athena Lemnia, by associating a head in Bologna with a statue in Dresden. His two main literary sources for this were Pausanias (1. 28. 2) and, more important, Lucian.[57] In this case the identification of the object went hand in hand with its attribution, and it is interesting to note how the descriptions given by these two authors could still trigger off the search for an ideal physiognomy, in terms of the contours of the face, the delicacy of the cheeks, and the fine proportions of the nose: 'Seen from the front, the face forms a regular, elongated oval corresponding to the cranium. The forehead, cheekbones and chin are not prominent, but are joined by delicately curved lines. That is what Lucian means when he praises the Lemnia and adopts these features as an ideal of beauty.'[58] This quasi-physiognomical definition was also based on considerations of a stylistic nature, and in the passage that followed Furtwängler unquestionably used arguments of the Morellian type:

The Lemnia's ears merit special attention; they are finely worked, and the hair only just touches them at the upper edge. The ear is tiny, with a long, narrow lobule which is clearly differentiated from the upper cartilage. Copies of the Parthenos head, insofar as they permit a comparison, seem to have similar ears; we can therefore conclude that this form was the one preferred by Phidias. This is interesting, because on the Attic monuments of the Periclean epoch we find a broader, shorter type of ear, with a wide socket and a short lobe; in this type, the distance between the end of the lobe and the upper edge of the socket is normally very small, and certainly not larger than the total width of the ear.[59]

Adolf Michaelis and Salomon Reinach were in no doubt that Furtwängler had been influenced by Morelli where method was concerned.[60] In essence his theories represented a consistent effort to reconstruct a history of sculpture based on the most notable individual artists, and it is here that we can draw a parallel with his book on Greek vase-painting. The visual and philological method which he developed for sculpture may not have been the same as the one he used for vases, but by applying attributionism to pottery as well as sculpture he showed that he had a similar notion in both fields of what the history of art should be, that is to say the history of the best artists, those who had left their mark on their age. We can see from the subtitle he gave to *Griechische Vasenmalerei* ('A selection of the finest painted vases'), that he wanted to show the development of Greek and Italiote pottery from the beginning of the sixth to the fourth century BC, by giving a selection of the finest pieces conserved in the museums of Europe (at least a quarter of them in the Munich collections).

[57] Pausanias (1918: 1. 28. 2); Lucian (1925: 267).   [58] A. Furtwängler (1893: 29).
[59] Ibid. (31).   [60] Reinach (1907: 310).

On the question of how much creative ability could be ascribed to the craftsman potters, Furtwängler did not go nearly as far as Hartwig. In his opinion, vase-painting drew directly on the model of major painting; the drawings on vases were copies, sometimes freely adapted from superior models, but copies all the same. This view was very much in keeping with his desire in his archaeological research to reconcile knowledge gained from books and analysis of painted objects themselves, and it also explains his policy of providing illustrations resembling real paintings. To sum up Furtwängler's contribution we can do no better than to quote a statement of Pottier's, in which he gave a fairly clear idea of how vase-painting was seen in official circles at the turn of the century:

Its main importance is that it restores to us the evolution of a body of painting which has disappeared for ever in the original, but which lives on in the mark that it left on secondary works, in the same way as a star which is invisible to the most powerful instruments betrays its presence by the attraction it exerts over other celestial bodies.[61]

Although there was an appreciable disparity between their aims, Hartwig and Furtwängler opened up a field of essentially visual and empirical type of research, the aim of which was the discovery of individual artists. The main difference between this and the method which since the time of Otto Jahn had been the model for the study of pottery was that the signature was no longer seen as an adequate basis for judgement; it needed to be supplemented by the study of style. In this respect we can draw a fairly clear dividing-line between, on the one hand, archaeologists such as Klein and Pottier who still believed that vases should be classified according to inscriptions, and on the other, Hartwig and Furtwängler, whose emphasis on the notion of individual style paved the way for someone like Beazley. The idea of attributions to *Meister mit Notnamen* (names of convenience) was further encouraged by the example set by art historians researching into the painting of the Northern Schools, where the extreme rarity of documents led to this type of attribution.[62] This approach was widely followed in the first half of the century by men such as Ernst Langlotz, Ernst Buschor, and Andreas Rumpf. It was therefore no coincidence that when John Beazley, the master of attributions in the twentieth century, brought out his first exhaustive work on the red-figured style of Attic vase-painting, he, at the instigation of Bernard Schweitzer, a professor at Königsberg University, and like Morelli before him, published it in German.[63]

---

[61] Pottier (1906: 445).   [62] Reynaud (1978).   [63] Beazley (1925).

Two Works by Pottier

THE LOUVRE'S *CATALOGUE OF ANCIENT VASES*
AND HIS CONTRIBUTION TO
'DAREMBERG AND SAGLIO'

'The consequences of war,' he said, 'are never-ending. I learn in a letter from my excellent friend William Harrison that French science has been despised in England since 1871, and that the Universities of Oxford, Cambridge, and Dublin affect to know nothing of the manual of archaeology by Maurice Raynouard, even though it is likely to be of more use to students than any other work of its kind. However no one wants to take lessons from the vanquished. And if anyone is to listen to a professor on the subject of the characteristics of Aeginetan art or the origins of Greek pottery, he must belong to a nation which excels in making cannons. Because Maréchal de Mac-Mahon was beaten at Sedan in 1870, and General Chanzy lost his army in Maine in the same year, my colleague Maurice Raynouard is being turned away from Oxford in 1897. Such are the slow, roundabout and inevitable repercussions of military inferiority. It is only too true that the fate of the Muses depends on the grimacing face of war.'

Anatole France, *Le Mannequin d'osier* (1897)

We shall now leave aside the study of individual artists for the time being, and turn our attention to two other aspects of research at the end of the nineteenth century: the museum catalogue and the encyclopaedic dictionary of classical antiquity. This departure from our main theme will enable us to present the figure of Pottier, and his principal contributions to the science of vases in the period roughly speaking prior to Beazley's work. This preliminary insight into Pottier's scientific orientation will also be a useful preparation for our examination in Chapter 6 of the way in which Beazley's work was received in France.

Our study of this topic will highlight the influence of German archaeology and science in the period following the Franco-Prussian war in 1870. Owing to the nationalism which sprang up as a result of France's defeat, the reaction of the French to this German influence was far from straightforward.

It was commonly felt that Germany owed its victory largely to the quality
of its science and education, and from that time on, many writers and men
of science in France were to show a marked concern for the influence of
thought on the running of the country.[1] Pottier was receptive to this way
of thinking, even with regard to archaeology. In the unpublished report
which he wrote in 1888 on his scientific mission to Germany and Austria he
made it very clear that museum collections had a vital role to play in France's
attempt to compete with Germany for intellectual prestige. The case of
'Daremberg and Saglio' was even more striking owing to its value as a collective enterprise. It was planned in the 1850s, but did not really begin to be
published until after the 1870 war. It then employed several generations of
researchers until soon after the First World War, and on its completion was
saluted by the chief collaborators (one of the foremost of whom was Pottier)
as a just reward for the concerted efforts of French science.

THE KEEPER OF ANTIQUITIES

Edmond Pottier was born on 13 August 1855 in Saarbrücken in the Prussian
Rhineland, to Ferdinand Pottier, a civil engineer, and his wife Anne (née
Servier). He can be regarded as a model product of the social and intellectual
advancement of a middle-class family in the nineteenth century. His paternal
grandfather was a Post Office clerk, while his father held a diploma from
the École Centrale des Arts et Manufactures. His father had been a founder
member in 1848 of the Société des Ingénieurs Civils, and had gone to Saarbrücken to work as a mechanical and electrical engineer for the Eastern
Railways. Three years after Edmond's birth his parents moved to Passy, which
at that time was a town in its own right just outside Paris.

   Edmond Pottier described himself as 'a man of the middle class' in *La Pensée libre*, a fascinating book for those interested in exploring the attitudes of
a representative of the secular, scientistic freethinking which was mainstream
under the Third Republic in the 1880s.[2] Along with the founding of the
Republic, or rather its progressive consolidation, the most significant event
for Pottier's generation was undoubtedly France's defeat in the war of 1870.
An interesting example of the sentimental patriotism that resulted from it
can be found in a French speech with which Pottier won first prize in the
Concours Général (a competitive examination for secondary schools), thus
crowning a brilliant school career at the Lycée Condorcet. The subject of
the competition (Charles V's speech after the death of Jean le Bon) could be

[1] See Digeon (1959).
[2] Pottier (1918: 7). The records at the library of the Maison du Grand Orient de France do not show
whether Pottier, like many other freethinkers, was also a freemason; see Lalouette (1997: 18).

related more or less directly to France's position at the end of the war, and Pottier clearly jumped at the opportunity:

There are better days ahead, believe me; as France recaptures her military glory, she will add to the power of her arms the benefits of civilization, and as she takes up the pursuit of her glorious destiny once more, she will offer the world the admirable spectacle of a nation lifted up by itself and by its king. With the help of God I shall succeed in my task; for the moment it is my labour; one day it will be my glory.[3]

Pottier had a prestigious career as a student of the arts: after three years of study at the École Normale Supérieure in rue d'Ulm (1874–7), he took fourth place in the *agrégation de lettres*, and went on to study at the École d'Athènes (1877–80).[4] There were fewer archaeologists studying ancient Greece at that time than now, and they formed a homogeneous group of academics and museum experts. Almost all of them were products of the École Normale ('normaliens') and the École d'Athènes ('Athéniens'), such as Albert Dumont, and two other intellectual leaders of Pottier's generation, Georges Perrot and Léon Heuzey. Pottier openly paid tribute to Heuzey and Dumont:

I have had the good fortune in my life to meet two men united by sure bonds of friendship, and also by remarkable similarities of profession, taste and character: Albert Dumont and Léon Heuzey. I am delighted to bring them together once more by remembering with the same affection and gratitude these two masters who had a decisive influence on me and determined the direction of my whole career.[5]

Albert Dumont was a good example of the vocation inspired by the events of 1870, and he in his turn inspired many of the Athéniens who crossed his path: so much so that the 'Dumont-worshippers' (Théophile Homolle, Paul Girard, Jules Martha, Edmond Pottier, and several others) were nicknamed 'Mamelukes'.[6] After 1870, when he published a thesis in French on the chronology of the Athenian archons, Dumont devoted most of his scientific activity to the cause of national regeneration through the creation of competitive institutions and the modernization of teaching methods. 'Germany has at least twenty-two chairs set aside for this teaching [archaeological], we in France have two. Wherever the Greek and Roman plastic arts are studied, there is a cast museum. Every university has one of its own, and they all have catalogues which are the simplest and most reliable histories of art.'[7]

Dumont was also responsible in 1875 for setting up the École Française in Rome, which at first was conceived as just an offshoot of the École

---

[3] Pottier (1872: 59); cited by Cagnat (1935: 5).
[4] On the ÉNS: Duchêne (ed.) (1994); Sirinelli (1994). On the ÉFA: ÉFA (1996).
[5] Pottier (1922*a*: 331); see Carbonell (1976: 134–43).
[6] Radet (1901: 200).   [7] Dumont (1874: 774).

d'Athènes. It can safely be assumed that this new school was felt to be urgently necessary as soon as the Instituto di Corrispondenza Archeologica (founded in Rome in 1829) came under the direct control of the Royal Academy of Science in Berlin, following an edict from King Wilhelm I of Prussia on 2 March 1871. Since its foundation this Institute had been international, but it now became an exclusively national and in 1874 imperial establishment, while at the same time a German Institute was also being created in Athens. Political events could have a direct effect on the foundation and organization of foreign archaeological institutions; this was also true of Dumont's reforms at the École d'Athènes, which, founded in 1846, was the first institute to have been set up in that city. During his time as director of the École (1875–8), Dumont set up the Institut de Correspondance Hellénique, the collection of the 'Bibliothèque des Écoles françaises d'Athènes et de Rome', and the *Bulletin de correspondance hellénique*, which is still the official organ of the École today. These reforms, as well as those that he made of the teaching there by giving priority to technical studies, were clearly intended to counteract the influence of the newly created German Institute.[8]

At the end of his time in Athens, Pottier, along with Salomon Reinach, was given the job of excavating the necropolis at Myrina on the coast of Asia Minor, near Smyrna (1880–2). There he discovered hundreds of terracotta figurines from the late Hellenistic period, which rivalled the finds of Tanagra in Boeotia, and were to prove an outstanding addition to the collections at the Louvre. At the same time as these excavations were going on he taught as a senior lecturer in Greek language and literature at the Faculté des Lettres in Rennes and then in Toulouse. In 1883 he submitted his two theses, one in French and one in Latin; the first was on Attic white lekythoi, the other on terracotta pieces found in tombs.

The beginning of 1884 marked a turning-point; Pottier left higher education, went to the Louvre as an independent assistant, and stood in for Léon Heuzey at the École des Beaux-Arts as a lecturer in archaeology and history of art.[9] It was not until two years later that he was made a salaried assistant, and that appointment coincided with a reorganization of the departments. On 20 August 1881, to mark Heuzey's appointment as curator, a department of Oriental antiquities had been created by separating it from the main department of antiquities. On 30 January 1886 the ancient pottery section was removed in its turn and joined to the Department of Oriental Antiquities. This arrangement, far from being insignificant from a scientific point of view, lasted until 1924, when Pottier asked to retire so that he could devote all his energies to the *Corpus Vasorum Antiquorum*.

---

[8] Radet (1901: 191).   [9] Merlin (1934).

Nor was it immaterial that Pottier should have been in charge of the ancient pottery in an institution such as the Louvre, since the acceptance of vases into a prestigious museum was likely to confirm their status in the eyes of society as a whole.[10] This would explain the failure of a plan to set up a technical museum for pottery, following the purchase by France in 1861 of the collection of Marchese Campana, the greatest collector of the time.[11] The arrival in France of thousands of vases provoked a debate as to where they should be housed. Opinion was divided between those who favoured setting up a technical museum modelled on London's Victoria and Albert Museum, and others who claimed the collections for the Louvre. Feelings ran so high that the debate about where the vases should go actually caused deep rifts between various coteries in the world of fashionable society and politics surrounding the emperor. The stakes were too high; the second group prevailed, although a Napoleon III museum did exist for a time in the Palais de l'Industrie. Pottier's opinion on this affair suggested a certain self-interest, although it may be felt that he was bound to side with the Louvre given the position he held there: 'Nor should we regret that we have been asked to give these works of art a home that is worthy of them, and that this wish has been carried out in princely fashion, since the luxurious nature of the installation has helped to accentuate the importance of the whole collection.'[12]

THE LOUVRE'S *CATALOGUE DES VASES ANTIQUES*

One of the best ways to 'accentuate the importance of the whole collection', as well as the 'works of art' that formed part of it, was to compile a *catalogue raisonné* of vases. The plan for such a catalogue probably went back to the purchase of the Campana collection, since Wilhelm Fröhner, a somewhat eccentric German and a member of Napoleon III's intimate circle who read aloud to the emperor, was engaged in 1862 to write the notes on the Greek vases in the collection.[13] Fröhner had time to compile a catalogue of *Inscriptions grecques*, as well as a *Notice de la sculpture antique*, but the war of 1870 put an end to his career at the Louvre, and for the time being to the idea of the catalogue. After a delay of about fifteen years, Pottier's arrival meant a new start for the project, this time on a much more secure basis. In October and November 1887 Pottier travelled to Germany and Austria to study the organization of collections of ancient vases in the public collections there. On his return, he wrote an extensive report on this mission, which remained unpublished even though a public official suggested that it should be published in the *Journal*

[10] Schnapp (1985: 72–3).
[11] Nadalini (1993); H. and A. Borowitz (1991).
[12] Pottier (1894: 223).   [13] Hellmann (1992: 252).

officiel, and that there should be an offprint of a thousand copies for distribution to the Chamber of Deputies and the Senate.[14] The official justified his request by referring to the interest that had been aroused the previous year by a report by Frédéric Montargis (one of Pottier's fellow-students at the École Normale Supérieure) on the organization of the teaching of aesthetics and art history in Germany.[15] Pottier's report was not published, perhaps because documents of the same type were already available, notably Olivier Rayet's report on the comparative state of European collections, which was inserted after the report of the budget commission written by Antoine Proust for the fiscal year 1887.[16] In any case, these documents testify to the lively interest in national collections that existed at the time.

What the official who recommended Pottier's report for publication must have recognized was that, although he did not shy away from mentioning 'the regrettable inferiority of our acquisition budgets', 'the gaps in our current catalogues', and 'the absence of cast museums', his tone was resolutely optimistic. The same was true of a letter he wrote to Heuzey:

All in all, we in France greatly exaggerate the lead that other countries may have over us in these matters. The vase museum in Munich is not even classified and they have made no progress since the days of O. Jahn. Unpublished material is just as common there as it is here. [. . .]

I do not believe that any museum in Germany can offer a whole body of work and catalogues on a collection of terracotta to compare with ours. As for the vases, we have a gap which can rapidly be filled by a brief catalogue, and our classification is done. In sum, people abroad are noticing how harshly we denigrate ourselves, and how much harm it is doing. We are so good at repeating that we have achieved nothing and that other countries are ahead of us in everything that we would end up believing it ourselves if we did not go and make the comparison on the spot. I can see no serious gap except in our lack of the cast museums which are so widespread and valuable in Germany.[17]

The *Catalogue des vases antiques* finally started to be published in 1896, and it was not as brief as Pottier had given to understand it would be in his letter, since it ran to three volumes.[18] It consisted of a *catalogue raisonné* and a historical section, each of which depended on the other; the historical part was vital to an understanding of the strictly descriptive part, and the whole work was intended to serve as a manual of the history of painting and drawing in

[14] Pottier's unpublished report on an archaeological mission (1887) to study museums in Germany and Austria (Munich, Vienna, Dresden and Berlin); Louvre: Department of Etruscan, Greek, and Roman Antiquities. Cf. letter to the administration (Paris, 29 July 1888); Paris, Archives Nationales, F²¹ 4437.

[15] Montargis (1887).

[16] Rayet (1887); cf. Paris, Archives Nationales, F²¹ 4007ᴮ.

[17] Letter to Heuzey (Vienna, 30 Oct. 1887); Paris, Institut de France, MS 5774.

[18] Pottier (1896–1906).

the ancient world. The classification system was both geographical and chronological; the origins of vases were dealt with in the first volume, then Ionia, and finally Attica. In the third volume, which was devoted to Attic pottery, vases were grouped according to style and schools. This was based on a fairly vague principle, and went no further than the establishment of broad groupings by workshops and chronological series. The classification was based on vases bearing signatures or the names of ephebes, but there were also anonymous vases which were fitted in with the others on grounds of style. With the catalogue in mind, Pottier had carried out a comprehensive reorganization of the Campana gallery, so that the alphabetical divisions would correspond to those given in the work, which also served as a basis for the numbering system of the general list of vases.

The geographical order of origin

To understand what was original about Pottier's catalogue, we need to go back in time. In the first half of the nineteenth century sales catalogues were normally ordered thematically. The change to a geographical order, according to origin and/or region of production, represented an important new departure in the cataloguing of vases. The decisive impetus for this had been given in the middle of the century by Otto Jahn in his catalogue of King Ludwig I of Bavaria's collection in Munich. Jahn expressly recommended to archaeologists that they should carefully note the origin of vases at the time of discovery, instead of inventing it as many of his predecessors had done:

In general they did no more than indicate certain differences of style, describing beautiful black gloss pottery as *Nolan*, free style vases as *Apulian*, those in a rather crude style with pale colours and a matt finish as *vases of the Basilicate*, and black-figured vases as *Sicilian*, and they believed that they were authorized to draw conclusions from these criteria as to the origin of the vases, which was only precisely recorded and indicated in exceptional cases.[19]

Although Jahn himself may not always have been in a position to indicate origin, the principle had now been established. The place of discovery was not necessarily the same as the centre of production, but it was normally a good geographical indicator. Since Jahn could not rely on indications of origin, it was even more difficult for him to build up a framework of geographical reference. Furthermore, as Dietrich von Bothmer points out, Jahn did not have an official position at the museum in Munich, and must therefore have had to come to terms with the random way in which vases were presented in

[19] Jahn (1854); cited by Reinach (1891: 10 n. 2).

Leo von Klenze's Alte Pinakothek when he visited the museum in September and October 1853.[20]

Despite its faults, Salomon Reinach considered Jahn's book to be 'the model for all *catalogues raisonnés* that have been published since', in particular those of St Petersburg, Naples, and Berlin, and of course the British Museum and the Louvre.[21] Since centres of production could not be identified as a matter of course, the way in which these catalogues were organized is a good indicator of the problems that arose and the progress that was achieved in the classification of pottery.

Heinrich Heydemann's catalogue of the Naples museum was divided into three parts corresponding to the history of the collections. The first part dealt with the old Bourbon Museum, the second with the Santangelo collection, and the third with vases from Cumae.[22] Heydemann was in a similar position to that of Jahn, and as a result did no more than describe the content of the exhibition rooms. Ludolf Stephani, on the other hand, was part of the curatorial team at the Hermitage Museum, and had probably carried out a partial reorganization of the collections there in preparation for the catalogue, which was published three years earlier than the Naples one.[23] The description of the five exhibition rooms dealt in turn with the most ancient vases, vases from Cumae, black-figured vases, Nolan vases, and the antiquities of the Bosphorus. It should be noted that in the middle of the century the British Museum curators, Samuel Birch and Charles Newton, had taken a bolder approach by adopting broad geographical and chronological divisions for their catalogue.[24]

The real breakthrough came, however, with Adolf Furtwängler's catalogue of the Berlin museum; here, for the first time, was an example of how a large collection (more than 4,000 vases) could be classified by a system which took into account the technique, region of production, date, and shape of the vases.[25] This meant that the vases had to be attributed to their respective centres of production, and also that the collections needed to be organized according to the same geographical system. Within the subdivisions corresponding to the regions of production, Furtwängler did not merely classify vases by shape and type of ornamentation, he also grouped certain vases according to the stylistic affinity that he was able to recognize between them. This ability to distinguish the hands of different painters, including those of

[20] Bothmer (1987: 193–5).   [21] Reinach (1891: p. ix n. 2).

[22] Heydemann (1872).   [23] Stephani (1869).

[24] Birch and Newton (1851–70), vol. 1 (1851). Divisions are as follows: 'Early Italian ware'; 'Black Etruscan ware'; 'Red Etruscan ware'; 'Miscellaneous varnished ware mostly of the early period'; 'Italian vases of archaic Greek style'; 'Vases of transition style'; 'Vases of finest Greek style'; 'Black vases of the best period of fictile art'.

[25] A. Furtwängler (1885).

unsigned vases, and to group them accordingly, opened up a new museographical approach, which was also evidence of the new trends in the study of pottery which were examined in the previous chapter.[26]

In his catalogue, Pottier congratulated himself on the progress that had been made in grouping pottery; for him, this was 'the most pleasing result of modern research', because the layout of the series in separate units made it possible to establish 'a chronology based entirely on a rational classification'.[27] He also recorded the most recent progress made in the science of vases, which 'often enables us to attribute with near-certainty to a given workshop a work which the maker has not taken the trouble to sign'.[28] A misunderstanding arose, however, concerning the notion of the maker; Furtwängler believed he was discovering an individual artist, whereas Pottier thought it more prudent to confine himself to the notion of a workshop. In a more general sense, Pottier's catalogue differed from Furtwängler's in one essential respect; the geographical system was not based on centres of production, but on where the vases were found. Pottier, who had completely reorganized the exhibition rooms according to this system, justified his choice by emphasizing the lessons that could be learned from the very fact that objects had been discovered in such and such a place:'By studying each room separately, we can see what products were made in or imported into a particular region.[. . .] By seeing products found in the same area grouped together, we can take in at a glance the artistic and commercial history of that area.'[29]

Ultimately, what characterized his museographical method was that he used the museum as a laboratory. By adopting a comparativist approach, he sought to lay out evidence before the archaeologist or the ordinary visitor of the sort of pottery that different cultures had produced at a given time, whether or not under the influence of imported models.

THE *ALBUM DE VASES*

It is remarkable that the primary objective of the museum catalogue was not, right from the start, to illustrate the objects described in the text. An exception to this, admittedly, was the *Musée grégorien étrusque*, which was published in 1842 and nevertheless was the first catalogue to be fully illustrated with engravings. It was not organized in any order of classification, however, and as a result the commentary accompanying the plates had to be written at a later date to fit in with the illustrations, as in the old style of publication where the plates were produced before the text.[30]

---

[26] Cf. Bothmer (1987: 197).   [27] Pottier (1896: i. 57).
[28] Ibid. (58).   [29] Ibid. (67).   [30] Vatican (1842).

As a general rule then, vase catalogues before Pottier's contained few illustrations. We may find this surprising, given that in addition to the traditional methods of reproduction (essentially engraving), archaeologists had begun as early as the middle of the century to use photography during their explorations abroad.[31] The explanation, no doubt, is that there were practical difficulties and/or problems of cost. At the end of the century, however, thanks to the progress made in the field of photomechanical reproduction (notably with the introduction of half-tone engraving), the situation changed completely. The new British Museum catalogue, which appeared not long before Pottier's, marked a significant step forward, since it contained a number of phototype plates, and even some illustrations within the body of the text.[32]

Ultimately, Pottier's most original contribution to the concept of a catalogue of vases lay in his desire to illustrate a sizeable portion of the vases in the museum.[33] Whereas the British Museum catalogue contained only ten plates (if that) in each fascicle, the albums of the *Vases antiques du Louvre* showed about fifty plates each, thus enabling more than 300 vases to be reproduced in every album.[34]

The album differed from the catalogue in that the latter was aimed at a wide public, whereas the former was intended more particularly for specialists who needed a comprehensive source of information about the vases in the Louvre. Following the numbering system in each room, the text gave minutely detailed descriptions of these vases, and also of all vases that had been published before, with references to the relevant bibliography. Thus there could be no doubt that the principle of illustration was the determining factor here: 'I am more and more convinced that it is essential to have a picture of the object alongside the words describing it, and that without illustrations, the best descriptive catalogues remain an almost useless instrument in the hands of researchers, despite all the time and trouble that have been spent on them.'[35]

As a keen photographer, Pottier was fascinated by the problems posed by photography in its scientific application. References to this can be found in his correspondence with Heuzey, where he recalls the heroic times when it was necessary to take several hours over one object in order to obtain a satisfactory image, with all the specific problems resulting from the positioning of the vases and the reflection of light on the glaze. Despite this, he writes, these attempts were worthwhile, because when they were successful 'the precision of the lines and drawing that one gets is absolute. One no longer has the

[31] Bustarret (1991).   [32] Walters, Smith, and Forsdyke (1893–1925).
[33] Bothmer (1987: 199).   [34] Pottier (1897–1928).   [35] Pottier (1901: ii, preface).

inevitable interpretation of the artist and then on top of that, of the engraver as well.'[36] Here Pottier clearly showed the great advantage that photography had over drawing: that it faithfully reproduced the real appearance of the vase. This advantage was both scientific and artistic; scientific because the photograph was so accurate, and artistic because it was so faithful to the original. As progress continued in the technical process of photomechanical reproduction, it was not long before photography had the further substantial advantages of speed and lower cost. Although Pottier still used drawings to illustrate some of the vases in the first fascicle, all the reproductions in the other two were photographic.

One final point to note is that, in more senses than one, the *Vases antiques* albums were the forerunners of the editorial and scientific enterprise which Pottier was to carry to a successful conclusion after the First World War in the *Corpus Vasorum Antiquorum*. As he himself wrote in the first volume: 'Nowadays most of the great Museums publish descriptive catalogues accompanied by numerous illustrations; this is the best way of gradually building up that *Corpus Rerum* whose much-desired completion will, along with the *Corpus Inscriptionum*, be the great achievement of modern archaeological science.' The idea, it seems, was spreading fast. In 1888, at the time when Salomon Reinach was bringing out his 'Bibliothèque des monuments figurés', a series of works whose ambitious aim was to bring together all the known illustrations of archaeological objects, such as statues, bas-reliefs, paintings, and vases, the Academies of Berlin and Vienna had also tackled the problem and begun to publish series on terracottas, sarcophagi, and funerary bas-reliefs. There were of course significant differences between these projects. Reinach's illustrated lists did not aim to produce any hitherto unpublished material; they were simply intended to bring together in one single publication images that had been scattered over various works and periodicals which were sometimes not easily accessible. The corpus projects, on the other hand, were of a much more exhaustive and systematic nature. Whatever approach they adopted, however, all these various enterprises flowed from a single desire that was widespread at the end of the century: to make available to archaeologists one special publication in which they could find all the objects that particularly interested them. In the context of the exaggerated nationalism of those years, it is not surprising to discover that this work on archaeological lists and publications was subject to intense competition between the various institutions and learned societies, as can clearly be seen in the course of one of Pottier's letters: 'Despite the Franco-Russian festivities, it is mainly the Germans that I have on my back at the moment, Winter, Reisch; Winter has come for the

---

[36] Letter to Heuzey (n.p., n.d); Paris, Institut de France MS 5774.

Corpus of terracottas that the Berlin Institute is starting. Another one that we won't be doing!'[37]

A NATIONAL WORK: THE 'DAREMBERG ET SAGLIO'

There are at least two reasons for our interest in Pottier's collaboration in the *Dictionnaire des antiquités grecques et romaines*, the publication of which went on for almost half a century (the first fascicles came out in 1873, the analytical tables in 1919).[38] First, he was closely associated with the practical production of the dictionary; in 1884, on the recommendation of Perrot, he was appointed as an assistant editor to Edmond Saglio, a role which became more and more important as the work advanced. The original idea for the project was Daremberg's, but he took no active part in it, and Saglio remained the real head of the editorial enterprise until his death in December 1911, when Pottier took on the editorship of the dictionary, assisted by Saglio's son-in-law Georges Lafaye (who had also been in the same year as Pottier at the École Normale Supérieure). Once Lafaye and Pottier had been appointed as editors in a new contract with Hachette signed on 23 October 1914, they took over officially and saw the project through to its conclusion. The second reason relates more precisely to Pottier's contribution as a scientist; not only did he write 177 of the entries in the dictionary, but seventy of them are directly concerned with vases. In these he discussed the question of the names used to describe Greek vases, a problem which was of great concern to the archaeologist-philologists of the nineteenth century.

A difficult birth

Started after the defeat of 1870 by men who were obsessed by the idea of asserting the intellectual vigour of the nation, the *Dictionnaire des antiquités grecques et romaines* was the product of the efforts of several generations (and more than 174 collaborators) to maintain the good standing of French science. As he handed over the final fascicle of the dictionary containing the analytical tables to the Académie des Inscriptions et Belles-Lettres, Pottier presented the completion of the enterprise as the successful outcome of a 'patriotic and scientific undertaking': 'It gives me great pleasure to think that this work, begun after the disastrous reverses that France suffered, and intended to affirm the intellectual vitality of our nation, has been completed at a time of victory, and that it contains within it the efforts

---

[37] Letter to Heuzey (Paris, 21 Oct. 1893); Paris, Institut de France MS 5774.
[38] Daremberg, Saglio, and Pottier (1877–1919).

of a whole generation which has worked to uphold the good name of French scholarship.'[39]

The fact that the beginning and end of this great collective work coincided with two symbolic dates in the history of France could hardly be seen as mere coincidence, and indeed it was generally regarded as the work of fate.[40] As a result, the genesis of the enterprise in the mid-1850s rather tended to be forgotten about, and any mention that was made of it in passing was usually derogatory: 'Considering the decadence of French archaeology in the Second Empire, it is not surprising that the first fascicles of the *Dictionnaire* were of such poor quality.'[41]

Although this view of Reinach's was not entirely free of bias, there can be no doubt that the dictionary's early days were not easy. It was on 25 July 1855 that Charles Daremberg signed a contract with the Hachette publishing house, for the writing of a *Dictionnaire des antiquités orientales, grecques, latines et du Moyen Âge*. At that time Daremberg had made a name for himself by his translations of the Greek physicians, and had close links with the Institut de France; in particular he had been sent with Ernest Renan on an important mission to Rome, and had been the librarian at the Mazarine since 1852.[42] The connection with Louis Hachette may have been made through Émile Littré, a childhood friend of Hachette's, with whom he was also on good terms.

Since its foundation in 1826, the Librairie Hachette had undertaken the publication of several dictionaries; the most famous of these today is Littré's work on the French language (completed in 1873), but before that there had been the *Dictionnaire grec-français* (1841) by Charles Alexandre, which was the first great venture of the new publishing house (and the forerunner of the Bailly), and also Nicolas Bouillet's *Dictionnaire universel d'histoire, de mythologie et de géographie* (1842). Bouillet's book is important, because it was its success that started the great collection of Hachette dictionaries.[43] The 1855 contract stated that it should serve as a model for the *Dictionnaire des antiquités*, and it was agreed that the author should be paid advances, a practice that was peculiar to the new publishing house. The dictionary was scheduled to go to press in five years' time.

Eight years later, after a considerable delay, it was decided that the section on Christian antiquities which was now complete should be published as a separate work.[44] After two more years, in accordance with a contract signed

---

[39] See *Comptes rendus de l'Académie des Inscriptions et Belles-Lettres* (report on the meeting of 26 Sept. 1919: 377).

[40] Lafaye (1917).   [41] Reinach (1911: 458).

[42] Gourevitch (1990).   [43] Mistler (1964: 59).

[44] Contract (signed on 16 Oct. 1863); Paris, Hachette Arch.; cf. Gourevitch (1993: 82–7).

on 25 March 1865, Daremberg appointed Saglio as his assistant, and put him in charge of revising articles, labelling plates (of which there were now 3,000), and correcting proofs. Edmond Saglio had been working for several years on the dictionary, but he now became Daremberg's official collaborator, while Daremberg himself was taken up with his research into the history of medicine. He undertook to complete the dictionary for Hachette by 1 April 1867. Further delays once again prevented him from doing so, however; 1867 and 1868 went by without copy being delivered, and it was not until the end of 1869 that Daremberg and Saglio started to hand over the first of it. The printing was finally due to begin in 1870, when it was halted by the political circumstances already described.

The expansion to fifteen years of an editorial job that was originally expected to take five had cost a great deal of money. The first limit of 24,000 francs, which was already an enormous sum at the time, had been far exceeded; the new cost was estimated at 75,000 francs on 1 April 1872, when a fresh contract was signed, stipulating that the *Dictionnaire*, from which Eastern antiquities had meanwhile been dropped, would consist of two quarto volumes, each of 1,600 pages, and that it would initially be published in fascicles, to appear every three months. Daremberg died shortly afterwards, in October 1872, and Saglio was left in sole charge of the editing for twelve years, until the arrival of Pottier. The first fascicle came out in 1873. After quite a delay, this was the true beginning of a scientific and editorial enterprise which was to go on for more than another forty-five years.

A singular history and a collective destiny

In the foreword to the first fascicle, Saglio set out the aim of the work: to summarize 'every aspect of public and private life in the ancient world' in the practical form of an alphabetical dictionary. It was intended for scholars, the educated public, and artists alike, and it contained 'the testimony of Greek and Latin authors', 'commentaries by modern scholars', and as far as possible 'illustrations of the objects'. The dictionary's method was in general well received by the critics, who were also impressed by a combination of two qualities which enhanced the value of the whole work: 'Thus the authors have succeeded in combining the advantages of our clear, precise method of exposition with the creative approach that is so commendable in the scholarly writings of foreign literatures.'[45]

Although the *Dictionnaire* was not strictly speaking an encyclopaedia of classical antiquity, the work soon began to develop along those lines, and to

---

[45] See *Séances et travaux de l'Académie des Sciences morales et politiques* (report on the meeting of 23 Aug. 1873: 891).

offer something in just about every field except the sciences proper. Some of the main scientific collaborators, such as Gustave Humbert, Exupère Caille-mer, François Lenormant, Gaston Boissier, Fustel de Coulanges, Georges Perrot, and Amédée Hauvette, were involved in the enterprise from the out-set, and in some cases continued to work on it to the end. More important, however, the *Dictionnaire* acted as a catalyst on a whole generation, and unless we understand this we will find it hard to grasp why, for intellectual and other reasons, the dictionary grew to five times the size foreseen at the outset, in other words how it could have gone from a plan for two volumes, each of 1,600 pages, to ten volumes comprising a total of over 8,200 pages (and 7,500 illustrations). Pottier, with his usual modesty, told how the story had unfolded:

Starting in 1878, M. Saglio went to Rome and made contact with the École Française at the Farnese Palace; he felt that his personal friendships with men of his own age were not sufficient and that he needed to turn to the younger generation. [. . .] And so now the *Dictionnaire* had a new breeding-ground for collaborators. I hope I have been of some service to M. Saglio in adding to and enriching that breeding-ground; but let us not forget that it was he who had the idea in the first place. In this laboratory many young scholars, who have now become authorities, went through their training in good hands and found the opportunity to put their qualities to good use.[46]

However briefly we may have summed up the episodic history of the *Dictionnaire des antiquités grecques et romaines*, there is no denying the significant disparity that exists between the beginning and the end of this vast work of collective scholarship. It is clear that the dictionary was originally inspired by a rationalist, encyclopaedic, and universalist spirit which stemmed from the main current of liberal thought in the nineteenth century. In the process of its creation, however, it became preoccupied above all with national issues, essentially in connection with 'the German crisis', to use Claude Digeon's expression. Furthermore, the fact that this interplay of competing influences had in the end been of benefit to classical studies was something of which Pottier was very much aware: 'The scientific competition between France and Germany is far from over, and one cannot but rejoice in a peaceful strug-gle which is of benefit to everyone.'[47]

The real names of Greek vases

We need only glance at the dictionary's general table of contents to see how ambivalent attitudes to vases can be. We find them under the heading of 'fur-niture, utensils, tools', which, if we count the other entries written by Pottier

---

[46] Daremberg, Saglio, and Pottier (1917: 7).   [47] Pottier (1902: 19).

that come under this heading, contains a total of about a hundred entries by him, some of which may admittedly appear in several places. By listing vases under this heading, Pottier seemed to be stressing the utilitarian nature of pottery, as he also did in his writing. Despite this, in the analytical table which he organized, the rubric 'fine art' has an entry for 'painted pottery', listing the article 'Vasa' which he wrote in collaboration with Charles Dugas, and cross-referring to the 'furniture, utensils, tools' heading for information on individual shapes.

It must be said that ancient literature does not throw much light on the matter. The ancient authors, in particular Athenaeus and the grammarians of the Late Empire, wrote about vases in their explanatory glosses; archaeologists therefore had a number of texts to which they could refer in their attempts to find the real names of Greek vases. The first systematic attempt was that made by Theodor Panofka, in a scholarly work which discussed the evidence provided in over 700 ancient texts.[48] In 1833, however, Jean-Antoine Letronne published a series of articles in the *Journal des savants*, in which he completely demolished Panofka's theories.[49] Indeed, Letronne regarded Panofka's attempt as a complete failure, and considered that the search for the names of Greek vases was

still at the same point where it was when he took it up; he may even have set it back, since by his general error concerning the meaning of the ancient glosses, and the inaccurate interpretations he has given to passages from Athenaeus and other authors, he has set it off on the wrong track, from which it has had to be removed so that it could be restored to the point [at which] it was found.[50]

Letronne also decided on mature reflection that in most cases it was impossible to achieve anyway, but he tempered his scepticism by proposing a radical solution. Although vases could never be classified by their real names, it would be possible to use a method borrowed from the naturalists:

I can see only one possible way of classifying such a variety of shapes as these; as I have said, it would mean using an artificial method, analogous to that used by naturalists. For example, if I had time I would take those ancient terms whose *general* sense is known; I would turn them into the names of classes which I would divide into *specific* denominations, based on distinctive features such as types of ornamentation, workmanship, and so on. The three or four hundred types of vases that are known to us could all be included in this and form an artificial nomenclature which would have the same advantage as any other, that of making it possible to name and recognize any object of a constant character.[51]

[48] Panofka (1829).   [49] Letronne (1883: i. 334–432).
[50] Ibid. (429).   [51] Ibid. (430).

Archaeologists had in a sense given their seal of approval to Letronne's proposal when they distinguished the volute krater from the calyx krater by distinctive features of workmanship in the shape of the handles. In his article 'Krater', Pottier recorded this 'established convention, to which we have no objection, but about which it is essential to have reservations'.[52] His reservations about modern authors' common use of conventional names concerned the fact that in a sense they were betraying the ancient texts, and that 'antiquity certainly did not limit the krater to these types'. One senses a certain reluctance on his part to accept this conventional terminology, as if he found it difficult to admit that it was not possible to make texts and works of art correspond precisely with one another, or as if the role of the critic should be limited to recording the impossibility of this perfect union between texts and relics. He was obliged to bow to the evidence; in the majority of cases, what the ancient authors said was of no great help to archaeologists: 'In short, all this evidence given by authors is of little help to us, and throws our minds into some confusion rather than enlightening us.'[53]

In certain cases Pottier was in a position to get round the uncertainty caused by the imprecision of authors, as in the case of the kotyle, where he was able to cite the example of two vases with this word incised on them. There was no room for doubt here, since the objects themselves provided the basis for the nomenclature. It could hardly be expected, however, that objects would provide enough names for themselves to constitute an exhaustive list, or even one that simply covered the commonest shapes. And even had they done so, Pottier was prepared, like Letronne, to acknowledge that it was not always possible to rely on the inscriptions incised on vases: 'We cannot even rely on the κρατῆρες inscriptions that are engraved on the foot of certain vases, because according to Letronne these graffiti merely denote orders for vases which the potter incised on the first vase that came to hand to remind himself, and they do not necessarily refer to the vase itself.'[54] The situation was problematical, since the ancient authors could not be relied upon, and even incised inscriptions were not an indisputable criterion. Pottier was therefore obliged nine times out of ten to confine himself to two observations: (1) the name in question denoted a certain shape of vase as it was commonly known in archaeological language, and (2) Letronne had clearly shown that to the ancients it was a generic term overlapping with other words. We shall take just one example, the *olpe*: 'We have grown accustomed in archaeology to giving this name to a particular type of oinochoe with a round lip and high handle. Letronne demonstrated that this classification is arbitrary. The texts

[52] Daremberg, Saglio, and Pottier (1887: 1554).
[53] Ibid. (1550).   [54] Ibid. (1554).

concerning the *olpe* prove yet again how elastic the terms were that the
ancients used to describe their vases.'[55]

In fact, Pottier found himself in an very awkward position with regard to
the general method advocated by the dictionary, because where vases were
concerned the entries were chosen according to the names given by ancient
authors. And although he was quite well aware that it was not sensible to rely
on these authors to provide the real names of Greek vases, he could not quite
bring himself to give up trying, in the words of a rival dictionary, the *Dictionary of Roman and Greek Antiquities* by Anthony Rich, to 'illustrate systematically, and word by word, the language of ancient literature by the works of
ancient art'.[56] When the texts and objects could indeed be made to match,
then 'all this information takes on life and colour', an expression of Pottier's
which can be compared with this extract from Rich:'When these are discovered, a sudden light would flash upon the mind, dispelling doubts, creating
conviction, and enabling the observer to say with self-satisfaction—this was
called by such a name, that was employed in such a manner.'[57] This relentless
search for the real (for every word a tangible referent) was one of the characteristics of what may be described as positivist archaeology. Because this was
too difficult to achieve in the case of the names of Greek vases, archaeologists
had resigned themselves to accepting conventional names, which at least
had the advantage of offering a precise nomenclature. What will concern us
in the next three chapters will be the process by which archaeologists came
to favour a similar approach to the identification of vase-painters.

[55] Daremberg, Saglio, and Pottier (1907: 1023).   [56] Rich (1849: p. vi).
[57] Ibid. (v); Daremberg, Saglio, and Pottier (1896: 1026).

3

A Brief Glance at Art History

THE NOTION OF INDIVIDUAL STYLE IN THE WORK OF MORELLI AND BERENSON

Everything remains to be done, do you hear me, mon cher Maître, everything! . . . I have come to the conviction that there are not ten paintings in a hundred that are by the artist to whom they are attributed, not ten . . . The most dubious of all are those that are signed . . . I know. There is Vasari. But to start with Vasari is a text that needs revision, and in any case it is full of fables . . . There are the archives. They are full of forged documents . . . Look at the note inserted by that Abbé Pierotto fellow in the margin of the Caleffino manuscript. But now Criticism is here, Criticism, Queen of the World as it has more right to be called than fortune does, with its infallible processes. They are the processes of Science.

P. Bourget, *La Dame qui avait perdu son peintre* (1910)

We shall resume our investigation into the history of connoisseurship by examining the thinking of Giovanni Morelli and Bernard Berenson. There seems little doubt that, although archaeologists were of course capable of realizing for themselves that many of the styles of drawing they observed on vases could be attributed to individual artists, works such as those of Morelli (whose influence on Furtwängler has already been mentioned) must have spurred them on to go further down the road of attributionism. That was after all what Pottier was suggesting when he declared that the history of Greek vase-painting would one day have 'fixed contours and a precise classification, like the history of Italian painting from the fifteenth to the sixteenth century'.[1]

Berenson, who started his career as a disciple of Morelli's, contributed just as much as the Italian, if not more, to the emergence of the scientific connoisseur as a prestigious figure at the turn of the century. He was responsible for the famous Lists of painters, which in many ways were similar to Beazley's. It should be noted that Beazley did not see fit to mention

[1] Pottier (1902: 22–3).

Morelli or Berenson in his writings, but regardless of personal considerations, and the differences between their respective fields, there is no doubt that his notion of the science of the connoisseur was strikingly similar to theirs.[2]

MORELLI AND THE SCIENCE OF ART

In his *History of Art Criticism*, or more precisely in a chapter entitled 'Philologists, Archaeologists and Connoisseurs of the xixth and xxth Centuries', Lionello Venturi claims that, of the various ways in which the historical-philological trend in art criticism manifested itself in the nineteenth century, it was research into individual artists that brought about the greatest advances in the discipline: 'Philological criticism of art showed its best qualities, not in the organisation of universal histories of art, nor in the materialistic treatments of technique and iconography, nor even in evasions towards the history of culture, but in researches into the individual. The *catalogue raisonné* of the works of each artist was the masterpiece of the philological history of art.'[3]

It may be that, as a disciple of Croce, Venturi could not but think highly of this type of research, but despite that he had no time for Morelli, whom he regarded as much too materialist. Yet Morelli (who wrote under the pseudonym Lermolieff) was one of those who did most to further this branch of art criticism; he was famous for his efforts to open the way to a 'science of art', based on a method by which he could confidently identify the artist responsible for a drawing or painting through the meticulous examination of apparently insignificant details such as the shape of the hands or ears.[4] By the time of his death in 1891 this brilliant connoisseur enjoyed a considerable reputation both as an art critic and in politics, his other great passion, as a Senator of the Kingdom of Italy.

Morelli's supporters have emphasized that he revolutionized the method used by his predecessors, by applying to it the anatomical knowledge that he had acquired in his youth. He did indeed study medicine at Munich University (1833–6) and although he never practised as a doctor, he specialized in comparative anatomy at Erlangen University (1837–8). The symbolic name of Cuvier, whom Morelli regarded as 'the jewel of our age', immediately comes to mind, since Cuvier maintained in his theory of the correlation of parts that it was possible to deduce the whole of a living organism from a fragment of it, in accordance with the basic anatomical principles of the inter-

---

[2] See Kurtz (1985). Beazley mentioned Morelli's name in a letter to Plaoutine (25 Dec. 1934); Louvre: Department of Etruscan, Greek, and Roman Antiquities.

[3] Venturi (1936: 233).　　　　[4] Cf. Anderson (1987); Agosti *et al.* (1993).

dependence of organs (Rudolph Wagner, who had studied with Cuvier, was one of Morelli's professors at Erlangen).[5]

The idea of applying a theory concerning living organisms to the identification and classification of works of art may appear preposterous; less so if one considers the tremendous vogue enjoyed by the biological sciences during the second half of the nineteenth century. That, moreover, was what Venturi criticized the Italian connoisseur for:

It is necessary to remember the infatuation for experimental science in the years between 1850 and 1880 in order to succeed in understanding, not only how a man of talent could have been able to construct such a theory, but also how such a theory could have had a great international circulation, and an influence, even favourable to the scholars of art history.[6]

Once again it is hard for us to imagine how much importance was attached to the issue of attribution, especially in Italy, Germany, and England, in the late nineteenth and early twentieth centuries, when decisive steps were being taken towards establishing the distinctive elements of individual style.[7] These advances were not only due to Morelli's work, even though it was spoken of (by Lady Eastlake) as a 'revolution';[8] also vitally important were Crowe and Cavalcaselle, the joint authors of monumental works on Flemish and Italian painting.[9] Morelli accused them of making unscientific attributions which were deduced from an overall impression, but he also acknowledged that the critical research for his first work was primarily based on his disagreement with them:

I have taken advantage of this opportunity to give an insight into my experimental method as it is applied to the study of fine art, and I have devoted a few pages to my definition of a history of art in Italy, as opposed to the *New History* of Messrs Crowe and Cavalcaselle. In short, my opuscule will essentially be a critique of their books.[10]

Principles and method

Morelli justified his criticism of overall impression, which was aimed not only at Cavalcaselle but at German connoisseurs such as Waagen and Bode, by saying that it was impossible to use this method with works which were damaged or repainted, as they so often were. Worse than that, however, they were making an error of method in the actual observation of paintings:

I have sought to demonstrate here [in the book] that the general impression of a work of art is not enough; that in order to recognize a great master with certainty in his

---

[5] See Pau (1993).   [6] Venturi (1936: 238).   [7] Castelnuovo (1989: 412).

[8] [Eastlake] (1891: 238).   [9] Crowe and Cavalcaselle (1864–6).

[10] Letter to Layard (Milan, 7 Aug. 1879); London, British Library, Add. MSS 38963. Lermolieff (1880).

works of art one needs above all to be acquainted with the *forms* that are characteristic of that master, and that in order to recognize and actually be able to appreciate those *forms* one needs to have learned the grammar of artistic language.[11]

This notion of artistic grammar is crucial to an understanding of his philological conception of the history of art. It should be noted, however, that Morelli was certainly not as systematic as he would have liked it to appear, and that he allowed himself on more than one occasion to be guided in his identification of a painter by his intuition or by the quality of the painting. On one occasion, for instance, he claimed that the spirit of Giorgione had suddenly enabled him to discover the painter of the portrait of a lady in the Borghese Gallery in Rome.[12] This trait of his was not lost on the art critic Claude Phillips, the author of an otherwise eulogistic review of the first volume of *Kunstkritische Studien*, who found it, to say the least, amusing in view of the Italian connoisseur's theories.[13] Morelli's correspondence also shows that, in the controversial case of the *Concert in the Park* at the Louvre, it was as much his knowledge of Titian's artistic personality as the distinctive features of his pictorial technique that made him identify Giorgione as the painter of the picture:

I shall admit that I believed it until now to be the work of Titian, for the simple reason that I had not yet devoted sufficient study to the spirit and technique of his rival from Castelfranco. [. . .] Titian is always heavier than his emulator, the forms of his hands, legs and arms are very different from Giorgione's forms—the tone of the landscape is also not the same in the work of the two masters.[14]

Be that as it may, his criticism of the overall-impression approach went hand in hand with his view of documents. In both cases, he believed, there was the same lack of method: 'Have not all connoisseurs, from Vasari to the present day, used the two expedients already mentioned, in other words that of intuition, the so-called overall impression, and that of the written document, to judge works of art?'[15] He maintained that one should not rely on external criteria such as literary tradition or archive documents to make judgements about attribution, but on the work itself: 'For the connoisseur, the only true document [. . .] in the final analysis, is the work itself.'[16] This may suggest that Morelli had too much confidence in the gifts of the observer, and at the same time too little trust in documents. Nevertheless there is no denying that the pre-eminence of the naked eye and of direct contact with the work was one of the most innovative aspects of the Morellian approach,

[11] Letter to Layard (Milan, 26 Dec. [1885]); London, British Library, Add. MSS 38965.
[12] Morelli (1994: 320).   [13] Phillips (1890: 308).
[14] Letter to Layard (Bergamo, 23 Oct. 1875); London, British Library, Add. MSS 38963.
[15] Lermolieff (pseud. of Morelli) (1890: 26).   [16] Ibid. (32).

a distant echo of which can be found in Beazley's assertion that the work of art is 'the court of last instance'.[17]

Another relevant factor here is the invention of photography, which undoubtedly played a crucial part in the evolution of connoisseurs' attitudes. In the absence of photographic prints enabling them to make multiple comparisons, earlier critics had had no option but to rely on general impressions, and to work by means of synthesis towards comparisons based primarily on the quality of the work, or on more questionable criteria. With the arrival of photography, and the opportunities for comparison that it made available to critics, this method underwent a lasting if not permanent change. It was Morelli who insisted that it was equally necessary to carry out an analytical conversion of what the eye could see, based directly on the technical and heuristic changes brought about by the extensive use of photography.

This need to make use of photography emerged implicitly when, having stated that it was very important to pick out the 'material trivia' in a master's work that betrayed his personality, Morelli was careful to point out 'of course, it is not enough to see one or a few of his works; one needs to see a large number of them, from every period of his artistic production.'[18] This kind of comparative work on the corpus of an artist could only be achieved by the extensive use of photography, as was even more apparent in the case of Beazley: 'The process of disengaging the work of an anonymous painter is the same as that of attributing an unsigned vase to a painter whose name is known. It consists of drawing a conclusion from observation of a great many details; it involves comparing one vase with another, with several others, with all the vases the enquirer has seen.'[19] At a later stage the need for direct contact with works of art and the concern to adopt a global approach led to photography being used as an instrument of student assessment. We know that Beazley was continually building up these photographic archives, which suggests that they were indispensable to his work as a connoisseur.

Poetry is like painting

Morelli wanted to achieve a science of art which would enable him, by meticulously examining the individual forms and material details of works of art, to understand them in an organic way.

It is precisely the study of all the particular details that go to make up the form of a work of art that I would like to recommend to those who do not merely intend to be

---

[17] Beazley (1946: 26).   [18] Lermolieff (1874: 8).   [19] Beazley (1918: pp. v–vi).

verbose amateurs, but wish to experience the real pleasure of hacking their way through the tangled jungle of the history of art and arriving, if possible, at the science of art. As there exists a spoken language, so too there exists a language which expresses itself in forms.[20]

It was by means of language, acting as a sort of intermediary between writing and the plastic arts, that a real knowledge of works of art could be achieved. Morelli justified this need to know the grammar of art by classifying the artistic event as a language event, and likening it to a sign language which had an inherent relationship with articulated language:

This relationship between articulated language and sign language or, to put it more clearly, between spoken language and painted or sculpted language, between the form in which the same mind expresses itself through articulated language and that through which it expresses itself and makes itself understood in the language of art; there is nothing, I say, about this relationship between the two modes of expression that is external or accidental; it is inherent.[21]

There was nothing really outlandish about this view of the artistic event as a means of expression similar to language; in a sense it was a scientific version of the famous classical theme *ut pictura poesis*, which art critics had readily turned to their own purposes by reversing the proposition and saying that painting was like poetry.[22] This humanist theme enables us to relate our discussion to classical studies, and more particularly to Percy Gardner, Beazley's predecessor in the chair of Classical Archaeology and Art at Oxford University. In 1889 he produced a pamphlet called *Classical Archaeology at Oxford* which was intended to arouse the interest of Oxford's scientific community in the teaching of archaeology, and to promote the idea of integrating it into the degree course in Literae Humaniores. In it he wrote that if one were to ask what the relationship was between classical archaeology and literature, 'the answer is that the plastic and poetic arts grow from the same root, and send out shoots in the same direction.'[23] What Gardner wanted was to reaffirm the methodological importance of philology, the positivist approach to textual criticism, by showing how useful archaeology can be to the study of ancient history. Even so, the theoretical and practical implications of this are not dissimilar to those of the Morellian method. This connection becomes clearer when we look at how Salomon Reinach compared the two approaches in his review of Berenson's book on *Lorenzo Lotto*:

It is essential to bear in mind that three-quarters of the attributions given on the labels in our galleries are nothing more than the hypotheses of connoisseurs of the old

---

[20] Lermolieff (1890: 96–7).   [21] Lermolieff (1891: 7).   [22] See Lee (1967).
[23] Gardner (1889: 10); cited by Boardman (1985: 53).

school. They have no more authority than the corrections or additions introduced into the Greek and Latin authors by the editors of the Renaissance. Art criticism that is scientific, or aspires to become a science, regards them as null and void; in this respect it is no more foolhardy than philological criticism, which is turning away from printed books to appeal to the evidence of manuscripts.[24]

Morelli only tried to apply his method to paintings and drawings from the late fifteenth and early sixteenth centuries, and to works which could be analysed; indeed he believed that his method was not universally applicable, and that it ceased to be effective for anything after the death of Raphael. Thus his technique of building up profiles of artists, almost like a handwriting expert, was valid essentially for the stylized periods of the Italian Renaissance, from its early stages to the end of the High Renaissance.[25] Logically, then, there was a good chance that this method could be successfully applied to vase-painting, where the style of drawing corresponded to a highly developed system of graphic conventions.

If, as those who believe in a Morellian notion of experimental science would suggest, a theory should be judged above all by its results, there is no doubt that his method produced some spectacular upheavals. The example often quoted is Giorgione's now world-famous *Venus* in Dresden, which was catalogued at that time as a copy of a lost Titian painted by Sassoferrato. Of the sixty-three alterations proposed by Morelli in his study of the Dresden collection, the curator, Karl von Woerman, accepted no fewer than fifty-six in the museum's new catalogue of paintings, thus confirming the Italian connoisseur's authority where attribution was concerned.[26] Less important alterations were made in the Munich and Berlin museums, but Morelli could feel satisfied that his research had borne out his theories, that is to say that only a 'scientific' methodology could enable works in museums to be classified according to style. What were the immediate implications of this dramatic change of names? How important is it to know the identity of a painter? This is an elementary and yet crucial question, to which it is difficult to give a brief answer. First, it is impossible to avoid the question of the artist's identity completely. As Bachelard said: 'Nature really wanted to do chemistry, so in the end it created the chemist.'[27] Certain works are crucial for the light that they shed on the artistic personality of the painter, and by some sort of osmosis the whole impact of the work is often transformed when there is a change of name. Such was the case, to take another famous example, with Giorgione's *Tempest*, which remained completely unknown for more than

[24] Reinach (1895: 271).   [25] Previtali (1978).

[26] Letter from Morelli to Layard (13 Jan. 1888); London, British Library, Add. MSS 38965.

[27] Cited by Chastel (1980: 8).

three centuries, until it was established in 1855 that it was the work of the Venetian painter.[28]

Although the Morellian method bore the stamp of positivism, it was by no means without importance. Morelli's modernism lay in his adoption of a rigorous method whereby he could attempt for the first time to define an individual style in a scientific manner, by disregarding the overall impression and concentrating on the study of apparently insignificant details. His influence extended far beyond the limited circle of connoisseurs of Italian painting, and we know that it became widespread among the researchers of the Viennese school.[29] It was in fact through the Viennese connection that he had his greatest stroke of luck, since Freud considered that there was a strong analogy between Morelli's interest in the unconscious gesture in the act of painting and the technique of psychoanalysis.[30] This link was the basis for the historian Carlo Ginzburg's 'clue paradigm' theory, according to which the end of the nineteenth century saw the emergence of a new explanatory model for the human sciences.[31] The reader is referred to the conclusion of this work for a general discussion of this theory and the essential problems it poses.

In the field of archaeology, when Pottier decided to include drawings of eyes and ears in the Louvre catalogue, thus showing the stages through which the painting of these anatomical parts had developed, he was in effect adopting Morellian criteria for the identification of vase-painters. Archaeologists could not ignore such a tool in a discipline where the only evidence they could have as to the identity of painters was derived from the pieces themselves. Of all Morelli's successors, such as Bernard Berenson, Gustavo Frizzoni, and Jean-Paul Richter[32] (whose daughter Gisela was a well-known figure in classical archaeology as Curator of the Department of Greek and Roman Antiquities at the Metropolitan Museum in New York from 1925 to 1948), Beazley was in my opinion one of those who remained closest to his technique of analytical conversion of what the eye could see. Both men shared the same philological conception of the history of art; they both had an unflagging interest in technique, and a partiality for direct contact with works.

Morelli's books were translated in Great Britain as early as 1883, and he had influential supporters there such as Lady Eastlake, the widow of Charles Eastlake, former director of the National Gallery, and Austen Henry Layard, the excavator of Nineveh, whom Morelli had helped to build up a large collection. With regard to this, Francis Haskell has stressed the impor-

---

[28] Haskell (1976: 15).   [29] Sciolla (1993).
[30] Freud (1985: 102–3).   [31] Ginzburg (1989).
[32] The correspondence between Morelli and J.-P. Richter, at the Biblioteca Hertziana in Rome, has been published, but more than half of the content has been omitted: G. and I. Richter (eds.) (1960).

tance of the change that took place in the role of the collector's adviser; previously this had been a job for artist-dealers, but now it was taken on by connoisseur-dealers.[33] Evidence of this new development in the second half of the nineteenth century could be seen in arbiters of taste such as Theophile Thoré, Sir John Charles Robinson, and Bernard Berenson, who acted as advisers to the Pereire brothers, Sir Francis Cook, and Mrs Isabella Stewart Gardner respectively. The change did a great deal to enhance the status of the connoisseur, who now had the aura of prestige associated with one who moves in the narrow circle of the social élite, but it also sometimes had more questionable implications concerning the link between scholarship and self-interest. This was true in Berenson's case, the details of which have been picked over with ease owing to his celebrity.[34] His dubious behaviour may well be explained by his unbridled desire for an ever more dazzling social career. It does not eclipse the prestige that he brought to this role at the turn of the century; it is no accident that the figure of the scientific connoisseur emerged in the literature of the time, in Paul Bourget's *La Dame qui avait perdu son peintre*. The author was careful to state in his preface that he detested the *roman à clef*, yet it is more than tempting to see a link here with Berenson.

A highly respected painter, Léon Monfrey, visits the Varegnana Palace in Milan, where he finds a *Portrait of a Lady* which bears a strange resemblance to a young woman with whom he is madly in love. This portrait has always been believed to be by Leonardo until a young critic and pupil of Morelli's, Georges Courmansel, rebaptizes it and attributes it to one Amico di Solario (whose real name, supposedly, is Cristoforo Saronno). Monfrey happens to meet Courmansel, and they both go to see the Marchesa Ariosti, who has another portrait of a lady to sell, also painted, according to Courmansel, by Amico di Solario. Monfrey immediately recognizes it as a forgery which he himself painted twenty-five years before when, as a mere dauber, he was struggling to survive in Rome. If there is a 'clef' to be found in this story, it is in the irony of the Monfrey's fortuitous revenge, since Courmansel's error concerning the forgery seems to invalidate his theory about the painter of the Varegnana portrait as well. Courmansel refuses to believe it, however, being convinced of the infallibility of his method: 'This painting is not a forgery. It is from the beginning of the sixteenth century. It is from Lombardy. It is by Cristoforo. These are not hypotheses. This is evidence, and its results are as certain as those of a geometrical theorem.'[35]

---

[33] Haskell (1976: 85); on the relations between Morelli and Layard: Lennon (1993). See also Anderson (ed.) (1999).

[34] Simpson (1987).   [35] Bourget (1910: 112); see Saisselin (1985: 164).

BERENSON BETWEEN PURE VISUALITY AND
ATTRIBUTIVE PHILOLOGY

Bourget's novel was published in 1910, at a time when Beazley was just beginning his research but when Berenson had already achieved almost everything
on which his reputation as a connoisseur and aesthete is based. Most authors
agree that the acme of his career as an art critic was in the 1890s.[36] He began
in 1895 with an essay on the Venetian painter Lotto, which he intended as a
new model for the monograph on an artist, advocating that any attempt to
sum up the artistic personality of the painter must be preceded by analysis
according to the canons of the new criticism. In the same year another event
took place which did just as much if not more to establish Berenson's reputation: the exhibition of Venetian paintings at the New Gallery in London.
Berenson wrote a pamphlet about it in which he radically contradicted the
attributions in the official catalogue.[37] No less than 80 per cent of the names
on the labels were changed; of the 120 paintings in the exhibition, only
fifteen were not altered. The revisionist nature of the pamphlet brought
Berenson to the forefront in the role, by now a familiar one to the reader,
of the iconoclastic connoisseur. This personal success is all the more easily
explicable when one considers that the main interested parties in this
upheaval were the collectors themselves.

At the end of the century there was indeed a massive influx of money into
Europe from the great American collectors, who were determined to procure
the very finest European paintings and antiquities on the market. Berenson
stepped in quite swiftly on their behalf, and did a great deal to convert these
wealthy patrons to a taste for the Italian Renaissance.[38] At the time of the
London exhibition, Berenson was already working on behalf of Isabella
Gardner, and he was to build an impressive collection of paintings for the
museum which she was creating at the time at Fenway Court in Boston. At
the same time Berenson very much wanted to widen the circle of collectors
who were likely to be interested in his expertise, as can be seen in a letter he
wrote to Mrs Gardner:

With all the experience I have had in buying and the control I could easily have
of the market, advising about pictures is the path marked out for me. [. . .] I could
sell ten times as much as I do now without taking more trouble if only I had a
larger circle of friends. [. . .] I want America to have as many good pictures as
possible.[39]

[36] e.g. Schapiro (1961: 59); K. Clark (1981: 114).
[37] Berenson (1895a = 1901–16: i. 90–146).
[38] Brown (1979: 17–24).
[39] Letter to Mrs Jack Gardner (Haslemere, [9 Aug. 1902]); McComb (ed.) (1965: 69).

The market in ancient art, which was mentioned in the previous chapter in connection with the figure of Edward Warren, was similarly affected by the strong interest of American collectors in European masterpieces, and this leads me on to the relationship between Warren and Berenson, which started during their years together at Harvard. Whereas Warren came from a rich family of industrialists which was long-established in America, the same was far from true in the case of Berenson. Having spent his early childhood in the ghetto of Butrimonys, near Vilnius in what is now Lithuania, he arrived in America at the age of 7, and was able to go to Harvard thanks to the help of wealthy benefactresses. Warren was also one of his patrons at university, although it seems that at this point he did no more than act as guarantor. It may have been the young Berenson's good looks that led him to do so, but what is certain is that the two young aesthetes shared the same ideals of classical beauty and the same enthusiasm for everything to do with the ancient world. When Berenson finished his degree course at Harvard, Warren shared the cost of his travel to Europe with Mrs Gardner, and both men spent some time in Oxford, Berenson in 1888 in order to try to meet his spiritual master, Walter Pater, Warren to study Classics.[40]

It now appears, according to Colin Simpson, that during his early lean years in Europe, Berenson regularly received financial help from Warren.[41] In fact, Warren's patronage was on a par with that of Isabella Gardner. We can understand why Berenson's book on Lotto was dedicated to Warren, who would very much have liked his protégé to become a specialist in the ancient world. It should be noted that in 1918 Beazley's work on red-figured vases in American museums was also dedicated to Warren (and to John Marshall). Beazley's links with Warren were much closer than that, however; he compiled the catalogue of Warren's collection of ancient gems at Lewes House, contributed to the first biography of Warren with a chapter on his activities as a collector and connoisseur, and also wrote two biographical notices in which he described the figure of the great American collector in flattering terms.[42]

The Lists of painters

The 1890s also saw the publication of Berenson's *Drawings of the Florentine Painters*, which Kenneth Clark regarded as his masterpiece, and even as having inspired his own vocation as an art historian.[43] Above all, however,

---

[40] Barolsky (1984).   [41] Simpson (1987: 57).

[42] Beazley (1920); *The Times* (7 Jan. 1929); *Oxford Magazine* (24 Jan. 1929); in Burdett and Goddard (1941: 331–63).

[43] Berenson (1903; the MS was complete in 1897); K. Clark (1974: 76).

Berenson's fame rested on his four volumes on the 'Painters of the Renaissance' which were published in England and the United States between 1894 and 1907. These were devoted to the Renaissance painters of Venice, Florence, and central and northern Italy, and consisted of long introductory essays, followed by the famous Lists of the principal artists of the Renaissance.[44] These Lists were organized rather differently from Beazley's; Berenson provided an inventory of each artist's corpus, in alphabetical order according to where the works were conserved, and briefly stating their subject matter. Beazley's lists, which appeared considerably later, gave much more information, especially by means of bibliographical references. One point that both men had in common was that they regularly updated their lists as they acquired further knowledge about the painters.

These revisions were sometimes painful, as in the case of Berenson's most famous creation, the Amico di Sandro. He invented this artistic personality by giving him a conventional name that expressed the stylistic affinities between his works and those of Botticelli.[45] He included him in the second edition of the Lists of Florentine painters, but eventually had to reconcile himself to dividing his works between Botticelli in the 1480s and the early Filippino Lippi.

Berenson's Lists did not receive the unanimous approval of art historians; Roberto Longhi had no qualms about comparing them to railway timetables. Nevertheless, Kenneth Clark emphasized that 'the prestige of the lists led to the triumph of Connoisseurship, and for almost thirty years this particular branch of scholarship—the giving of names—had a prestige similar to that of textual criticism in classical studies'.[46]

The obvious ambition of these Lists to be exhaustive shows that research had now moved on to a new stage; Morelli had never thought it sensible to try to pin a name on every piece in a museum. Indeed, in a letter to Jean-Paul Richter, he begged him not to give in to 'the mania for trying to give a name to every picture', and he also declared: 'Only novices in the science of art, or charlatans, try to give a name to every work of art.'[47] As for Berenson's own view of his vocation as a connoisseur, one of many occasions on which he explicitly alluded to it was in *Sketch for a Self-portrait*, the autobiography which he wrote after the Second World War. Using a dialogue in the Morellian mode, he tells the story of a scene which took place in May 1890, when he was sitting on the terrace of a café in Bergamo—Morelli's home town—in the company of a colleague, Enrico Costa:

[44] Berenson (1894; 1896; 1897; 1907).   [45] Berenson (1899 = 1901–16: i. 46–69).

[46] K. Clark (1981: 115).

[47] Letter to J.-P. Richter (Milan, 19 Nov. 1877); G. and I. Richter (eds.) (1960: 17); Lermolieff (1890: 57).

You see, Enrico; nobody before us has dedicated his entire activity, his entire life, to connoisseurship. Others have taken it as a relief from politics, as in the case of Morelli and Minghetti, others still because they were museum officials, still others because they were teaching art history. We are the first to have no idea before us, no ambition, no expectation, no thought of reward. We shall give ourselves to learning to distinguish between the authentic works of an Italian painter of the fifteenth or sixteenth century, and those commonly ascribed to him. Here at Bergamo, and in all the fragrant and romantic valleys that branch out northward, we must not stop till we are sure that every Lotto is a Lotto, every Cariani a Cariani, every Previtali a Previtali, every Santa Croce a Santa Croce; and that we know to whom of the several Santa Croce's a picture is to be attributed etc. etc.[48]

It may be that this declaration should not be taken literally, given that it was written at a time when, as he took stock of his own life, he was perhaps inclined to embellish the tale, and that it therefore tells us more about him as an old man than as a young aesthete. If we do take it literally, however, the suggestion is that once the path had been opened up by Morelli, it was a question of scrupulously marking out the territory, metre by metre, with geometrical precision, in order to carry out an operation which Morelli had supposedly neglected. If we now turn to Beazley, we find a rather similar picture to do with the desire for exhaustiveness. The essay in question is in his book on red-figured Attic vases in American museums. It should be explained that just before the First World War, Beazley went to America to visit the museums there, very much for the traditional reason that a connoisseur's knowledge depends first and foremost on having direct contact with works of art by visiting public and private collections. This trip provided him with the material for his first work, which presented itself as a guided tour of the museums of America, although it was in fact a general history of the red-figure Attic style of the fifth century BC: 'I have tried to find out who painted each [vase]. I have not been able to assign every vase to its author, although I do not consider that an impossible task, but I have managed to put in place most of the more, many of the less, important pieces.'[49]

Fin de siècle *aestheticism*

Whilst Beazley largely achieved the task he had implicitly set himself in that preface, in other words to discover as many painters as possible, along with the corpus of vases which could be shown to be theirs, Berenson was, it seems, prevented from doing so by issues quite other than the recognition of artists' identities. He gave the reasons for this in *Sketch for a Self-portrait*, where, in a self-consciously Proustian tone, he said that if he had not allowed himself

---

[48] Berenson (1949: 51).   [49] Beazley (1918: p. v).

to be carried away by connoisseurship, he could have become the aesthete that he longed to be, a second Goethe. A passage in a letter he wrote to Mary Costelloe sums up quite well the rather stuffy cult of classical beauty that existed at that time. It concerns the portrait of a young man: '*Beauty is supreme*, and its greatest manifestation is in the perfect ephebe, so rare a creature that one can count them on the fingers of one hand.'[50] The conventional image of the ephebe goes back to ancient Greece, for which we know that he had a real fascination; and the fact that he never wrote anything about Greek civilization is really very surprising. He talks about this passion in his memoirs: 'I ought to have been a Greek scholar. I do not mean a grammarian but a student of Greek letters, thought and art in all their phases through the twenty centuries of their vigour. I should have been happier that way.'[51] He went even further in this worship of Greece, and admitted that the least object of that origin merited his unqualified admiration: 'I can now look only at the masterpieces of European art from the Carolingian period to our own day. Yet I can be indulgent to the humblest and even meanest product of Greek art.'[52]

Berenson conveyed his aesthetic thinking in his writing; it was already clearly apparent in the introductions to his volumes on 'Painters of the Renaissance'. The well-known expressions that he used to define the spectator's response to works of art echo the views of his Harvard psychology master, William James, the idealism of Pater, and Adolf von Hildebrand's poetics of the figurative arts. The nature of this response is the aesthetic pleasure that a work of art gives through 'ideated sensations'. It is a matter of knowing what creates these effects in a particular art form, since the nature of the response varies from one type of art to another, as do the methods that are used to produce it.[53] Berenson defined several of these intellectual sensations according to the nature of the response which each type of art aroused in the observer, such as the 'tactile values' of Florentine painting, and the 'spatial composition' of Roman painting.

Berenson's aesthetic discourse, which was innovative if only because it avoided the hasty generalizations of contemporary philosophers, deserves to be gone into in more detail; here we are drawing attention to it mainly because it establishes a significant difference between him and Beazley, who had mixed feelings on this subject, and in any case never wrote anything equivalent. We can simplify the matter by saying that Berenson was more of a philosopher, and Beazley more of a philologist. It is interesting to note, however, that these personal preferences affected each man's conception of what

---

[50] Letter to Mary Costelloe (23 Oct. 1890); cited by Brown (1979: 40).
[51] Berenson (1949: 83).   [52] Ibid. (84).   [53] Cited by Salvini (1988: 33–4).

a connoisseur's job was. The following anecdote is illuminating. During a trial in which his qualities as a connoisseur were put to the test, Berenson was earnestly asked by the judge to justify his opinion of the attribution of a painting by Leonardo:

'You've given a good deal of study to the picture in the Louvre?'
  'All my life, I've seen it a thousand times.'
  'And is it on wood or canvas?'
  'I don't know. [. . .] It's as if you've asked me on what kind of paper Shakespeare wrote his immortal sonnets.'

Francis Haskell, recalling this episode as reported by Ernest Samuels, Berenson's biographer, rightly says that

the clever boutade [. . .] is perhaps more revealing of his approach to connoisseurship than we might expect. After the travels of his early days, his work on the Lists and on the certificates he wrote for dealers was very largely done on the basis of photographs, which played a greater part in his life than in that of any connoisseur before his time; and the effect of the photograph is, of course, to detach the image from the means whereby it has been created.[54]

Berenson's aestheticism was closer to the neo-idealism of someone like Croce than to Morelli's materialist positivism. It is therefore not surprising that he and Morelli should differ on some points of method. We find for instance that his view of the role of overall impression in the attribution process was in a sense a reaction against Morelli's. It was clear in his 'Elements of Connoisseurship' (an essay written in 1894 but not published until 1902) that the subjective element had returned to favour. Running through the various Morellian criteria, Berenson remarked that 'in the case of the nude, therefore, as in all the other cases we have been discussing, the ultimate test of the value of any touchstone is *Quality*'.[55]

Unlike Morelli, Berenson maintained that although the connoisseur's analytical abilities must of course be taken into account, attribution could not be a science, since it was based primarily on qualitative judgments which inevitably involved a degree of subjectivity.[56] In fact, Berenson's notion of attribution was a reflection of his interest in the critical definition of artistic personalities, and by the same token of his aesthetics. Where method was concerned, however, one of the important results of this line of argument was the belief, which may be justified in the case of Italian painting, that an artist would always maintain a certain level of artistic quality throughout his career, and that this would be apparent in all his work.

---

[54] Haskell (1987a: 596).   [55] Berenson (1901–16: ii. 134; see also 144–5, 147).
[56] Similar conclusions in Offner (1972).

As regards the role of literary tradition and archives, however, Berenson had declared himself as adhering more or less to the Morellian orthodoxy. However, the claim that the work of art must be the only criterion for attribution was no longer viewed as original or infallible. The Amico di Sandro episode was a good example, although it was not the only one of its kind, and we know of other examples of Berenson's tendency to favour the work over the document at all costs; it had led him to transfer a number of drawings by Michaelangelo to Sebastiano del Piombo, to the detriment of the Vasarian tradition.[57] The science of the connoisseur was subject to error, and in the final analysis there was no substitute for a document or, to a lesser extent, a signature.

It should be noted that in the study of pottery this dialectic was impossible to achieve, since there was no documentary evidence by which the validity of Beazley's stylistic assertions could be verified. Since the only means of verification were themselves stylistic, the argument was almost bound to become circular. There was of course a limited number of signatures on vases, and Beazley's predecessors had logically relied on these inscriptions to build up a picture of the painters' works. Beazley, however, was to attach greater importance to style than to any form of signature. In fact, the only real way in which he could verify the validity of his method was, where possible, to reconstruct vases from fragments scattered around different museums, thus proving the coherence of his attributions, as he did in 1933 in his *Campana Fragments in Florence*.

The comparison with Italian painting is limited by the fact that the two disciplines do not use the same instruments of knowledge, but it has perhaps enabled us to account for the prestige that this type of research conferred on the cause of connoisseurship. Morelli undoubtedly paved the way for Beazley, and their methods were strikingly similar, although in the systematic nature of Beazley's attributions and the principle of the Lists itself, he was closer to Berenson. What is most remarkable is that a type of research that was taking place somewhat in the margins of official art history should have had such enormous success. Its popularity went on into the 1920s: 'It is difficult for anyone who was not concerned to imagine the mania for "attributions" which flourished in the inflationary '20s. It was like the railway mania of the 1840s, or to take a closer parallel, it was like the trade in relics in the fourteenth century.'[58]

---

[57] K. Clark (1981: 117–19).   [58] Ibid. (120).

4

Beazley's Background

A STUDY OF A YOUNG MAN WHOSE EDUCATION WAS NOT NEGLECTED

> Wot do I want? Fects! FECTS! Nah, Rum's a *fect*:
> Rum's somethin' solid in a wobbly world.
> It's cheap. It's there. It's never fur aw'y.
> It nips yer stummick, an' it 'eats yer blood;
> Gives ye the notion that you're still alive . . .
>
> W. Mackenzie, 'Bagster, French-polisher, Descants' (1911)

Like Morelli, Berenson, and most connoisseurs of the time, Beazley acquired most of his training for himself by going to museums. It should be explained straight away that he had the best possible education in Classical Greats at Oxford University; not only was he very much a product of Oxford, he also spent the whole of his adult life there, from October 1903 until his death on 6 May 1970.[1] At the beginning of the century, however, there was no real teaching of art history or archaeology on offer at the university.

The task of looking into Beazley's background and setting his student years in context will not be an easy one, since we have very few accounts of his life prior to 1910. The attempt will be worthwhile, however, if we can show that he had other essential interests apart from classical philology, such as Italian Renaissance painting and poetry. It is our view that his association with poetry is a kind of intellectual lever which enables us to grasp some important aspects of the special relationship he had with Attic vase-painting and -painters.

LITERAE HUMANIORES

John Davidson Beazley came from an educated middle-class background; his father was an interior decorator and his mother a nurse. He was the first of two children, born in Glasgow on 13 September 1885. Bernard Ashmole has noted that his father must have taught him a great deal about artistic

[1] Bothmer (1970); Ashmole (1970) = in Kurtz (ed.) (1985); Robertson (1971).

craftsmanship, and adds that his mother, a woman of character, was 'the main-stay of the family in many vicissitudes'.[2] One of these vicissitudes was no doubt the move to Brussels in 1897; his father took the family to live there so that he could retrain professionally as a glass-maker, while John stayed in England to continue his studies. In 1896 he went to King Edward VI School in Southampton, then moved in 1898 to Christ's Hospital in London. From his earliest years he was an excellent pupil, and at Christ's Hospital he moved into the élite, as a 'Classical Grecian'. With what might have been seen as 'effortless superiority', he carried off most of the prizes awarded by the school, as he was to continue to do at Oxford. The following is a summary of the honours he received:

Christ's Hospital. 1902, Thompson Classical Gold Medal, awarded to the 'Scholar most proficient in Classics'; Richards Gold Medal, for the 'author of the best set of Latin Hexameters'. 1903, Montefiore Prize, awarded 'to the most proficient of all the Grecians in Classics and Mathematics conjointly'.[3]

Oxford. 1904, Ireland and Craven Scholarships. 1905, Hertford Scholarship. 1907, Derby Scholarship; Gaisford Greek Prose Prize.[4]

Already a past master in the art of versification, 'that specialised training in writing Greek and Latin poetry which enables a man to gain scholarships and earn his living as a don',[5] Beazley was admitted to Balliol College. Oxford is of course a collegiate university, that is to say that it is organized on the principle of autonomous colleges, each with its own administration, finances, and accommodation. The university awards degrees and organizes lectures and final examinations, but it is mainly the college they belong to that determines the nature of the students' daily lives, their rooms, and virtually all the teaching they receive. The feeling of belonging and identification was even stronger at Beazley's time than now, because the differences between the colleges were more marked, and each college had its own very individual character and atmosphere.[6]

Between 1903 and 1907 Beazley read Literae Humaniores. The course consisted of five terms devoted to the detailed study of Greek and Latin language and literature (Classical Moderations or Mods), followed by seven terms in which Greek and Roman history were studied in combination with ancient and modern philosophy (Final Classical Schools or Greats). For a student who achieved First Class Honours in both examinations, the door was open to the highest posts in the Civil Service, the Church, and of course in education.

---

[2] Ashmole, in Kurtz (ed.) (1985: 57).   [3] Allan (1924: 167–71).
[4] Beazley (1907).   [5] Flecker (1910: 77).   [6] Hunter-Blair (1908).

Effortless superiority

Having already said that membership of a college was of prime importance, we must now turn to Balliol, which at the turn of the century was one of Oxford's most prestigious colleges. Its reputation attracted the social and intellectual élite of England; in 1900, 80 per cent of the students were from England alone, and one in four was an Etonian.[7] Balliol owed its renown outside Oxford largely to the figure of Benjamin Jowett, the translator of Plato's dialogues, Thucydides, and Aristotle's *Politics*, Regius Professor of Greek, and Master of Balliol from 1870 to 1893. He is generally regarded as the most famous educator of the late Victorian era, and his particular achievement was the reintroduction of the tutorial system, one of the special features of the Oxford system of teaching, which at his time had tended to fall out of use. The feeling of belonging to and identification with Balliol remained with students long after they had left, and this needs to be borne in mind as we consider some famous words that were spoken by Herbert Asquith, Leader of the Liberal Party, when he became Prime Minister in 1908. During a dinner organized by some old members of Balliol, Asquith declared that the members of this college could be distinguished from less fortunate souls by their 'tranquil consciousness of effortless superiority'.[8] This caused quite a stir, for obvious reasons. George Beardoe Grundy, Professor of Ancient History at Corpus Christi, did not fail to allude—in a very Victorian autobiography— to Balliol's remarkable ability 'to invent stories about itself and its members', but also acknowledged that when he had been elected a fellow of Corpus Christi in 1903 Balliol had been generally regarded as the best college in Oxford.[9] In Beazley's case, it went without saying that he should choose Balliol, since F. H. Merk, his teacher at Christ's Hospital, was himself a former member of Balliol and an 'Old Blue'.[10]

These remarks about Balliol applied especially to Jowett's generation; Asquith himself was a student of the celebrated Hellenist. For Beazley's generation things were somewhat different, including the way in which the students viewed themselves. There is evidence of this in *An Edwardian Youth* by Sir Lawrence Jones, who studied at Balliol at the same time as Beazley, from 1904 to 1908:

These, then, were the Fellows of Balliol fifty years ago, who in some ways maintained, in others greatly modified, the Jowett tradition. They maintained it on the purely academic side by the system of giving personal attention, through *tête-à-tête* sessions, to all men of promise. They changed it—and in this the Hartleys, Urquharts, Baileys and Lindsays must have most of the credit, under the pervasive humanity

---

[7] J. Jones (1988: 229).   [8] *The Times* (23 July 1908).
[9] Grundy (1945: 67; 102).   [10] On Merk, see Middleton Murry (1953).

of Strachan-Davidson and 'A. L.'—by a new emphasis upon personal relationships and the art of living. [. . .] I believe that, but for the Great War, my own generation of Balliol men would have walked the world with a different sort of reputation from that of 'effortless superiority'.[11]

Jones's remarks were in a sense corroborated by Maurice Bowra, who said of Beazley that he 'never put on the airs of a great man',[12] and more recently by the great historian of ideas Isaiah Berlin (born in 1909), who described how the figure of Beazley appeared among the teachers of his generation:

The dons of the twenties and thirties, those whom Evelyn Waugh, for instance, describes in his novels, came as a general rule from middle-class or even relatively modest backgrounds. There were few aristocrats among their ranks. David Cecil was an exception. But quite a few of their students were members of the aristocracy, with whom they were on excellent terms. The result was that as time passed and they went on rubbing shoulders with them, they often ended up deluding themselves that they belonged to the same milieu as they did. They became more open, invited them to dinner, shared jokes with them, in short took on the mentality of the eternal student. And those men were snobs. But not the great academics like Gilbert Murray and Beazley, who was a genius of the first order.[13]

Beazley's tutors at Balliol were the Latinist Cyril Bailey, and Arthur Wallace Pickard-Cambridge, who specialized in Greek drama. These are the two names mentioned by Bernard Ashmole, but it should be noted that the name given in the Balliol College Register is not Pickard-Cambridge but John Alexander Smith, a Hegelian metaphysicist who was one of the first to introduce Croce's ideas to Oxford.[14] It is not hard to see why Smith was omitted; in a lecture on the training of archaeologists which he gave at London University during the Second World War, Beazley spoke with acid irony about modern philosophy, which he would gladly have replaced in the degree course by an introduction to archaeology:

At Oxford in the four-years classical course there is little place for archaeology. A man may take the most important period of Greek sculpture as a special subject in Honour Moderations, and many do; this means that for five terms he is studying Greek sculpture as one of many classical subjects. One of the alternatives is Homeric archaeology. In Greats it is open to candidates to offer an archaeological subject, but not one in a hundred does. (I have sometimes wondered whether it might not be possible to make some knowledge of archaeology an alternative to that smattering of modern philosophy, obligatory in Greats, which confuses so many minds, some temporarily, and some for good; but this would be tampering with the sacred edifice of Litterae Humaniores.)[15]

---

[11] L. E. Jones (1956: 39–40).   [12] Bowra (1966: 249).   [13] Berlin (1991: 67).
[14] Elliott (ed.) (1934: 273); Ashmole, in Kurtz (ed.) (1985: 57).   [15] Beazley (1943 = 1989: 99).

It was not from his university education that Beazley gained the knowledge that was to give him his reputation as a connoisseur. A chair of archaeology had indeed existed at Oxford since 1885, and Percy Gardner, the second
holder of this chair and Beazley's predecessor, had succeeded in introducing
some reforms into the Literae Humaniores degree course, notably the special
Mods examination in Greek sculpture which he brought in in 1890. It seems,
however, that when he tried several years later to have the same subject examined in Final Schools, his proposal met with strong opposition.[16] Beazley took
Gardner's course on sculpture, but it is almost certain that Gardner did not
look favourably on the recent practice of attributing pieces of sculpture to
their presumed authors and carrying out spectacular reconstructions.[17] His
attitude to the attribution of vases emerges clearly in his autobiography:

These vase-paintings have of late been the subject of very minute study and classification, and no one could deny their great freshness and charm. But this study has
mainly been concerned with questions of style and technique, and has less regarded
the broader questions of mythologic rendering, and of the course of life and physical
training. We have to look not only *at* the vases but *through* them at Greek art and
civilisation.[18]

In view of this it would seem unlikely that Gardner's teaching did much to
foster Beazley's interest in connoisseurship of vases. As our knowledge stands
at present, the most likely hypothesis remains that he began to take a close
interest in them through reading the works of specialists such as Hartwig and
Furtwängler.

THE CONNOISSEUR OF THE EARLY RENAISSANCE

Sir Lawrence Jones also says that it was Cyril Bailey who introduced him to
classical music and painting, and taught him to think of aesthetics not as a
hobby but as an integral part of life. He reveals that, like every lover of the
early Italian Renaissance, he knew his Berenson very well:

The only painting—or rather fresco—of which I took home a reproduction to hang
in my rooms at Balliol was Guido Reni's 'Aurora', a choice which probably reflects
nearly enough my untutored taste at nineteen. I imagine my great-grandfather
would have made much the same selection, unless he had picked a Carlo Dolci
instead. But on a later vacation, when I joined my parents in Florence, I knew better.
For, in the meantime, there had been many an evening in Cyril Bailey's rooms, spent
in turning over our host's collection of photographs of Renaissance paintings [. . .]
Besides, I had read my Berenson, and could look out for 'tactile values' with a docile

<hr />

[16] See Grundy (1900).   [17] Cf. Gardner (1926: 26–45).
[18] Gardner (1933: 55); see Boardman (1985: 46–50).

and obedient eye. Botticelli held, I think, for my generation the position that Piero holds today; he was the touchstone of a good taste that none could call in question.[19]

In a sense, Jones's testimony also holds for Beazley, who had a great liking for the early Renaissance. He, moreover, was not content to be a mere amateur, and had acquired a thorough knowledge of fourteenth- and fifteenth-century Italian and Dutch painting. We learn about this passion from James Elroy Flecker, a close friend of Beazley's while they were both studying at Oxford. During the summer of 1908, Beazley and Flecker met in Italy to embark on a 'Grand Tour' of the Italian cities: 'We saw *all* the pictures in Italy,' Flecker wrote to his friend Frank Savery.[20] While discussing Beazley's many gifts as a connoisseur, Ashmole tells how he acquired a picture (reproduced as Pl. 13 below) which he believed to be by the Sienese painter Simone Martini:

In 1910 he was with Gow in Paris studying in the Louvre. Concentration on Greek art had not prevented his acquiring an extensive knowledge of other forms of art— Italian and, especially, Flemish painting, and together they bought a little picture which they judged to be by Simone Martini. It was eventually found to be from a polyptych of which other panels had been acquired by Langton Douglas, and believing that the panels ought to be reunited, they sold it to him; it is now in the Lehman collection (Metropolitan Museum of New York) and is thought to be a copy by Lippo Vanni of a figure by Simone Martini.[21]

The panel shows St Ansanus, and was acquired by Beazley and Gow from a secondhand dealer on the banks of the Seine, of the sort that can still be seen today lining the walls by the river. We do not know exactly when they sold the picture to R. Langton Douglas, the art critic and dealer, but it cannot have remained in their possession for long, since it changed hands again in 1916 and passed into the collection of Philip Lehman, one of the greatest American collectors of Italian Renaissance painting of his time. Berenson, who played a very active part in building up the collection of Lehman's son, believed that the painting was by Lippo Vanni, a pupil of Simone Martini's. Nowadays, however, the balance is tipping back in favour of Simone Martini, at least if we are to go by what Frederico Zeri and Pope-Hennessy say in their respective catalogues of the Lehman collection.[22] It cannot necessarily be assumed that Zeri and Pope-Hennessy are right, but Beazley's penetrating intuition is no less remarkable for that. Pope-Hennessy also mentions that there are two photographs of the picture in the archives of the Harvard Center for Renaissance Studies founded by Berenson in the I Tatti villa,

[19] L. E. Jones (1956: 130–1).   [20] Cited by Sherwood (1973: 81).

[21] Ashmole, in Kurtz (ed.) (1985: 59).

[22] Zeri (1980: 94–5); Pope-Hennessy (1987: 21).

one of which has an annotation on the back showing that it was sent by Beazley.[23]

That Berenson's name should appear here is in no way surprising, given his extraordinary celebrity at the time. What is more interesting is to discover that Beazley may have been familiar with his work from a very early stage, as would appear to be indicated by the fact that he owned the first volume of *The Study and Criticism of Italian Art*, in the second edition of 1903. This book, which is now in the Ashmolean Museum, contains a handwritten dedication: 'To Jacky from me' (he was known as 'Jacky' or 'Jack' to his family and friends). This would seem to suggest someone close to Beazley, and in view of the date of the edition we thought at first of Flecker, who had accompanied him on his pilgrimage through the cities of Italy. Dietrich von Bothmer, however, to whom we sent a copy of the dedication, believes that it is clearly in the handwriting of Marie Ezra, whom Beazley married on 13 August 1919.

THE POETRY LOVER

Be that as it may, it is to the figure of James Elroy Flecker that we would now like to turn our attention. Flecker was a poet and dramatist who died too young (in 1915, at the age of 30) to achieve all he might have done and take his place among the outstanding literary figures of the first half of the century. His best-known works are a collection of poetry, *The Golden Journey to Samarkand*, and a play, *Hassan*, which Flecker did not live to see performed, but which was very well received when it was put on at the Haymarket Theatre in London in 1923. George Bernard Shaw, Gilbert Murray, and T. E. Lawrence all thought highly of Flecker's talent.

In 1913, in the preface to *The Golden Journey to Samarkand*, Flecker declared himself a disciple of the Parnassians; a specialist might well add the names of Swinburne, Baudelaire, the early poems of Oscar Wilde, Aubrey Beardsley, Housman, and . . . Beazley. Indeed, the influence of Beazley on Flecker's poetry was frequently emphasized by their contemporaries. The two men met in February or March 1904, and were very close during their student years. They both wrote poetry, and they took part in drama together. Beazley's connection with poetry is somewhat problematical; after publishing some of his poems, one of which appeared in the volume *Oxford Poetry* in 1913 he stopped writing them and refused even to speak about the subject: 'In later life he would never speak of his poetry, and it was not possible to discover how much he had written or why he abandoned it.'[24]

[23] Mariano (1965); Beazley's name does not appear among Berenson's correspondents.
[24] Beazley (1911a; 1913); Ashmole, in Kurtz (ed.) (1985: 59).

Flecker's various biographers have emphasized Beazley's influence on his poetry. The most recent biography, by John Sherwood, goes into their relationship as students at Oxford in some detail. This was made possible by the fact that he was given access to the Flecker family's papers, including letters from Beazley to Flecker from which he prints some interesting extracts. I have not seen the letters, but assume that unless they have been destroyed, they must still be in the family's possession. Sherwood writes: 'Nor is there any clue to the exact nature of his relationship with Beazley. It took place, however, in an aura of bisexuality.'[25] It should be noted that as a general rule, 'mild homosexual romances' were quite common in the extremely cloistered world of the colleges; Lawrence Jones goes so far as to write that 'the notional gap between man and girl made it difficult for either to regard the other as a simple fellow-creature'.[26]

It is clear that when Flecker met Beazley in the spring of 1904 he fell completely under his spell. Shortly afterwards, in the Easter vacation, they went to Wales together. In a letter, Flecker described Beazley in flattering terms:

He is an encyclopaedia, but a fascinating one. He reminds me of Shelley, as portrayed by Hogg! especially when he lies on the hearthrug, his head almost in the fire, with his long light hair, slight frame and pensive face. The description sounds as if it is out of a novel, does it not? Indeed such a fellow is not often to be met with outside of a novel or romance. He is shy, free from all touch of conceit and healthy-minded withal, with a voice like a bell.[27]

And a little later: 'He is far and away the most interesting fellow I have ever met in my life: he is the only man now living that I can think of whose intellect makes me feel ashamed and calls up all the admiration of which I am capable.'[28]

A drawing by Reginald Wilenski, an art historian somewhat younger than Beazley, and also a Balliol man, shows Beazley in 1911 at the age of 26. Not only was Beazley both good-looking and intelligent, he was also much more mature than his friend. Frank Savery noted that when Flecker arrived in Oxford, he 'was extraordinarily undeveloped, even for an English Public School boy'.[29] He came from an extremely devout, puritanical family and was very close to his parents, whereas Beazley, with his parents on the continent, had been living a more or less independent life for several years, and had the reputation in Oxford of being an agnostic. No doubt the fact that Beazley professed agnosticism was enough to make Flecker do likewise in his turn:

---

[25] Sherwood (1973: 35).   [26] L. E. Jones (1956: 37).
[27] Letter to Sedgwick (Easter 1904); Sherwood (1973: 36).
[28] Letter from Flecker to his parents (June 1904); Sherwood (1973: 38).
[29] Quoted in Flecker (1930: p. vi).

'It might interest you to know that I have at length definitely become an agnostic, with a firm belief in the immortality of the soul.'[30] Flecker's parents took this very badly and laid the blame for it on Beazley, who from then on was considered *persona non grata* by Flecker's mother. She even took great care to try to erase all mention of Beazley from the biography of Flecker published by Geraldine Hodgson in 1925.

It should also be said that at that time, Beazley was no shrinking violet. John Sherwood quotes a note (undated) scribbled in Beazley's hand, which, although not very academic, is full of fun and exuberance:

No we did *not* go to Wytham, George and I, no we did *not* find lovely girl in inn, no we did *not* make overtures, no I was *not* rebuffed (horribly) at second appearance owing to precipitation, no she did *not* say to me 'don't you think you'd better take it out again?' after fruitless gropings (it = my hand), no we did *not* part on equally good terms, no George is *not* going to meet her on Sunday, no she has *not* lustrous eyes and the sweetest smile, no no my name is not John.[31]

These biographical details give some idea of the spirit that presided over a magazine called *The Best Man* which was produced jointly by Beazley and Flecker early in the summer of 1906. It did not survive beyond one issue, and is the only evidence we have of a literary and artistic collaboration between the two men. Some of the drawings and written pieces in it come from a notebook called the 'Yellow Book of Japes', which they kept for a while as a record of all the literary witticisms that occurred to them, and which was well known to some of their contemporaries as being of a rather scandalous nature. The written pieces in *The Best Man* were almost all by Flecker, the drawings by Beazley. The cover, which was bright red, showed a picture of a diabolical creature, a slender black figure with a face drawn in outline which was somewhat reminiscent of the drawings of Aubrey Beardsley. The 'Yellow Book of Japes' was probably also a reference to the famous review *Yellow Book*, which printed the drawings by Beardsley that gained him a certain notoriety. The drawings on the inside pages of *The Best Man* were accompanied by limericks, for which Flecker's talent was renowned. In the earliest biography of Flecker, there is a fairly salacious one which he would have been hard-pushed to publish, complete with illustration, in *The Best Man*:

> If Daremberg bedded with Saglio
> And the scene were engraved in intaglio
> And worn in a ring
> By our popular King
> What delight it would give his seraglio![32]

---

[30] Letter to Sedgwick (Easter 1904); Sherwood (1973: 36). [31] Cited by Sherwood (1973: 35).
[32] Goldring (1922: 34); the limerick is by Flecker and a friend from Cambridge (not named).

Beazley's influence on Flecker became even more clear after the discovery among the Flecker family's papers of a notebook in which Flecker copied out twenty-eight poems by Beazley. Sherwood writes: 'Beazley's youthful verse appears to have been influenced mainly by Housman and Yeats. It is unequal in quality, though no more so than early Flecker. At its best it reveals a distinctive poetic personality, difficult to mistake for Flecker's though one is conscious of a common attitude to words and images.'[33] We have had the good fortune to discover another notebook, this time in Beazley's own handwriting, which contains twenty-five of his poems, most of them unpublished.[34] The manuscript indicates that it was donated to the Bodleian by E. A. East of Blackwell's on 6 August 1975 (Edward East was the former head of the rare books' department at Blackwell's bookshop). No definite indication is given of the dates of the poems, but the first poem in the notebook ('Waste') mentions the narrator at the age of 20, which would place it in 1905. Moreover, Flecker wrote his 'Invitation' in 1909, which shows that by that time Beazley had all but, if not completely, stopped writing poetry. This would suggest that, if the poems in the notebook are arranged chronologically, they were written between 1905 and 1909. Sherwood works on this assumption in his biography of Flecker, having picked up the allusion to the narrator's age in 'Waste'. He cannot be far wrong where the dates are concerned, but it should be noted that the poems in the notebook at the Bodleian are not necessarily in chronological order; on the contrary, the way in which they are arranged seems to reflect Beazley's concern for the overall composition of the book. Be that as it may, Douglas Goldring adds an interesting detail concerning the habit that both poets had of copying out their poems: 'Both Flecker and his friend, J. D. Beazley, had a habit of writing out their poems very neatly in tiny little manuscript books and presenting them to the lady of the flat. Several such volumes were in circulation among our group and are still, I hope, in existence.'[35]

Sherwood also describes the influence that Beazley had over Flecker at this time:

Beazley's main functions at Oxford were twofold: he provided a climate of creative excitement and enjoyment in which the lyrical mood could flourish; and even more important, he was the candid friend and discriminating critic whom Flecker badly needed to have standing by his elbow. It was due to Beazley's critical influence that he began to revise and refine, instead of pouring out a torrent of indifferent work. [. . .] it was Beazley who set him on the way to becoming a sound craftsman.[36]

[33] Sherwood (1973: 44).
[34] Oxford, Bodleian Library, MS Eng. poet. f. 32 (four poems have been published).
[35] Goldring (1922: 59).   [36] Sherwood (1973: 45).

A letter which Beazley wrote to Flecker in mid-August 1906 gives some idea of the very precise literary advice he gave him, and his style is not in fact far removed from that which he was to adopt later in works of a more scientific nature, in particular in his reviews of the *CVA*. Commenting on the first attempts at 'From Grenoble' and 'Rioupéroux', two poems connected with Flecker's experiences in France, Beazley wrote:

Why 'turns colder than the moon'? I don't like the 1st line v. much, perhaps because I can't make out the place name. Change 2nd couplet of 1st verse. You don't want the mountains, do you? Rioupéroux also unimpressive first line. Line 6 jerky, in the wrong place. And I think change line 4, knocking out the repeated 'and there as I wandered' in favour of some additional touch which you must carefully choose.[37]

As already suggested, the assumption that Beazley stopped writing poetry around 1909 is based on a poem written in that year by Flecker, an 'Invitation to a young but learned friend to abandon archaeology for a moment, and play once more with his neglected Muse', in which he earnestly and elegantly entreats his friend to return to poetry, which he is neglecting a little too much for his liking:

> Must I alone keep playing? Will not you,
> Lord of the Measures, string your lyre anew?
> Lover of Greece, is this the richest store
> You bring us,—withered leaves and dusty lore,
> And broken vases widowed of their wine,
> To brand you pedant while you stand divine?
> Decorous words beseem the learned lip,
> But poets have the nicer scholarship.[38]

With regard to this poem, it should be noted that the archives of Christ Church still contain the handwritten text of a lecture on Flecker's poetry given on 10 June 1928 to the Pater society by Sydney Owen, a colleague of Beazley's at Christ Church, where he taught for seventeen years (from 1908 to 1925).[39] Owen mentions the 'Invitation' and provides explanations which make it possible to identify the literary figures described by Flecker in the poem. He complains that poets have become rare since Swinburne died, referring to him as 'the sea-born, the Ionian' because he was born in Bonchurch on the south coast of England; there are hardly any left apart from Housman, who wrote *A Shropshire Lad* (1897), and 'he dreams deeper than the oaks of Clun' (a place in Shropshire), which indicates that he is no longer very

---

[37] Letter to Flecker (Aug. 1906); Sherwood (1973: 63).
[38] Flecker (1916: 96–7).
[39] Owen, 'The Poems of James Elroy Flecker'; Oxford, Christ Church, MSS lxx. B. 13.

active; there is Kipling, 'our Tyrtaeus', the war poet, but his popularity is fading fast; finally there is Yeats, 'whose gown is black and crimson', like a magician's, to suggest his fantastical, esoteric poetry. All these identifications were in fact based on a letter which Beazley wrote to Sydney Owen one month before the lecture.[40]

Another interesting comment on Beazley's poetry comes from T. E. Lawrence, in a letter to Sydney Cockerell, the director of the Fitzwilliam Museum in Cambridge:'Beazley is a very wonderful fellow, who has written almost the best poems that ever came out of Oxford: but his shell was always hard, & with time he seems to curl himself tighter & tighter into it. If it hadn't been for that accursed Greek art he'd have been a very fine poet.'[41] It seems, however, that Lawrence was doing little more here than repeat the opinion of Flecker. Lawrence was of course capable of forming his own opinion of Beazley's poetry and personality; like most of his colleagues he was a great lover of poetry, and he had a particular reverence for poets. It is a little too much of a coincidence, however; it was Flecker who deeply admired Beazley and his poetry, and it was also Flecker who had to suffer when his friend grew more distant towards him.[42] Lawrence probably did not know much about Beazley; in any case, his name does not appear anywhere in the index of the monumental biography of Lawrence of Arabia (almost 1,200 pages) which was published in 1989.[43] On the other hand, Lawrence knew Flecker very well, having met him in Beirut in 1911, and the two men subsequently corresponded; Lawrence even wrote a pamphlet on Flecker.[44] When Lawrence died, Sydney Cockerell must have told Beazley about the remarks he had made about him, because we have a letter from Beazley to Cockerell dated 28 May 1935, in which he gives his own opinion of what Lawrence had said:'Lawrence was a generous man, and it was nice of him to speak well of my poems: but I assure you that he was mistaken: they were quite valueless.'[45]

The shared experience of poetry was the basis for the friendship between Beazley and Flecker, because it was when Beazley stopped writing poetry that he began to grow further and further away from his friend. At that time he was having to devote more and more time to his research into the artistic personalities of Attic vase-painters.'J. works because he loves work and it is his duty. Everything he does he does well.' Flecker did not know how right he

---

[40] Letter from Beazley to Owen, enclosed with the script of the lecture (Oxford, 10 May 1928).
[41] Letter to Cockerell ([Karachi], 27 May 1927); Garnett (ed.) (1938: 519).
[42] See letter from Flecker to Savery (17 Jan. 1914); Flecker (1926: 70).
[43] Wilson (1989).   [44] Lawrence (1937).
[45] Letter from Beazley to Cockerell (Oxford, 28 May 1935); British Library, Res. MS 123/A (Add. MS 52 704).

was when he wrote those words about Beazley to his mother, in an attempt
to heal the rift between him and his family.[46] The fact that he had stopped
writing poetry, however, did not of course mean that he had ceased to be a
lover of it.

VASE PAINTING IS LIKE POETRY

Martin Robertson has published the most interesting extracts from
Beazley's correspondence with his parents, Donald and Petica. One letter
stands out from this collection; written in May 1911, between his article on
'Kleophrades' and his essay on the Berlin Painter, it contains the following:
'I often wonder whether I am a pedant or a fanatic. I suppose a year ago I
was a fanatic and in a year's time I shall be a pedant. But one must have *Facts*
. . . ; Kleophrades is a *Fact*.'[47] As the suspension points in Martin Robertson's
quotation indicate, it is not complete. Here it is in its entirety: 'But one must
have *Facts*, see *Rowton House Rhymes* by Mackenzie lately published (recommend it to your little sister): Kleophrades is a *Fact* like Rum for Bagster
in Rowton rhymes.'[48] *Rowton House Rhymes* was a collection of poetry edited
in 1911 by William Mackenzie, and Bagster and Rum appear in a poem entitled 'Bagster, French-polisher, Descants'. Bagster's job as a French-polisher
leaves him time to think and talk, and indeed he is something of a philosopher. The poem is written in Cockney, and the scene it describes seems to
be set in a pub. Bagster soliloquizes in the presence of two fellow-drinkers
and the barman, Elfred, and he is probably already somewhat the worse for
wear, because he starts to ask himself great questions about life, notably what
it is that drives men to work. Some work for the love of a person who is dear
to them, others for money, but in the end most work simply in order to eat.
What a life! Working to have enough to eat, so that one has the strength to
go on working. In the end, 'Rum' is the only thing that helps to swallow the
bitter pill.

> Wot do I want? Fects! FECTS! Nah, Rum's a *fect*:
> Rum's somethin' solid in a wobbly world.
> It's cheap. It's there. It's never fur aw'y.
> It nips yer stummick, an' it 'eats yer blood;
> Gives ye the notion that you're still alive . . .

In short, it is up to each individual to find something that gives his life meaning. Although the importance of this poem should not be exaggerated—the

---

[46] Letter from Flecker to his mother (June 1904); Hodgson (1925: 78).
[47] Robertson (1976: 32–3).
[48] Letter from Beazley to Mrs Robertson (Oxford, 16 May 1911); Oxford, Beazley Archive.

allusion to Petica's sister shows that he was being light-hearted—it does nonetheless shed new light on Beazley's letter. Before reading Mackenzie's poem, I took Beazley's letter to mean that his work could be compared to a foundation course in the history of art; in other words, research into individual artists was the indispensable basis of any form of history of art, even if it was archaeological and concerned vase-painting ('one must have *Facts* . . . ; Kleophrades is a *Fact*'). This interpretation seemed to be corroborated by what he said about the Kleophrades Painter: 'A general discussion of Kleophrades must be postponed until we have studied the work of some of his more important contemporaries, especially those who applied themselves to the decoration of the larger kinds of vase.'[49] But what his reference to the poem tells us is more simple and direct: research into artistic personalities is the scholar's home ground, the territory he covers in his day-to-day work, and from which he gains a certain professional satisfaction.

Had he been less self-critical, Beazley might have done as Housman did and pursued a dual career as scholar and poet.[50] It has been claimed by Richard Jenkyns that at this time scholarship and poetry no longer went together as successfully as they had done a century before, and that, whereas at the beginning of the nineteenth century they had still been regarded as related fields, a hundred years later they had come to be seen as rivals.[51] There can be no doubt that this view needs to be challenged, at least where Beazley is concerned. The evidence suggests that he was always deeply interested in poetry.

Two examples should suffice to illustrate this. While Harold Acton, the historian, collector, aesthete, and poet was studying at Oxford in the mid-1920s, he became friendly with Beazley and his wife, who were happy to spend time with brilliantly gifted undergraduates like him. Acton mentions his relationship with the Beazleys in his *Memoirs*, and what he says about Beazley himself is more than a little reminiscent of his influence on Flecker: 'So high were Jacky's standards that one went from him purified, resolved to write something worthier of such a mentor.'[52] It should be noted that around the same time another poet who was to become famous, Louis MacNeice, spent some

---

[49] Beazley (1910: 39).

[50] This is what Ashmole implies (in Kurtz (ed.) 1985: 58) when he quotes E. S. G. Robinson, who knew Beazley when he was at Christ Church: 'He [Beazley] thought it would be amusing to polish up my verse composition; perhaps a reaction from his deliberate abandonment about this time of writing English verse. We took Housman's "Shropshire Lad" and turned many of its poems into Latin elegiacs. He would go through my copy with skill and kindness, then, in a few minutes, with idiomatic and effortless ease, produce his own version.'

[51] Jenkyns (1980: 344).

[52] Acton (1948: 142). Acton neglects to say that he used to accompany Beazley in his travels through Europe; see Rowe in Chaney and Ritchie (eds.) (1984: 64).

time with the Beazleys. It is not certain, however, that MacNeice was aware of Beazley's activities as a poet; he only knew them through Mary Ezra, who was Marie Beazley's daughter by her first marriage to David Ezra, and whom MacNeice married not long after they met.[53]

More evidence came fifteen years or so later, this time in relation to philology, and to Denys Page's editions of Greek poetry recorded on papyrus. In one of his prefaces, dated 1940, Page thanked Beazley so warmly as to leave no doubt about his mastery of Greek metrics: 'And late, but not too late, Professor J. D. Beazley performed a miracle of deep and painless surgery on every page: to him above all my readers I owe whatever state of convalescence they may find in this volume; they will never know how ill it was before.'[54]

There is even a direct allusion to be found to the parallel between vase-painting and verse in a review by Beazley of one of the volumes of Edmond Pottier's *CVA*. One of the early criticisms of the *CVA* was that it tended to publish vases with modern restorations:

Is it really impossible to have the vases cleaned before publication? This is an obvious question, but though I have been asking it for years I have never received an answer. Not everyone likes vases and vase-paintings that are half ancient and half modern; the modern side by side with the ancient, and concealing it or travestying it. Suppose that a schoolboy took a text of a Greek play, supplied the missing parts in doggerel, and altered the old wherever he chose, regardless of metre or sense; and suppose that an editor, professing to publish the text of the play, should publish the schoolboy's version instead? I hear the answer—'just what many editors of the classics do.' But would the technical commission of the Budé Association be completely satisfied? And here, remember, the text which can be recovered, with a dash of sponge, is not a copy of a copy of a copy, but *the poet's autograph* . . . [my italics].[55]

If vase-painters were to be thought of as poets, it was only right that one should at least make the effort to find out about their personalities. Since most painters remained anonymous, however, this might appear to be a very arduous, if not impossible task. Yet it was in this area that Beazley gave the fullest expression to his demiurgical abilities, by creating from nowhere an onomastics which itself was far from devoid of poetry. We can see this Alice-in-Wonderland universe in names such as the Flying-Angel Painter, the Swing Painter, the Brown-Egg Painter, the Group of the Skinny Griffins, the Painter of the Woolly Satyrs, the Class of the Seven Lobster-Claws, The Fat-Runner Group, etc. As Charles Calhoun remarks: 'No one has ever said that the most intense scholarship could not be, every now and then, fun.'[56] Calhoun's high spirits do, however, need to be tempered by an awareness that Beazley's

[53] Stallworthy (1995).   [54] Page (ed.) (1970: p. xvii).
[55] Beazley (1928).   [56] Calhoun (1987: 12).

humour may tell us as much about his poetic universe as about vase-painting. From the historiographical point of view, the parallel with *Alice in Wonderland* is illuminating, since Lewis Carroll was not only the poet that we know, but also a gifted logician and mathematician. It would seem then that scholar-poets were not in fact uncommon in Oxford in the second half of the nineteenth and early twentieth centuries. If nothing else, the success of Housman's *A Shropshire Lad* should be enough to convince us that there was nothing unusual about it, especially where classicists were concerned. But whereas Housman was anxious to make it absolutely clear that there was a supposedly watertight barrier between philology and poetry, this does not seem to have been at all the case where Beazley was concerned.

A tender-hearted Ajax

We shall now turn our attention briefly to Exekias, a painter and potter who worked in Athens in the third quarter of the sixth century, and was the most outstanding individual artist of that period. His case demonstrates how Beazley's poetic culture could be reflected in his writings.

In a lecture which he gave to the British Academy in 1928, he spoke for the first time about black-figured pottery as a whole, and also about the work of the artist who 'in many respects [was] the greatest of black-figure painters'.[57] Some of these remarks may appear sibylline if we do not bear in mind the particular preoccupations of the speaker: 'His signatures are beautifully neat: and as a lover of form he signs in a faultless trimeter: the spondee in the fourth foot, with which he has been credited, is due to a clever emendation by a modern scholar.'[58] On two vases by this artist the signature is iambic; one of these is a neck-amphora in Berlin, the other an amphora in the Vatican.[59] No doubt Beazley's remark shows what philology can bring to the study of artists' signatures, but how should we interpret it more generally? Are we to believe, as Aristotle did (*Poetics*, 1449^{a}24–8), that the metrics observed in Exekias' signature reflect a commonplace speech habit which was transposed here into writing? Or that on the contrary, the versification was entirely conscious and should be seen in relation to the calligraphic perfection of Exekias' signatures? Beazley appears to have opted for the second solution.[60] The hypothesis is plausible if not finally demonstrable, as was another supposition of Beazley's, that the picture of *Achilles and Ajax playing dice* on the famous Vatican amphora was based on a lost poem. It must at least be admitted that neither idea was entirely gratuitous.

---

[57] Beazley ([1929]: 18).   [58] Ibid. (17).

[59] Berlin 1720 in *ABV* (143 no. 1); Vatican 344 in *ABV* (145 no. 13).

[60] *Contra* Saerens (1995: 38).

Sometimes even the artist's style itself is eloquent. Let us consider another amphora by Exekias, also a masterpiece, in this case an early one, which is conserved in Boulogne. The main face of the vase shows a theme which would later become well known through Sophoclean tragedy, the preparations for the *Suicide of Ajax*. In explaining that Exekias was the only archaic artist to show not the dead hero or the moment of his death, but the preparations for the final act, Beazley may have been thinking of Lessing's *Laocöon*, which itself refers (not very faithfully, it seems) to what Philostrates says in his *Life of Apollonius of Tyana*, about Timomache's *Furious Ajax*: he praises the painter for having chosen the moment of greatest dramatic intensity, which never coincides with the performance of the act itself.[61] The most remarkable passage, however, was that in which Beazley noted Exekias' predilection for painting pictures of Ajax, son of Telamon and most courageous of Greeks, in terms which show that he was still a poet at heart: 'There is something in Exekias of Ajax; so that he could admire and understand the hero, slow, and strong, and at heart delicate.'[62]

A remark of this kind must raise the issue of just how subjective a critic is entitled to be. Martin Robertson is very clear on this: 'Some Edwardian lady is recorded as saying that being kissed by a man without a moustache is like eating an egg without salt; and value judgments are to me the salt in art history.'[63] Perhaps we should simply say that as a gentleman, Beazley had the courage of his convictions, and was not afraid to reveal them. The idea that criticism was entitled to a certain degree of subjectivity was a part of his way of thinking which gave his work more coherence than might be apparent at first sight. His aim was to construct an exhaustive global history of Attic black-figure and red-figure pottery. For this reason, he did not concern himself only with the great masters such as Exekias and the Berlin Painter, but also with all the other more modest artisans who worked in the workshops of the Kerameikos. By so doing he pioneered an approach which from then on formed an integral part of the study of pottery. We now have names for the pupils, imitators, and successors associated with the great artists; and the fact that he called one of them 'the Worst Painter', and another 'the clown', shows that he did not place all painters on the same artistic plane. The ability of art criticism to create its own scale of values, subjective though it may be, given that it is always more or less a matter of individual judgement, is an inevitable and even necessary dimension of the art historian's practice. In this respect we subscribe to the view of Ernst Gombrich: 'The neglect or even denial of values seems to me the greatest danger in that trend towards the dehumanization of the humanities.'[64]

---

[61] Lessing (1874: 31). [62] Beazley ([1929]: 20–1).
[63] Robertson (1985: 28). [64] Gombrich (1984: 25).

The discourse of art criticism is subsidiary to the overall discipline which we refer to here as art history. What is ultimately of interest to us in Beazley's work is what he understood by that term. What did he mean by a history of the art of Attic pottery? How did he conceive of that field of research, which he had created virtually alone? Since Beazley took great care never to develop a theory on this subject, we need to study the logic of his thinking if we are to see how it was related to the traditional approaches of art history, but also to conclusions that may be drawn as to the methods by which Greek vases were produced in the Kerameikos. We shall attempt to give some answers to these questions in the next chapter.

5

The Workshop and the Circle, the Painter and his School

A HISTORY OF THE ART OF ATTIC VASE-PAINTERS

I was brought up to think of 'style' as a sacred thing, as the man himself.

Sir John Beazley

Apart from those painters whom Beazley identified very early on, such as the Kleophrades Painter and the Berlin Painter, Beazley took little trouble to explain the reasons for his attributions. We therefore need to examine his work on those two painters; this will help us not only to analyse his method, but also to identify clearly the radical changes that he introduced to the study of pottery from the very beginning of his research. On the Berlin Painter he published one of the few articles in which he explained his ideas about the connoisseurship of vases in detail. His conclusion was a sharp reaction against erroneous interpretations, which he saw as distorting any overall picture one might have of the production of painted vases in Athens, and also any sense of the status of the painters.[1]

Despite this, the influence of the pre-existing model of Italian Renaissance painting could be seen in his use of terms such as 'master', 'school', and 'manner'. With regard to these, Beazley did sometimes hesitate over what terminology to use, changing his mind as his knowledge of the painters and pottery increased. A parallel can be drawn here with changes of attribution, since essentially they involved the same kind of problem, that of making a distinction between the works of the painter and those of the workshop, between the copy and the imitation.

BEFORE THE METHOD

The article on 'Kleophrades' was the first that Beazley wrote about a painter, but before that an article was published in which he dealt with three vases

---

[1] Beazley (1922).

at the Ashmolean Museum.[2] This is worth mentioning, since various writers have seen in it (*a*) a reflection of the impasse in which the study of pottery found itself at the beginning of the century and (*b*) the beginnings of Beazley's method. Cornelia Isler-Kerényi notes the failure of the traditional method to achieve any coherent result, as can be seen from this attempt to solve various problems by studying three vases which have nothing in common except that they happen to come from the same place, and in support of her argument she quotes a statement made in 1953 by Andreas Rumpf (1890–1966): 'Es ließ sich nicht verkennen, daß um 1900 ein toter Punkt erreicht war' ('There could be no doubt that around 1900 things had come to a standstill').[3] Martin Robertson claims to see the beginnings of the method in a postscript to the 1908 article. Beazley quoted several vases in connection with one of those discussed in the article, a small-column krater from the beginnings of red-figure, and added the footnote: 'These kraters all belong to the same period and exhibit the same artistic tendency, a tendency which finds higher expression in the cups and amphorae of the time.'[4] It would seem that he was not yet very far advanced in his research, since with regard to the krater he merely said: 'The style is not individual, and it cannot be assigned to a particular artist.'[5]

A word on iconography. Beazley described a painted image on a black-figure pelike, showing a satyr sitting on a rock in the centre of the picture and holding a sort of abacus. To his left was another satyr, and to his right a male figure, perhaps Hermes. Although this was just one single scene, Beazley gave an ingenious interpretation of it, which he would later dismiss with no comment other than a laconic 'unexplained'.[6] Without prejudging his reasons for retracting, we may note that the excessive ingenuity of this interpretation was in contrast with the elegant economy of simplicity which, according to Henri Metzger, would be one of the main features of Beazley's hermeneutics.[7] What he did initially was to link the picture with a lost satyric drama about the marriage of Hermes. When he gave up that explanation he was forced to let the image float without literary moorings, and indeed we know that this was something he greatly disliked having to do, in which respect he was very much like the archaeologist-philologists of the nineteenth century.

---

[2] Beazley (1908). [3] Isler-Kerényi (1980: 13 n. 32).

[4] Beazley (1908: 318); Robertson (1971: 429–30).

[5] Beazley (1908: 317). He would later assign the vase to Myson; Oxford 561 in *ARV*² (241 no. 52).

[6] Oxford 563 (Eucharides Painter) in *ABV* (396 no. 21); reproduced as Pl. 14 below.

[7] Metzger (1987: 110).

THE KLEOPHRADES PAINTER AND HIS WORKSHOP

As the first of four great artistic personalities which Beazley unveiled to the public before the First World War, the other three being the Berlin Painter, the Pan Painter and the Achilles Painter, the Kleophrades Painter belongs to a second generation of red-figure painters from the beginning of the fifth century BC. Unlike the others, 'Kleophrades' had been known since 1829, thanks to a cup in the Cabinet des Médailles, bearing a signature on its foot in the form ΚΛΕΟΦΡΑΔΕΣ ΕΠΟΙΕΣΕΝ ΑΜΑΣ.......Σ.[8] The Duc de Luynes had published it in 1840 in the catalogue of his collection.[9] In 1893, Hartwig grouped eight vases around the Paris cup, and Hauser later added the Vivenzio hydria in Naples, with the beautiful painting of the Ilioupersis.[10] Following Gerhard's example, Hartwig had reconstructed the fragmentary inscription as *Amasis egraphsen* (painted by Amasis), and had thus created the painter Amasis (II), not to be confused with the first Amasis, another well-known black-figure potter and painter (Hartwig did not make the distinction by adding a number, as Klein did in his *Meistersignaturen*[11]).

The painter's name, or rather the form it takes when transcribed as a signature, is of some importance to our discussion, since it was the focus of certain aspects of Beazley's stylistic approach. He preferred Jan Six's restoration of the Amasis inscription to Hartwig's; Six believed that the gap indicated a patronym: *Amasidos uios* (son of Amasis). Since then this has been shown to be correct, and we now have three signatures which enable us to identify Amasis as the father of Kleophrades.[12] In adopting Six's solution, Beazley found himself without a painter's name, but this did not trouble him:

In any case the manufacturer from whose workshop the cup came was called Kleophrades. [. . .] It is possible that the man called Kleophrades not only manufactured it, but painted it with his own hand; but it is equally possible that someone else painted it. The name of the painter, however, is of little importance; what interests us is himself and his style. We may conveniently use the name Kleophrades to signify 'the painter of the cup in the Cabinet des Médailles which is signed by Kleophrades as manufacturer', just as we speak of the 'style of Brygos', although Brygos signs exclusively with ἐποίησεν.[13]

The traditional interpretation made no clear distinction between the potter's work and that of the painter (as we can see from the expression 'style of Brygos'). Beazley would avoid this source of confusion by systematically adopting conventional names (Painter of X or Y). Even so, this process

---

[8] Cab. Méd. 535, 699 and other frr. in *ARV²* (191 no. 103).   [9] Luynes (1840: pl. xliv).

[10] Hartwig (1893: 400–20); FR (ii. pl. 34).   [11] Klein (1887: 149).

[12] Six (1888); Bothmer (1985: 230–1).   [13] Beazley (1910: 38).

of symbolic divestment ('the name of the painter, however, is of little importance') did not happen as a matter of course, since Beazley felt obliged to return to the matter several times. He needed to offer something else to make up for it, and this new instrument, which was more subtle and, paradoxically, more reliable, was known as style. Here again Beazley could appeal to Hartwig, who said of the Kleophrades Painter: 'Wenn auch der Name des Meisters der Schale der Sammlung Luynes nicht unbestritten feststeht, so wird uns doch, wie wir sehen werden, seine Individualität greifbar aus seinen Werken entgegentreten' ('Even if the name of the master who painted the cup in the Luynes collection is not undisputed, nonetheless, as we shall see, his individual personality will become clearly apparent to us from his works').[14] Hartwig showed him the path he must follow if he was to move decisively on to a new stage.

I would now like to discuss a pelike in Berlin (reproduced as Pl. 15 below), which Beazley included in his list of 1910, and which bore two signatures in the form *Epiktetos egraphsen*.[15] *Egraphsen* usually denoted the painter, so the pelike should not normally have appeared in the list of works by the Kleophrades Painter, since Epiktetos is named as the author of the picture. Initially he did not deny that Epiktetos was the author; he merely noted the similarities, and inserted the vase into the list on the grounds that it 'shows the influence of Kleophrades'.[16] It was not until 1925 that he included the vase among the works of the Kleophrades Painter: 'Trotz der Inschrift reihe ich diese Vase unter den Werken des Kleophradesmalers ein. Vorsichtiger wäre es gewesen, auf meiner früheren Meinung zu bestehen, daß sie eine Nachahmung des Kleophradesmalers von Epiktetos sei; doch hat mich erneute Untersuchung überzeugt, daß sie gar nichts Epiktetisches, nur Kleophradisches hat and daß es unlogisch wäre, sie von den Spätwerken des Kleophradesmalers irgendwie loszureißen' ('Despite the signature, I am classing this vase as a work by the Kleophrades Painter. It would have been more prudent to hold to my earlier opinion that it was an imitation of the Kleophrades Painter by Epiktetos; further investigation has convinced me, however, that it bears no resemblance to the works of Epiktetos, only to those of the Kleophrades Painter, and that it would be illogical to make any attempt to separate it from the late works of the latter').[17] Later it was thought that a second Epiktetos existed, to be distinguished from the equally well-known contemporary painter of the same name. This would have meant that the name Epiktetos (II) was the real name of the Kleophrades Painter.[18] In the end John Boardman solved the puzzle, by demonstrating that the signatures were modern.[19] This

---

[14] Hartwig (1893: 402).   [15] Berlin 2170 in *ARV*[2] (185 no. 28).
[16] Beazley (1910: 61).   [17] *AVS* (71 no. 23).
[18] G. M. A. Richter (1936).   [19] Boardman (1981).

neatly illustrates the sort of trial-and-error methods archaeology has to use in order to move forward; but it is also a good example of the ways in which the connoisseur's art can be of service to the study of forgeries, which is in fact one of its own fields of competence.

The workshop and the circle

In the 1910 article, the Berlin pelike 2170 was one of a series of vases for which Beazley had a special fate in store. Denying their status as autographed works, he placed them peripherally as being within the painter's sphere of influence. He did, however, make a distinction between two types; some came from the workshop and some from the circle. Words are of some importance here, and we need to examine the vocabulary that he used to distinguish between the two.

First, a revealing example of what he says about workshop pieces: 'This vigorous work we may assign to the hand of Kleophrades himself; the following two vases are from the same workshop and copies of his designs.'[20] As one would expect, when we come to the circle we find that he uses terms with a different meaning: 'In connexion with the Louvre pelike we must consider a fragment in Athens. [. . .] Graef attributed this pelike to the same hand as the Florence kotyle, N. 19*b*; at any rate it belongs to the circle of Kleophrades, and the scene recalls the Louvre pelike and the Florence stamnos. But the work is too stiff and the lines too hesitating to allow us to assign it to the master's own hand.'[21] On the one hand then, we have copies produced in the workshop based on the master's designs, and on the other, vases that can be linked to the painter himself, within a circle which is under his influence. The Berlin pelike 2170 is one of these: 'The ears, the wrist-lines, the heads and proportions recall Kleophrades. Epiktetos, who came under the influence of Douris in his later years, must have been brought into close relations with Kleophrades.'[22]

The mention of Douris' influence on Epiktetos is a reference to Furtwängler, and more precisely to the second volume of *Griechische Vasenmalerei*, which had been published the previous year. Beazley would of course have kept up with Furtwängler's publications, in which he found not only great similarities with his own aesthetics, but also more precise analyses of the way in which the work of the Kerameikos workshops was organized. In the text to which Beazley was referring, Furtwängler discussed a cup in the British Museum with the double signature of Epiktetos and Python (reproduced as Pl. 16 below).[23] Since Python had also worked for Douris, he felt that it was

---

[20] Beazley (1910: 50).   [21] Ibid. (61).
[22] Ibid. (61–2).   [23] London E 38 in *ARV*[2] (72 no. 16).

logical to suppose that Epiktetos had gone to Python's workshop to copy a composition by Douris.[24] This takes us further away from the Kleophrades Painter, although the potter Kleophrades did also work for Douris.[25] What the parallel with Furtwängler shows is that when Beazley used the term 'workshop', it must have meant much the same to him as it did to Furtwängler. For the German it was the potter's workshop, whereas for Beazley it was the manufacturer's. It is difficult to know exactly what he meant by the term 'manufacturer'. In the case of the Cabinet des Médailles cup, this could equally well be the potter, the painter or the owner of the workshop from which the cup came. These conclusions may seem rather vague, but it should be made clear that even today we are very short of precise information about the conditions in which vases were produced in the workshops of the Kerameikos.

From the workshop to the school

In 1916 the possibility of publishing two vases in the Harrow School Museum gave Beazley the chance to move on to the work of a new artist, the Harrow Painter, and to complete the list of works by the Kleophrades Painter.[26] He had in fact already included the Harrow vase in his 1910 list, by associating it with two other vases which he classed as workshop pieces. He had changed his mind about them, however, and this was his opportunity to set the record straight: 'I must first say that the vases which I then counted as school-pieces I now consider to be by the painter himself, with the exception of the vase signed by Epiktetos, N. 26b; and the pelike N. 26c, which I said might possibly be by our painter, but which I now see is not.'[27]

The Berlin pelike 2170 remained unchanged, unlike another pelike which had once been on the open market in Rome. Beazley was later to attribute this piece to the Tyszkiewicz Painter, who took his name from the collector who owned the vase that was also named after him, a calyx krater in Boston.[28] In 1916 he said nothing about the presumed author of the pelike, except that it was by another painter, even though in the same year he wrote an article about the Tyszkiewicz Painter.[29] This hesitation may have been due to the fact that he had to rely on a drawing published by Gerhard, since the vase itself was already lost by that time.[30] We note from this that Beazley did attribute vases that were known to him only through drawings.

---

[24] FR (ii. 83).   [25] Berlin 2283 and Naples, Astarita 134 in *ARV²* (429 no. 21).

[26] Beazley (1916).   [27] Ibid. (125).

[28] Boston 97.388 in *ARV²* (290 no. 1). For Robertson (1992: 128) there is no special connection between the two painters.

[29] Beazley (1916a).   [30] Gerhard (1847: pl. clix).

In the 1916 article, the school-pieces regained their status as named works, but that change seems less significant than the fact that these same pieces had been included in the first article in 1910 under the heading of workshop pieces. In fact the term 'school-pieces' appeared as early as 1910, and since it replaced the other term without explanation from the author, we can assume that the two terms are interchangeable. This is also what emerges from Martin Robertson's analysis of the use of the terms 'group', 'workshop', and 'school':

The reason why he habitually used 'group' and not 'workshop' in the heading becomes apparent in the one case where 'workshop' does appear in a chapter-title: 'The Penthesilea Painter and his Workshop'. Here the first introductory paragraph begins 'This workshop . . .' and the second 'A feature of the school of the Penthesilea Painter is the frequent collaboration of two painters on one cup (which occurs elsewhere but seldom): in this workshop—here the term may be used without misgiving—it was quite customary . . .' He clearly inclined to believe that these 'groups' represented workshops, but felt it demonstrable in the one case only.[31]

Near or in the manner?

An initial analysis shows that 'school', 'group', and 'workshop' were more or less the same, even if Beazley sometimes thought differently. In any case he used these names to express a reality which to say the least was fluctuating. One might have thought that these changes only occurred in the early stages of his work, but in fact the same thing happened fifty years later. Thus in *Attic Red-figure Vase-painters*[1], a number of vases were classed under the heading 'manner of the Kleophrades Painter', whereas in the second edition of the work we find virtually the same vases, but this time listed as 'near the Kleophrades Painter'.[32]

The list in *ARV*[1] was divided into five sections. The first consisted of the oldest pieces, while the second and fifth referred to black-figure works; Beazley had realized quite quickly that the painter's work included a significant number of vases painted in the old technique.[33] The third section brought together two vases by the same hand, in the painter's very late style; and the fourth concerned a hydria of fairly mediocre workmanship which suggest the late style of the Kleophrades Painter, and his successor, the Boot Painter.

In *ARV*[2] the list had only four sections, and some vases in the first edition had disappeared; what had been section II, containing fragments of a

---

[31] Robertson (1989: p. xvi); cf. *ARV*[2] (877).

[32] Compare *ARV*[1] (129–31) and *ARV*[2] (193–4).

[33] *VA* (44); on the black-figured vases by the Kleophrades Painter, not dealt with here, see Kunze-Götte (1992).

black-figure plaque which it was said 'may be' by the painter, no longer appeared in *ARV²*, but in *ABV*, where they were 'at least near' the painter. The former section V, a series of Panathenaic amphorae linked with a similar series by the Kleophrades Painter, met the same fate, although their fortunes varied (three vases went into the list of named works, two became 'very close to him', while one disappeared completely). The arrangement of the three other old sections was slightly altered, but the lists remained identical. In the fourth section, Beazley added a series of black-figure neck-amphorae which were near the painter.

Given how few red-figure vases appeared on this list, we may wonder whether this was not simply because they were particularly difficult cases to judge. With regard to the difference in use of terms between *ARV¹* and *ARV²*, Martin Robertson may once again have pointed to the solution; in his view, Beazley preferred to restrict the use of 'manner' to areas clearly dominated by one indisputable artistic personality, such as the Kleophrades Painter. He was fully aware, however, that this heading covered a number of different realities:

I am conscious that the vases placed under the heading 'manner of' an artist are not always in the same category: the list may include (1) vases which are like the painter's work, but cannot safely be said not to be from his hand, (2) vases which are like the painter's work, but about which I do not know enough to say that they are not from his hand, (3) vases which are like the painter's work, but of which, although I know them well, I cannot say whether they are from his hand or not.[34]

Where the Kleophrades Painter was concerned, Beazley may have considered that the list of vases which he had placed on the first occasion under the heading 'manner' was too heteroclite to remain as it was, and therefore chose in *ARV²* to use the term 'near', which was meant to express more or less the same thing, but with the advantage that it had a more general meaning.

All these reflections on the connoisseur's vocabulary might seem superfluous, were it not for the fact that Beazley himself was at great pains to stress how sensitive he was about the tendency of some archaeologists systematically to misunderstand the results of his work:

My attributions have often been misquoted. In the former edition of *Attic Red-figure Vase-painters* I wrote that in the *Corpus Vasorum* misquotation appeared to be the rule although I did not know that it had been anywhere prescribed in black and white. I thought of omitting this sentence in the present edition (as possibly indicating a certain lack of calm): but recent experience of the *Corpus* has warned me that it would be foolish to do so. I may perhaps be allowed to point out that I make a distinction between a vase by a painter and a vase in his manner; and that 'manner', imitation, fol-

---

[34] *ABV* (p. x); Robertson (1989: p. xviii); on the history of the word 'manner' see Treves (1941).

lowing, workshop, school, circle, group, influence, kinship are not, in my vocabulary, synonyms. If I have written that a vase is in the manner of a painter, it pains me to read that I have attributed it to that painter; if I have written that a vase is by a painter, it pains me to read that I have ascribed it to the workshop of that painter; if I have written that a vase is not by a painter, it pains me to read that I have said it was by him. A scholar is free to disagree with what I have said, to ignore it, or to deride it; but if he quotes me, I hope that he will be so good as to quote me correctly.[35]

Beazley's biting humour cannot have been much appreciated by archaeologists who, because they had not had the good grace to follow his latest works to the letter, were exposed to the public ignominy of this damning review. It was no accident that these repeated clarifications were mainly to be found in reviews of the *CVA*, since he considered that this work had a duty to be an essentially scientific instrument, and thus to transmit information that was completely reliable. He was therefore shocked to see that colleagues were not capable of quoting him correctly. In some sixty reviews of the *CVA*, Beazley often had occasion to set the record straight, and his compatriots were not spared his irony either.[36]

One further example will suffice:

In this instalment of the Corpus, as in others, many of the references to my writings are inaccurate. Pl. 34, 4, I said not 'style', but 'school' of the Berlin painter. Pl. 37, 8, not 'style' but 'school'. Pl. 37, 10; I did not 'connect this with the works of the Nikon painter', but with a vase which bears the love-name Nikon but is not by the Nikon painter. Pl. 40, 1, not 'group of the Tithonos painter', but 'by him'. Pl. 40, 3, there is no discrepancy between the two passages. Pl. 41, 4, not group of the Nikon painter, but by him. Pl. 41, 7, attributed not to the Berlin painter, but to his school. Pl. 43, 6 not 'group of the Syleus painter', but by him. Pl. 47, 6, the same. Pl. 48, 7 not 'workshop' of the Kleophrades painter, but by him. Pl. 53, 1, the same. Many of these modifications are well-meant, but they unintentionally misrepresent me nonetheless.[37]

In the end it is hard not to feel that there was more than a trace of pedantry about Beazley's insistence on all these corrections. If we consider that in the case of the Kleophrades Painter, there was first the workshop, then the school, not to mention the manner and the vases near the painter, which would not appear until later, and that meanwhile all reference to the painter's sphere of influence had disappeared from *Attische Vasenmaler des rotfigurigen Stils*, which at the time of the review was the standard work of reference, we may feel that Beazley would not have lost face excessively had he shown less acrimony towards those archaeologists who were less nimble on their feet than he was.

[35] *ARV*² (pp. xlvi–xlvii).   [36] Beazley (1931*a*: 122).   [37] Beazley (1930).

One great source of annoyance to him, judging by the number of times he alluded to it, was any reference to the works of Joseph Clark Hoppin in connection with matters of attribution. After a monograph on Euthymides (which was the basis for the doctorate he wrote under the supervision of Furtwängler), and some research into the Pioneer Group,[38] Hoppin published manuals of red- and black-figure pottery which carried on the now dated practice, seen in works such as Klein's, of listing all vases bearing signatures (the main interest of these manuals being that they gave illustrations of all the vases).[39] Hoppin's lists were published around the same time as *Attic Red-figured Vases in American Museums* and *AVS*. There is an interesting parallel to be drawn here, between two different types of work, appearing alongside one another in the same area of research, but one of which was based on a strictly philological view of connoisseurship. Beazley was anxious to make the difference clear, sometimes refusing to refer to Hoppin's work as anything other than a 'Handbook of Signed Vases'.[40] In Hoppin's books we find no mention of manner, circle, or successor, in other words of all the conceptual tools that make the difference between the connoisseur and the mere compiler. In the end it is Beazley's desire to construct a global history of painters which remains fascinating, even if it does raise a certain number of problems. We shall now examine some of these in connection with the Berlin Painter.

THE BERLIN PAINTER AND HIS SCHOOL

Along with the Kleophrades Painter, the Berlin Painter is one of the most outstanding artists of the late archaic period.[41] Beazley wrote:

The Berlin painter (Painter of the Berlin Amphora 2160) issues from the group of Euthymides and Phintias; and the Providence Painter, Hermonax, the Achilles Painter were his pupils.

The earlier vases are the best, and among them are many of the masterpieces of vase-painting. In what I call the middle period the drawing grows conventional, and in the late period mechanical. In the late period it is not always easy to tell the artist's own work from imitations; and over each of the vases marked 'late' in the list this question arises.[42]

In a somewhat acerbic review, Mary Beard rightly emphasizes (in connection with Beazley) that words, far from being neutral, might well be loaded and to some extent create their own subject:

---

[38] Hoppin (1896; 1917).   [39] Hoppin (1919; 1924).
[40] Beazley (1922:83).   [41] Kurtz (1983).   [42] *ARV²* (196).

One of the main effects of Beazley's endeavours was to provide a Renaissance model for the history of Athenian vase painting. For not only did he create a gallery of artists, he found 'followers', 'pupils', 'schools'; he identified 'influence' between one painter and another; he talked of vases 'in the manner' of his famous painters. This language is revealing. It did more than call to mind the great masters of the Florentine Quattrocento; it converted what had been a subject of antiquarian interest into high-status art history.[43]

It is odd that Mary Beard does not mention the word 'master', since that is the one which most obviously refers to Renaissance painters. It is true that after using it a great deal in the early days, Beazley quickly abandoned it in favour of the more neutral expression 'Painter of X'.[44] The word 'master' was used in the article 'Kleophrades', but it gained in importance by its presence in the title of his monograph on the Berlin Painter.[45] The term 'school' also appeared on this occasion, as opposed to 'workshop' and 'circle'; it is as if the ideas of master and school went together in his mind at that time.

I am half wishing to have my article back from Hill to throw the 'school-pieces' overboard; but after all no mistake they *are* schoolpieces and it is more honest to put them in although it makes the article less '*teres atque rotundus*'. I am convinced in these two articles—Kleophr. and the Berlin master—I have detached the two most important painters of big vases (i.e. non-cup) in developed severe painting (Euthymides dies young, as Furtw. said).[46]

The expression '*teres atque rotundus*' refers to a passage in Horace's *Satires* (2.7.87), in which it is the sage who is 'rounded and spherical', like a smooth ball that events simply flow over. Beazley's remark about 'half wishing' to have his article back from Hill may show that he realized he was putting himself in a delicate position by insisting on including the school-pieces at all costs, which he could easily have avoided by leaving them aside. The fact that he was determined despite everything to keep them in shows that for him they were just as important as the works of the master, if an objective account was to be given of the limited overall number of works that were available in collections. At that time he was in no doubt that the school-pieces he had had the chance to study really were what their name suggested: 'A further list of twenty-nine vases will follow. These are imitations. To say that they show the master's influence would be misleading; they are direct and conscious imitations: they copy his style, some of them so closely that it is difficult to distinguish them from the master's own work. Occasional stylistic variations

[43] Beard (1986: 1013).
[44] Beazley (1912; 1912a; 1912b; 1912c; 1913a; 1913b; 1914).
[45] Beazley (1911).
[46] Letter from Beazley to Mrs Robertson (Oxford, 9 May 1911); Oxford, Beazley Archive.

and crudity of touch betray the imitator.'[47] His opinion was to vary on this point, and he would regularly add pieces to the painter's corpus which he had believed at an earlier stage to be of his school.

Every edition of the lists contained vases of this sort, appearing under the heading 'manner' from the time of *ARV¹*, in which no differentiation is made between them, whereas in *ARV²* it is, although they are still presented very much as a composite whole. In the first section various vases from the painter's late period are grouped together, and in the second, four very late vases ('the Group of London E 311'), which Beazley had at first placed under the heading 'Art des Hermonax', then 'Manner of Hermonax', which indicates that he was wondering whether these might be early works by the Berlin Painter's pupil.[48] Another group that was formed around the London stamnos E 445 was also very late, showing stylistic connections with Hermonax. There then followed three hydrias which were imitations, the London E 180 hydria, and a series of vases with no figurative decoration, just ornamental motifs ('the Group of the Floral Nolans').

The role of the eye

Apart from the school-pieces which he regularly included in the painter's corpus, the list of named works was remarkably homogeneous. Beazley had a very clear idea of this painter's style, which was also true, to a lesser extent, of the Kleophrades Painter. Perhaps because these painters were the first two personalities he identified, he did not hesitate to contrast them in terms which once again show the parallel with Italian painting: 'He may be said to play a kind of Florentine to the Berlin painter's Sienese.'[49] He also wrote that the former was for him 'the painter of power' and the latter 'the painter of grace'.[50] Although he was later to describe the Kleophrades Painter as 'the most remarkable of the great vase-painters of the late archaic period',[51] we know that he had a preference for the Berlin Painter, and as a result undertook research which frequently gave him the opportunity to return to him.[52] It is worth mentioning, moreover, that at the time when he was working on his first article on the Berlin Painter, his enthusiasm for what he saw as the artist's Sienese qualities was such that, as mentioned in the previous chapter, he purchased a painting which he believed to be by Simone Martini.

It was therefore not at all surprising that Beazley should have used the case

[47] Beazley (1911: 277).   [48] *ARV¹* (323).
[49] *VA* (40–1).   [50] *VA* (35).   [51] *ARV²* (181).
[52] Beazley (1930); Beazley and Merlin (1936); Beazley (1961; 1964).

of the Berlin Painter to demonstrate the validity of his method. This essay, entitled 'Citharoedus' in reference to the presentation of a new vase by the painter which showed a citharode on the main face, was entirely characteristic of his way of proceeding, in that before attempting to demonstrate the theoretical basis of his method, he first showed how it was applied through the study of a particular object.[53] Induction being the connoisseur's favoured mode of analysis, he began by showing the lessons that could be learned from a comparison of the vase with a number of similar pieces. By describing these he was able to note the differences and similarities (in the painting of clothing and anatomy), which enabled him to establish that there was nothing arbitrary about the link between the pieces:

It cannot be maintained that the points in which these figures resemble one another or one of the rest are trifling, few, or restricted to one part of the figure. They comprise both the master lines which in archaic art demarcate the several parts of the body and of the drapery, and the minor lines which subdivide or diversify the areas thus demarcated. We may speak, in fact, of a coherent and comprehensive system of representing the forms of the human body naked and clothed.[54]

This system of rendering could be seen not only on those vases specially chosen for analysis, but on many others as well. Even so, it was not possible to say that the same system was used everywhere at that time:

The system of renderings described above stands in a certain relation to nature: the individual renderings are more or less inspired by nature, that is, by a desire to reproduce the actual forms of the body. But nature does not ordain that an ankle or a breast must be rendered in just this way and no other. Nor does nature insist that once you have drawn an ankle with black lines of a certain shape, you must put a vertical line on the chest, or a little arc in the middle of the deltoïd. But on the vases, the one rendering brings the other with it: where you find this ankle you find these lines, and the rest of the renderings, within reasonable limits, are predictable.[55]

What mattered to Beazley about the treatment of the image was not so much its figurative or decorative intention as the fact that it was the signifier of a second meaning, a message by implication relating to a personal system of rendering, which he naturally perceived first and foremost as denoting an individual artist: 'A system so definite, coherent, distinctive and in some respects so wilful, is most easily intelligible as a personal system: inspired in some measure by observation of nature, influenced and in part determined by tradition, and communicable or prescribable to others; but the child, above all else, of one man's brain and will.'[56]

---

[53] Beazley (1922); New York 56.171.38 in *ARV²* (197 no. 3).
[54] Beazley (1922: 80–1).   [55] Ibid. (83).   [56] Ibid. (84).

It is because art is entirely conceptual that, as Gombrich says, 'all representations are recognizable by their style'.[57] Likewise the possibility of recognizing the presumed author of a drawing or painting is bound to stem from
the psychology of the process of artistic representation. But the point at
which Beazley's approach became particularly interesting, because it was so
very precise, was when he claimed to be able, simply by having a trained eye,
to differentiate between the works of the artist himself, faithful copies of
them, and mere adaptations. This takes us on to an axiomatic discourse in
which Beazley expressed the subtle thinking of the connoisseur in algebraic
form:

First, the figure above us may be a substantive work, the man who executed it
having also designed it. If E be the execution, R the system of renderings, and
D the design, the work done by the executant may be roughly represented by
$E+R+D$.

Secondly, the figure may be a copy, the man who executed it not having designed
it, but having made a faithful reproduction of a model which was rendered in R. The
executant's share of the work may be represented by $E: R+D$ being the work of
another man.

Thirdly, the figure may be a translation, the man who executed it not having
designed it, but having reproduced a model which was not, however, rendered in R
but in another system: R being imported by the executant, whose share of the work
may be represented by $E+R: D$ being the work of another man.[58]

The argument that these three formulas did not cover every piece of painting produced in the Kerameikos was one with which he readily agreed. He
got round the difficulty by proposing that the third formula, which actually
represented the most difficult and risky type of case to judge, was in essence
the same as the first, since when the system was applied to some other kind of
design, it was likely to transform it to such a point that the end result was more
or less an autonomous work. What remained then were the first two types of
painting: the artistic production of the painter himself and that of his school.
Still on the basis of concrete examples, Beazley wrote several more detailed
analyses intended to show that vases with the same system of rendering actually had other features in common as well:

They showed, as a group, a liking for a certain choice and use of patterns, for certain
principles of decoration, for a certain relationship between colour and background,
for lines and curves of certain kinds. The system of renderings was not easy to separate from the other elements of design: it was, from one point of view, their vehicle,
and from another, a collateral expression of artistic will.[59]

---

[57] Gombrich (1960: 87).   [58] Beazley (1922: 84).   [59] Ibid. (90).

At the time when Beazley wrote his essay, the concept of 'artistic will' was being used by art historians to support two main lines of research.[60] Some saw it as referring 'to artistic phenomena as a whole, to all the works of one period, people or artist', while others believed that 'the expression "artistic intention" tends to be used for the most part to characterise a work of art taken in isolation'.[61] It was this 'artistic intention', as applied to the definition of an individual artist, that Beazley believed he could see in the organization of certain combinations of lines and surfaces, the choice of certain modes of composition, the arrangement of specific elements of ornamentation, etc. This was what enabled him to say with certainty that he could identify an individual artist.

I believe the best way of explaining the homogeneity of this group of vases is to suppose that it represents the work of a single anonymous artist, whom I have called, after his masterpiece, the painter of the Berlin amphora. I am ready to admit that some of the vases in the following list may be school-pieces, or, more precisely, faithful copies of the artist's drawings executed by subordinates at his instigation and under his supervision [. . .] I admit such a resemblance between the works of the Berlin painter and the works of older and of younger artists as may be accounted for by the necessary supposition that he learnt his craft from others, by the natural one that he trained assistants to follow in his steps. But between his masters—Phintias, or Euthymides, or both, or another—and his pupils—Hermonax and the rest—his personality stands out as distinct as that of Douris, or Epiktetos, or Euphronios, or Polygnotos, or any other vase-painter whose name has been preserved.[62]

This demonstration was not entirely free of ulterior motive. Its aim was to contest certain ill-founded conceptions, by showing that in most cases the person who had designed the vase really was the same as the person who painted it. If Beazley singled out Pottier as the perpetrator of these erroneous ideas, we may feel that his view carried a certain weight. In his catalogue of the Louvre, Pottier did indeed say that he believed the Kerameikos should be seen as a 'small industrial empire', where a few 'master painters', who took the trouble to sign their works, had command over a whole host of decorators who were inevitably of lowlier station:

It was he [the master painter] who in the vast majority of cases was the only true artist, whether or not he executed the work; it was he who composed the models, who took from great art everything he could find in it that was of benefit to his profession, and who bridged the gap between the élite of creative geniuses and the mass of workers.[63]

---

[60] Panofsky (1975). [61] Ibid. (200).
[62] Beazley (1922:90). [63] Pottier (1896–1906: iii. 705).

Beazley drew attention to the fact that this interpretation was based on an anachronism; Pottier was drawing a thinly veiled analogy with great modern industrial plants such as Creusot and Renault.[64] By demonstrating that it was possible, and in his view perfectly legitimate, to identify individual artists who were anonymous yet genuine, trained by 'masters' and then training 'pupils' in their turn, along the traditional lines of art history, Beazley was constructing a global theory which was in radical contrast to Pottier's. Just what Pottier's arguments were will become clearer as we look at how Beazley's ideas were received in France.

[64] Beazley (1922: 85).

6

The Reaction to Beazley in France

POTTIER'S CRITICISMS OF THE ATTRIBUTION OF VASES

I took this definition and this praise of Sainte-Beuve's method from M. Paul Bourget's article, because the definition was short and the praise justified. But I could have quoted twenty other critics. What everyone recognizes as original about him, and what he, quite rightly, recognized himself, was that he had created the natural history of minds, that in order to explain the intelligence of man's works and the nature of his genius he had looked to his biography, the history of his family and all his distinctive characteristics. Taine himself, who dreamed of a more systematic and better codified natural history of minds, and with whom, it must be said, Sainte-Beuve did not agree on matters of race, says exactly that in his praise of Sainte-Beuve.

Marcel Proust, *Contre Sainte-Beuve*

'Approval for Beazley's first articles at the beginning of the century was far from unanimous, especially in France where there was little support for attributionism. Edmond Pottier, the great connoisseur of pottery who was responsible for the *Corpus Vasorum Antiquorum* and the Campana Gallery at the Louvre, opposed Beazley's arguments on several occasions, thus exposing himself to the Oxford professor's acid irony.'[1] This brings us without further delay *in medias res*; although Pottier did not entirely determine the French reaction to Beazley, if we study his side of the argument we will see how the two men represented significantly different views of the science of vases, based on the conflicting notions of global history and biographical history. We can usefully begin our discussion by digressing into the field of literary criticism, where the same contrast is clearly seen in the figures of Taine and Sainte-Beuve. It seems that Pottier was greatly interested in Taine's 'ethnic and collective psychology', so much so that it probably influenced his own conception of the value of Greek art. Whether or not this was the case, he certainly believed that Beazley's biographical approach profoundly distorted its meaning.

[1] Frontisi-Ducroux and Lissarrague (1990: 205).

BIOGRAPHY AND MODERN INDIVIDUALISM

We shall begin this historiographical section with an extract from the Louvre's *Catalogue des vases antiques*. The fact that this was written at a time when Beazley had not yet started his research makes it all the more striking:

Our curiosity about history, whetted by the modern way of life in which individualism knows no bounds and demands an ever more omnipotent role, will not resign itself to not knowing the names of men who have created something useful or beautiful. Nowadays the whole history of art, whether ancient, mediaeval, or Renaissance, is tending to become the history of artists, to the great disadvantage of those questions of aesthetics and general evolution which ought to remain of paramount importance. If an artist's personality is to be of any importance to the history of art, we need to be certain that we know all his works, and all about the conditions in which he produced them, about his life, his circle, and his character. When the most laborious research leads to the discovery of one name or a date, this is certainly not to be despised; but we should see it for what it is worth and not make it the supreme goal of science. It can even be said that in many cases, especially with regard to antiquity, where information about individuals is very limited, the conclusions drawn by historians, which are almost always hypothetical and debatable, bear no relation to the effort expended for such small reward. And when it comes to industrial art and works that are for the most part imitations or copies of superior models, this matter is of even more secondary importance.[2]

This statement sums up perfectly the views that Pottier held on the attribution of vases. He felt very deeply that this practice was a passing fad, and that before long there would be a return to more interesting matters concerning aesthetics and evolution. It is difficult to know for certain what exactly he meant by these terms, but our most likely source of help is a famous theory of the time which is fundamental to our understanding of what Pottier was aiming to achieve in his study of pottery. It may be summed up by the triad of 'la race', 'le milieu', and 'le moment' (inherited personal characteristics, environment, and historical context), and its inventor was one of France's leading intellectuals in the last third of the nineteenth century, the critic, philosopher, and historian Hippolyte Taine.

The seed, the plant, and the flower

It was at the École des Beaux-Arts, in the context of a series of lectures during the 1860s on aesthetics and the history of art, that Taine developed his well-known theory that any artistic phenomenon must be explicable in

[2] Pottier (1896–1906: iii. 875).

terms of 'la race', 'le milieu', and 'le moment'.[3] These three factors, which he had believed since his student days at the École Normale to be the key to human history, formed a sort of 'moral temperature', which enabled us to appreciate the conditions that were necessary for the existence and evolution of art. His doctrine was to say the least extremely ambitious: 'Suppose that as a result of all these discoveries we were to succeed in defining and marking out the conditions for the existence of every art form; we would then have a complete explanation of fine art and the arts in general, in other words a philosophy of fine art; which is what we call an *aesthetics*.'[4]

At some points he was inclined to stress the importance of 'le milieu' to our knowledge of 'the feelings of a time', but he also considered that the study of 'la race' was often indispensable; in any case these scientific parameters were very useful tools in the study of ancient art, where the shortage of documents made it necessary to resort to other means of analysis: 'In the absence of detailed history, what remains to us is general history; more than ever, in order to understand the work of art, we are obliged to study the nation that produced it, the customs that created the need for it, and the environment in which it came into being.'[5]

Taine gave a series of lectures on the philosophy of Greek art, which in fact was a vague study of sculpture. He stressed that 'it was the physical structure of the region that left on the intelligence of the race the imprint that we find in its art and its history', and went on to conjure up 'a landscape of eternal summer', where there was 'balmy air' and 'a good and gentle sun'.[6] But Taine had never been to Greece, and had he seen fit to go and see for himself, he would have realized that the climate in Greece is often harsh, and that the mountainous regions are ravaged by storms in winter and scorched by intense heat in summer. This was rightly pointed out by Raymond Lebègue, who also suggested that Taine had based his image of the ancient Greeks on Plato's dialogues (which were the subject of his Latin thesis), and that as far as he was concerned all ancient Greeks were philosophers who spent all their time on the banks of the Ilissos discussing Beauty and Goodness.[7] His study of Greek sculpture was equally unconvincing; he barely touched on the works themselves, since for him antiquity was nothing more than 'a ruin', but that did not prevent him from concluding: 'After going round and round in ever-decreasing circles in pursuit of all the origins of the statue, we find ourselves in the still familiar empty space where its pedestal stood and from which its august form has disappeared.'[8]

---

[3] Taine (1865; 1866; 1867; 1869; 1869*a*); edited in one volume in 1882 (reissued 1985) under the general title *Philosophie de l'art*.

[4] Taine (1865: 19–20).   [5] Taine (1869: 3).   [6] Ibid. (32).

[7] Lebègue (1966: 4).   [8] Taine (1869: 200).

It would no doubt be wrong to caricature Taine's thinking; it gained much from his lively and powerfully evocative style, and was prolific and wide-ranging, and if we fail to appreciate this we will find it hard to see why it achieved such public acclaim. Taine believed that the coherence of his arguments proved beyond doubt that his experimental theories were sound; as Renan had remarked in his time, the notion of experimentation in the field of moral sciences was more often a matter of intimidation than of argument. This was not the only reference to the exact sciences; Taine's doctrine was modelled directly on biology: 'This sort of botanical analysis carried out on human individuals is the only means of bringing together the moral sciences and the experimental sciences, and in order for it to bear fruit we need only apply it to peoples, ages, and races.'[9] One of the weaknesses in Taine's theory is that it was merely a parody of a type of Darwinism. Darwin's ideas allowed for a connection between natural and moral science, and quite a number of thinkers in France were inspired by this, even though in general they misunderstood it.[10]

Taine's enormous influence lasted for several generations, and Pottier was not immune to it. It must be said that the vogue for Taine in the late nineteenth and early twentieth centuries was quite extraordinary, at least if we are to judge by the number of times his books were reprinted. Compared with his most popular works, his *Philosophie de l'art* can almost be regarded as a mere *succès d'estime*, even though the first volume of the series was in its fourteenth edition by 1913. His greatest success without question was *Les Origines de la France contemporaine*, a series of volumes which inspired a number of the reactionary elements that were in existence at the turn of the century. Broadly speaking Taine had two personae: on the one hand the writer of the *Origines*, and on the other the freethinker, battler against official spiritualism, and author of *Les Philosophes français du XIXe siècle* and *De l'intelligence*. Here again the change was brought about by the war of 1870, which led Taine to ponder over its deep-seated causes and to engage in vigorous criticism of the French Revolution and its principles. Some writers, while opposing the theories propounded by the author of the *Origines*, remained more or less loyal to the earlier Taine. One of these was the republican and positivist Alphonse Aulard (born in 1849), who was the first Professor of the History of the French Revolution at the Sorbonne: 'What tends to incline me in his favour is a bias of adolescence, from the time when I was studying at the École Normale and we saw him as one of the leaders of free research and free thought, as the modern of moderns, and I listened with a sympathetic and respectful ear to his lectures at the École des Beaux-Arts.'[11]

---

[9] Taine (1894: 59–60).   [10] See Conry (1974).   [11] Cited by Digeon (1959: 232).

Taine versus Sainte-Beuve

Taine's detractors frequently contrasted him with Sainte-Beuve, who also aspired to construct a 'moral botany', but whose approach to literature left considerable scope for biographical criticism. As Bourget wrote:

He wanted the literary analyst to try to understand a work before judging it, and first of all to place it in context and take careful note of every detail of the circumstances in which it was produced. Such a study involves research which cannot be too meticulous, into the biography of the author, his heredity, family, and friends, into the time he lived in, and the stages his work went through, all of which must be supported by verifiable documents.[12]

In the case of the ancient world, the problem took on a different form; no one could claim to have access to all the information they needed about an artist in order to shed light on his work. Sainte-Beuve acknowledged that his method did not apply to this period of history:

With the Ancients we do not have sufficient means of observation. To stand with a work of art in our hand and rediscover the man is impossible with most of the real Ancients, those of whom we have only half a picture. We are thus reduced to commenting on the work itself, to admiring it and dreaming through it of the author and the poet. In this way we can reconstruct the figures of poets and philosophers, the images of Plato, Sophocles, and Virgil, in a spirit of high idealism; that is all we can do given the incomplete state of our knowledge, the dearth of sources, and the lack of possibilities for finding information and going back in time. A great and in most cases unfordable river separates us from the great men of Antiquity. Let us salute them from the other bank.[13]

Even where contemporary artists were concerned, however, there were those who spoke out in condemnation of the idea that a work of art could be better understood in terms of extrinsic criteria, and that one should always see the man and the writer as one and the same. The strongest critic of this idea was Proust, who was largely responsible for Sainte-Beuve's fall from grace in the twentieth century, even though his essay, which was written for the most part in 1909 but left unfinished, was not published until much later.

'Sainte-Beuve's work,' wrote Proust,

is not profound. The famous method, which according to Taine, Paul Bourget and so many others, makes him the unrivalled master of nineteenth-century criticism, and consists of not separating the man from the work, of considering that in order to judge the author of a book, unless that book is 'a treatise of pure geometry', it does in fact matter whether one has first answered questions that appear entirely irrelevant to his work (how he behaved, etc.): of acquiring as much information as possible about

---

[12] Bourget (1907).   [13] Sainte-Beuve (1865: 15–16).

a writer, of collating his correspondence, of questioning the men who knew him, by talking to them if they are still alive, by reading what they wrote about him if they are dead: this method ignores something which a little self-examination will enable us to learn for ourselves; that a book is the product of another self than the one that we manifest in our habits, in society, in our vices.[14]

It is not our direct concern here to untangle the complex web of reasons given by Proust for his criticism of the biographical approach.[15] Suffice to say that although they were certainly tinged by personal considerations, they no doubt had more to do with his own aesthetics than with theoretical reflections on literature, and in that sense can be compared to the reasons advanced by that other great aesthete of the time, Oscar Wilde, for denigrating the taste of his fellow citizens: 'The British public, with its usual hypocrisy, prudery and philistinism, has failed to find the art in the work of art; it has searched in it for the man. Since it always confuses man with his creatures, it thinks that to create Hamlet one must be a little melancholy, and to imagine Lear, absolutely mad.'[16]

Literary, aesthetic, and individual motivations always come into play with any book that is not 'a treatise of pure geometry'. Of particular importance was the way in which Julien Benda echoed these factional squabbles in his *Essai sur l'esthétique de la présente société française*, published in 1918. Benda drew a rather pointed contrast between the two types of literary criticism embodied in Taine and Sainte-Beuve, making no attempt to conceal his preference for the former:

At the same time it has been claimed that criticism should concern itself only with the individual, that it should banish any notion of *classe d'esprit* or *genre*, any connection or law (this was the cult of Sainte-Beuve, or at least of the *Lundis* [*Les Causeries du lundi*, a series of weekly articles by Sainte-Beuve], which furthermore is perceived as having been even more individualistic than he was).[17]

Thanks to the students' borrowing register at the École Normale Supérieure library, we can see exactly what works by these two authors Pottier read while he was a student there. From 1874 to 1877 the number of entries for books by Taine equals the number for Sainte-Beuve; in addition to the *Philosophie de l'art* series, the other books by Taine that Pottier borrowed were his *Essai sur Tite-Live* and the third volume of the *Histoire de la littérature anglaise*; the works by Sainte-Beuve were the biographical *Notice* on Viguier, his *Étude sur Virgile*, two volumes (IV and VI) of *Port-Royal*, the first volume of *Portraits artistiques*, both volumes of his *Tableau*

---

[14] Proust (1954: 157).   [15] See Casanova (1995: intro.).
[16] Letter from Wilde to Edmond de Goncourt (17 Dec. 1891); Hart-Davis (ed.) (1962: 304).
[17] Benda (1918: 137).

historique et critique de la poésie française au XVIe siècle and Volume III of the *Causeries du lundi*. It may be that all of this was required reading for an arts student, but whereas Taine's influence on Pottier was to prove lasting, I do not believe that it is possible to find a single explicit reference to Sainte-Beuve in his later writings.

Two examples will suffice to illustrate this. Before going to the École d'Athènes, Pottier travelled through Southern France and Italy, using as his model an 'Itinerary of a journey from Paris to Rome' by the architect Charles Garnier. During this journey Pottier kept a diary in which he recorded his impressions of the various places he visited. On 3 December 1877 he wrote: 'When I got back to the hotel I was ferreting around in a little cupboard next to the dining-room when to my delight I came upon Taine's book, *Philosophie de l'art en Italie*, which I devoured forthwith.'[18] It was at the École des Beaux-Arts, however, in an introductory lecture on the study of Eastern civilizations at the beginning of 1884, that his allegiance to Taine's theories emerged most clearly:

Here of all places there is no need for me to stress the way in which an art is formed by climatic conditions, and the influence of the *milieu* in which a race develops, when these theories have been expounded so brilliantly in this very building by an eminent philosopher and historian. [. . .] Unless we continually bear in mind the climatic and ethnological conditions in which the Eastern races developed, we cannot hope to gain any understanding and appreciation of relics.[19]

On the concept of race

We need to give special attention to the word 'race', which Pottier used frequently, as did many scholars of the time. This concept was the favoured instrument of a type of anthroposociology which sought to go back to the scientific foundations of the naturalist by relating the physical and biological characteristics of man to his intellectual nature. The word itself, however, was open to several interpretations, and there was a tendency for confusions to arise which had more to do with history and linguistics than with anthropology, between race and language, race and people, and race and nation. One piece of writing by Pottier showed the kind of semantic and ideological aberrations that could arise from the use of such an unreliable concept, however great the author's desire to argue with rigour. When commenting on Sir Arthur Evans's discoveries in Knossos, Pottier remarked that even if we succeeded in deciphering the Cretan language, this would not teach us a great deal about their society:

[18] Pottier, 'Carnet de Voyage à Rome' (1877); Paris, Bibliothèque des musées nationaux, MS 305 (5–1).
[19] Pottier (1884:9–10).

We cannot make rigorous deductions from a language about the ethnic nature of those who speak it. We live alongside the Belgians and the Swiss who, although they speak French, are not of the same race as we are. [. . .] If we could decipher the Cretan inscriptions it would not tell us with certainty whether Minos was a Pelasgian, a Libyan, a Phoenician, or a Greek.[20]

Pottier shared the scientistic ideals of his time, when the concept of race was perceived as a scientific instrument of great precision.[21] There was a conflict here between two contradictory theses: polygenism, which argued for the plurality of the human species, and monogenism, the doctrine of common descent. Polygenism is at the root of evolutionist thinking, and Pottier saw it as playing an important part in defining the roles of East and West in the evolution of human history. Pottier believed that polygenism applied to archaeology, in other words he thought that decorative forms could have come into being independently of one another, in accordance with laws related to Darwinist determinism.[22] He opposed the standard tendency of the time to view the origins of art as being governed by man's instinctive feeling for beauty, and used Darwin and the study of folklore to support his argument that the origin of art was practical, and like every phenomenon must be seen first and foremost in a social context. Utility came before aesthetics. Here again Pottier had much to gain by referring to Taine, whose theories fell in so well with his view of evolution. We can see this in a letter he wrote to Duncan Mackenzie, Evans's assistant in Knossos:

Like you I believe that many forms of art are alike and appear to be related, but that that does not mean that any one is derived from another. Each was formed for overriding reasons to do with climate, region, and the customs of the inhabitants. This mania for affiliations is causing great disruption in archaeology. I could just as easily demonstrate that certain Peruvian and Mexican vases came directly from the Attic Dipylon style. I believe that each aspect of art and civilization must be studied 'regionally', which is not of course to deny the influence that peoples have on one another when they are neighbours.[23]

Around the same time, Pottier at one point explained his thinking by using a metaphor:

I believe that we must take notice, more than the theoreticians of both schools have done, of *polygenism*, of the ability that man has, everywhere in the world, under the influence of identical needs or instincts, to create similar forms. It is wrong to imagine an artistic creation as a luminous spark that flies out at a given point, then grows into a devouring fire, advancing with the wind that is pushing it along, always in the

---

[20] Pottier (1902a: 171).   [21] Simar (1922).   [22] Pottier (1907 = 1937: 33–50).
[23] Letter from Pottier to Mackenzie (Paris, 16 Nov. 1909); Oxford, Ashmolean Museum. On Mackenzie, see N. Momigliano (1999).

same direction. We forget that these fires flare up in many places at the same time, then spread, meet, and intermingle, the stronger absorbing the less strong, all undulating in various directions, sometimes going out there and then, sometimes making leaps over incredible distances.[24]

These theoretical debates between diffusionism and evolutionism, advocates of monogenism and of polygenism, were at the root of certain scientific leanings that are apparent in the *CVA*, even if Pottier did not particularly emphasize this point in his 'Project for a Corpus of Ancient Vases'. It was clear in any case that the question of artistic personalities played very little part in his thinking about what the aims of a science of pottery should be.

QUESTIONS OF METHOD

In 1917, in a review of Hoppin's book, *Euthymides and his Fellows*, Pottier took care to contrast the correct method (his own and Hoppin's) with the incorrect one used by Beazley. It is revealing that his opinion of Hartwig, of whom he had spoken highly in his catalogue, was now on the decline; had he not set a bad example? Pottier wrote even more categorically:

We must now wage war on the attribution of names, when they are not imposed by an absolute similarity of style. [. . .] We shall thus rid the study of pottery of a regrettable confusion between works that are authentic and beyond dispute by artists who have taken the trouble to sign, and anonymous paintings which may have been carried out in their workshops, whether by themselves or by their pupils, but which could also be copies, distant imitations, or indeed pieces produced by processes that were in use in many workshops in the same period. Antiquity had its Trouilleberts, who must not be mistaken for Corots.[25]

Trouillebert imitated Corot's paintings to perfection; his skill as a forger deceived many collectors, and one of his famous victims was Alexandre Dumas *fils*. As a curator, Pottier was of course aware of the problem of forgery, and frequently came up against it himself. His main concern, however, was to stress that attributionism told us nothing about the way in which the workshops of the Kerameikos were organized, and that it resulted in imitations being placed on a par with vase-paintings produced in a workshop known by a real name. It may at first seem surprising that Pottier should have rejected out of hand the very thing that formed the basis of the connoisseur's art, in other words the ability to distinguish the forgery from the original, the work of the master from that of the pupil, the workshop copy from the mere imitation. To understand the reasons for this, we need to examine two lines of

[24] Pottier (1909: 3–4).   [25] Pottier (1917: 441); Villard (1978: 15).

argument, the first of which stems from considerations of method, the second from his own aesthetic categories.

The considerations of method are easy to imagine, and we have already drawn attention to them; since we cannot fully understand the signatures on vases, it is wiser to confine ourselves to the notion of workshop and not seek to go beyond it. 'As long as a doubt remains, we shall be able to speak of a style commonly used "in the workshop" of such and such a master, or indeed we shall note the work of different hands in the same workshop, but in the absence of categorical signatures we shall not claim to identify the true author more precisely than that.'[26] Pottier resolutely followed the line of archaeologists such as Klein, who gave absolute preference to inscriptions as their basis for the classification of pottery. In his Louvre catalogue, Pottier had gone further than this by listing, along with vases that were securely attested by signatures, others that had stylistic affinities with them. Nevertheless he was always anxious to make a distinction between them, whereas in Beazley's case it was clear that he was completely disregarding this method of classification, and at the same time bringing about a confusion, which in Pottier's view was to say the least regrettable, between anonymous works and those that bore signatures.

The second argument was of an aesthetic nature, relating to Pottier's conception of the value of Greek art. Painted pottery owes its distinctive character to the fact that only human figures appear on it. Therein lies the secret of its originality and strength. The essential point in Pottier's view, however, was that these human forms were never simply paintings of individual people: 'Given over entirely to painting man, it knew nothing of the individual.'[27] What Pottier called 'the moral beauty of Greek art' resulted from this ability to go beyond the individual and paint moral entities. Looked at from this point of view, contemporary art was necessarily inferior, since it sought 'more and more for the individual, without penetrating to the human'. Pottier opposed individualism in all its forms, and called for a 'socialist art' which would return to the ancient tradition of 'losing the individual in the mass, for the good of the community'.[28]

To our knowledge this was the only occasion on which Pottier expressed a political opinion so openly in connection with art; in that sense, it is important to treat it with caution and not to exaggerate its significance. Nevertheless it was clear that Beazley's determination to place the accent on individual artists was in complete contradiction with what Pottier saw as the value of their art. He wrote monographs on Douris and Diphilos, in a collection which was to say the least in a well-established editorial tradition ('Les grands

---

[26] Pottier (1902: 29).   [27] Ibid. (225).   [28] Ibid. (226).

artistes, leur vie, leur œuvre'), but in the conclusion to his work on Douris he left no doubt about his view of the importance of individual artists in the development of the plastic arts in ancient Greece:

No doubt Douris had nothing to do with it. He had no idea; he didn't do it on pur‑
pose. He was the unconscious instrument of a great people and a great revolution.
That is what is wonderful about the works of the past. Time alone can show what was
beautiful and creative about them, even without their authors' being aware of it. The
creative force that brings them to life lies outside the individual; it springs from the
depths of the race that produced them.[29]

The importance of painters' work could not be reduced to the part played by individual artists, even major ones. The debate must therefore be raised to a higher plane, that of the nation that urged these painters to paint, the race from which they came, and the milieu that formed them. The argument has now come full circle, and there is no need to dwell on it any further, except to mention one final article of 1928 in which Pottier on this occasion attacked Beazley directly.

On style

In this, Pottier's most accomplished article, he devoted twenty pages or so to airing his grievances against Beazley.[30] The opportunity arose with the pub‑lication of a red‑figured krater in the Louvre (reproduced as Pl. 18 below), showing on its front two satyrs preparing to destroy a burial mound.[31] Pottier's argument did not concern iconography, but the attribution of the vase to Myson.[32] In *AVS*, the list of pieces attributed to Myson also included another vase in the Louvre, in this case a famous one, the amphora showing Croesus on the funeral pyre (reproduced as Pl. 19 below).[33] Pottier did not agree that all the works on this list were by the same artist, and tried to demonstrate this. In the case of the satyrs krater he was inclined to favour the Kleophrades Painter, although he did not consider it vitally important:

Thus to my mind all the details in the two paintings on this krater indicate an artist
who follows in the footsteps of Euthymides and Phintias, close to the painter known
as the 'Kleophradesmaler' [. . .] I do not know who the artist is and I shall not attempt
to name him; but in my view he deserves to be placed among the most expressive
artists working at the beginning of the fifth century BC, a time which spawned so
many great names.[34]

---

[29] Pottier ([1905]: 120).   [30] Pottier (1928 = 1937: 603–53, esp. 632 ff.).
[31] Louvre CA 1947; *ARV²* (240 no. 44); see Bérard (1990).
[32] *AVS* (97 no. 4); see Berge (1975).
[33] Louvre G 197; *AVS* (97 no. 1); *ARV²* (238 no. 1).   [34] Pottier (1937: 632).

His opinion of the Croesus amphora is also significant, especially since on this occasion he was very interested in the identity of the painter, no doubt because the vase showed one of the few historical scenes that were tradition-ally written about in ancient literature, in particular by Herodotus (1.86–91). In the Louvre catalogue, he favoured the Kleophrades Painter: 'We would be delighted to know who painted this beautiful painting. One might perhaps think of the workshop of one of Brygos' contemporaries, who developed the style of Euthymides and Phintias and whom M. Hartwig studied under the name of Amasis.'[35] The satyrs krater was not mentioned in the catalogue, since it was not acquired until 1913, but Pottier had published it briefly in the *CVA*, and there is every indication that he already had the Kleophrades Painter in mind: 'The style is very fine and belongs to the group in which the painter of an amphora in Munich worked.'[36] He was referring to the Munich amphora 2344, which Beazley attributed to the Kleophrades Painter.[37] He must have found this very puzzling, since in one case Beazley confirmed his judgement, while in the other he took a different stance on a piece which Pottier regarded as stylistically very close. In the absence of any solid basis on which to make an objective judgement, it is not for us to make a final decision on this case of attribution, but the episode is somewhat reminiscent of Furtwän-gler, who undoubtedly had the best eye before Beazley, but did not make a distinction between the works of the Kleophrades Painter and those of the Berlin Painter.

In the 1928 article he also used the specific problem of attribution as the basis for a discussion of wider issues arising from his desire to defend his own conception of attribution. Essentially it was a question of recognizing the unvarying linear features of a painter's style, ones which made it possible to make a judgement with certainty, and which were not to be confused with practical and technical criteria:

From these material details one needs to be able to discern the *style*, which is, I shall not say an 'imponderable', but a whole collection of beauties to be seen in the com-position, the originality of the motifs, the proportions of the bodies, the suppleness of the postures, the fineness of line, the combination of ornaments; all of which is not so easy to put across as a way of painting an eye, an ear or the folds of a tunic. That is the *mechanical* part of the job, and it is indispensable to the man who wields the brush; but it is not the true source of the artistic *personality*.[38]

It should be noted that Pottier cites Berenson in support of his argument, to be precise his 'Rudiments of Connoisseurhip', in which the American connoisseur states that formal details 'are not of the same importance in

[35] Pottier (1896–1906: iii. 1022).   [36] Pottier (1923: 13; pl. 24).
[37] Munich 2344 in *AVS* (70 no. 5); *ARV²* (182 no. 6).   [38] Pottier (1937: 636).

determining either the authenticity of a work of art or the personality of the artist, and that in the final analysis "quality" remains the essential principle which the connoisseur must be able to appreciate.—That is what we refer to here as "style".'[39] Pottier gives this as a quotation, but we have not been able to trace it, and believe that he chose to paraphrase the following somewhat unclear statement of Berenson's:

Although we have found that the quality can never be left out of consideration—indeed, that it is always the highest consideration—yet we note in the classification just made that on the whole the ratio of immediate applicability of a test is inversely as the importance of allowing for the question of quality: the more important the question, the less applicable; but we have also found that even in the most applicable test it is the qualitative rather than the formal element that gives them their value.[40]

Pottier refers not only to Berenson for the proper use of stylistic criteria, but also to Ernst Pfuhl, who in his *Malerei und Zeichnung der Griechen* treated the results of stylistic studies with great caution.[41] Thus Pottier is able to show a contrast between two notions of connoisseurship, the first (his own and Berenson's) based on the quality of the work and the psychology of the artist, and the other (supported by Morelli and Beazley) on the formal aspects of the image and the *ductus* of the painter.[42]

In this context we ought perhaps to quote the statement in which Beazley summed up his conception of style: 'I was brought up to think of "style" as a sacred thing, as the man himself.'[43] By this he meant simply that for him the word style referred to the painter himself, whereas others would prefer to use the word 'manner'. For Beazley, style was the very particular way in which each painter used his instruments to compose a picture, it being understood that the recognition of that hand had less to do with the perception of the graphic quality of the representation than with the features that were peculiar to that artist. He was also keenly aware of how difficult it was to give a convincing analysis of a painter's style, and perhaps it was this that prevented him from explaining his attributions more often than he did: 'To describe an artist's style is a difficult task, as everyone realises who has undertaken it. Just what is characteristic in his renderings often eludes expression, and over and above the renderings of separate parts there is something which can hardly be put into words.'[44] This lack of explanation did not lend itself to the exchange of views, and Pottier, who was genuinely trying to understand Beazley's method, must frequently have been disheartened by this curious logic which was so difficult to demonstrate.

---

[39] Ibid. (635 n. 1).   [40] Berenson (1901–16: ii. 144).   [41] Pfuhl (1923: i. 347–8).   [42] Pottier (1937: 634–6).   [43] *ABV* (p. x).   [44] Beazley (1917: 234).

It may be that in the long term, with regard to Greek pottery and the conditions that governed the artistic quality of its painting, the model that Pottier had in mind was that of Japan.[45] He found that the technique of drawing there was strikingly similar to that used in Greece, as evidenced by the art of painters like Hokusai and Utamaro. On the other hand Japanese prints of the seventeenth and eighteenth centuries were all of the same level of artistic quality, whereas Beazley's method showed that in Athenian pottery, even with the leading artists, such as the Berlin Painter, there were very noticeable differences of quality within the same corpus of images. 'It is my experience that Greek vase-painters were not always at their best, different in this respect from modern artists.'[46] Pottier's interest in the Japanese figurative arts must be seen in the context of the all-pervading interest in Japanaiserie at the time,[47] and we see something of this in one of several novels which his wife wrote under the pseudonym of Jacques Morel, *La Dette*; here she portrays a critic who specializes in Japanese art, Daniel Vitry, in whom some of Pottier's characteristics can no doubt be recognized.[48]

EPILOGUE

In conclusion, it should be made clear at what point Beazley's method began to be viewed differently. The turning-point no doubt came with the publication in 1933 of *Campana Fragments in Florence*, which showed how effective Beazley's experimental method had been in reconstructing fragments scattered around various museums, and with the death of Pottier in the following year (4 July 1934). In his biographical note on Pottier, Charles Picard continued to condemn 'the triumphant excesses of a certain method of classification of Greek pottery, by which it is attributed arbitrarily, and often regardless of the consequences, to more or less fictitious masters', but his remarks reflected an attitude which by now was rather backward-looking, probably because Picard himself was not strictly speaking a vase specialist.[49] Nicolas Plaoutine, on the other hand, the best connoisseur of the history of vase collections in the nineteenth century, immediately understood the import of Beazley's work on the Campana fragments in Florence. In this work, for which Beazley himself had to cover two-thirds of the publishing costs because at first it did not seem particularly appealing, he proposed several reconstructions of pieces whose fragments were spread around various museums. One example was the cup of Oltos, which appears on the book's frontispiece and whose *disjecta membra* were in six different museums,

---

[45] Pottier (1890 = 1937: 3–32).   [46] *ARV²* (p. xlvii).
[47] See Grand Palais (1988).   [48] Morel (pseud. of Mme E. Pottier) (1905).
[49] Lantier and Picard (1934: p. xi n. 1).

in Rome (Villa Giulia), Florence, Heidelberg, Brunswick, Baltimore, and Bowdoin College. These reconstructions testified to the coherence of Beazley's attributions, as Plaoutine told him in a letter: 'I am so glad to have your Campana Fragments, for it is the strongest proof that your system of attributing is correct. This pleases me especially because I believed in the soundness of your theories before you started your "reconstruction work", which is naturally a logical consequence, but nevertheless is most amazing.'[50]

Beazley's book drew on the first Florentine fascicle of the *CVA*, which was devoted in part to the fragments of red-figured vases in the Campana collection.[51] He was attempting to revise the *CVA* by renumbering the figures in the Florence fascicle correctly. This involved inserting seventeen overlays into the book; there was no other solution where fragments belonging to different vases were catalogued under the same number. He proposed a new numbering system of his own, and suggested to archaeologists that they refer to it in their bibliographical references. This might well have been badly received by those in charge of the *CVA*; in another letter from Plaoutine, however, we learn that when he showed Beazley's book to Georges Nicole, a collaborator at the Champion publishing house where most of the volumes of the *CVA* were published, Nicole was above all impressed by what it proved: 'I showed him your *Campana Fragments* & we had the Florence Corpus before us. He has admitted at last that the book is a triumph of your system which he did not recognize before.'[52]

That remark may well indicate the mixed feelings that Beazley's method had aroused initially, given that in France, as we know from Venturi, 'the connoisseur's activity has not been much developed'.[53] As regards Pottier, he did live to see Beazley's *Campana Fragments*, but as far as I know did not alter his opinion. In any case, his interest was very much focused on prehistory and the East, which were to take up a sizeable portion of the *CVA*. That was one of the original aspects of this enterprise which occupied the last fifteen years of his life, and which we shall present in the final chapter.

[50] Letter from Plaoutine to Beazley (Paris, 13 Nov. 1933); Oxford, Beazley Archive.
[51] Levi [1931].
[52] Letter from Plaoutine to Beazley (Paris, 16 Mar. 1934); Oxford, Beazley Archive.
[53] Venturi (1938: 271).

7

Pottier and the
Corpus Vasorum Antiquorum

A GENERAL INVENTORY OF ANCIENT CLAY VASES

> Putting together a *Corpus* of the trademarks of Roman potters is not in
> itself a mental operation of any more weighty existential value than that
> of the *Collector* imagined by Jean Capart, who gathered together, classi-
> fied, and identified the trouser buttons he picked up in the streets of
> Brussels; on the other hand, a *Corpus* like this is not an end in itself, and
> draws its justification from the use that a historian of the Roman Empire
> will make of it.
>
> H.-I. Marrou, *De la connaissance historique* (1954)

The *Corpus Vasorum Antiquorum* has an important place in the historiography
of vases in the twentieth century and in the creation of a science of pottery.
When Pottier conceived the project in 1919, his intention was to organize a
vast editorial and scientific enterprise on an international scale, whereby every
ancient clay vase conserved in a public museum or private collection would be
published. The *CVA* is still publishing fascicles today, and it now runs to more
than 300 volumes, thanks to the collaboration of more than fifty countries
working together within the Union Académique Internationale.

This alone would be enough to show that the *CVA* was produced in
response to a real need, although it has of course evolved since its beginnings.
In terms of its content the change is quite appreciable, since its creator originally intended that it should publish all the vases of the Mediterranean
world and the Near and Far East, the pottery of prehistoric Europe, undecorated vases, and so on. In fact, this over-ambitious project fell by the wayside,
and it was decided that the *CVA* should limit itself to the classical world, and
in particular to Greek vases, including those of the pre-Hellenic and para-
Hellenic periods. By the time this was made official in 1956 at a colloquium
in Lyons, it reflected what had in reality been the state of affairs for some
time.[1] In this respect, there is no doubt that the *CVA* did not fulfil all the

---

[1] *CVA* (1957: 10).

objectives envisaged by Pottier at the outset. It is worth examining what these were, however, in order to gain an idea of the scientific aims that lay behind the *Corpus*.

Another point that should be noted is the post-war context in which the *Corpus* was developed. When the UAI was set up in 1919 in order to facilitate projects such as this through close co-operation between the academies of the member countries, it decided to exclude Germany and Austria from the deliberations over the constitution of the new Union, thus duplicating the rulings of the Treaty of Versailles on the academic front. It was not until 1935 that these two countries were admitted to the UAI; the first German fascicle of the *CVA*, on the Bonn museum, was published three years later.[2] There is no need to dwell here on a situation whose repercussions were more serious elsewhere. It was clear, however, that the exclusion of Germany, which had played a significant part in creating a science of vases, was likely to lead to resentment, and indeed this was not long in coming to the surface.

l'union académique internationale

At the end of the nineteenth century learned bodies regularly held international conferences to discuss scientific projects that required the mutual help and support of the academies. Partly owing to the political and social internationalism of the time, there was also a climate of intellectual internationalism in which such meetings flourished. It was in this context that the first international conference on classical archaeology took place in Athens in 1905. This was of course attended by Théophile Homolle, the director of the Delphi excavations, who was to play an important part both in the formation of the UAI and in the deliberations over the *Corpus*. At the conference he expressed his concern to find 'means whereby to facilitate archaeological work, to make it more practical and more fruitful', and announced a plan for a *Corpus Inscriptionum Graecarum Christianarum*, to be carried out by the École française in Athens.[3] To make this type of work possible, academies grouped together within multi-national organizations such as the Association Internationale des Académies (1900–14), the direct ancestor of the UAI.

We shall not go into the details of the history of this Association, which brought together learned bodies from a dozen countries and met regularly every three years (the fifth and last meeting took place in St Petersburg in 1914). We need only note that it was set up by the Academy of Sciences in Berlin, which had produced the two epigraphical corpora of the Graeco-Roman world; a preliminary conference took place in Wiesbaden on 9 and

---

[2] Greifenhagen (1938).   [3] Chabert (1906: 133).

10 October 1899, and the drafts of the statutes were published there.[4] Although absent from the Wiesbaden conference, the Académie des Inscriptions et Belles-Lettres was officially invited to join the AIA, as was the Académie des Sciences Morales et Politiques. At the first official meeting in Paris in 1901, the Académie des Inscriptions, at the suggestion of the art historian Eugène Müntz, put forward a plan for a corpus of mosaics ('Plan for a Corpus of pagan and Christian mosaics up to and including the ninth century').[5]

The AIA's work was of course interrupted by the First World War, although it was not officially dissolved. From the autumn of 1918 on, contacts were renewed in the worlds of science and literature, and this time the Académie des Inscriptions was in a strong position. In October a Commission for international relations was appointed to consider new modes of association, and decide what course of action should be taken with regard to the learned bodies of Germany and its allies. As far as this second point was concerned, the message was unambiguous: 'The barbarity with which the war has been conducted and for which the whole nation, not excepting the intellectuals and scholars, is responsible,' meant that 'the Association Internationale des Académies, formed on the initiative of Germany and organized in accordance with its plans, with the imperialist aim of achieving scientific domination, cannot be maintained'.[6]

In March 1919, the Académie des Inscriptions invited several bodies to meet at a preliminary conference, which took place in May at the Bibliothèque Nationale in Paris, in the office of Homolle, who at that time was its director. The meeting was attended by representatives of seven nations (Belgium, the United States, France, Greece, Italy, Japan, and Romania), and the delegates decided on the creation of a new academic union, whose legal and administrative seat would be the Belgian Académie royale in Brussels, and which would meet at least once a year. Interacademic relations with Germany and its allies could not be resumed for the indefinite future.[7]

A second meeting took place 15–18 October 1919, once again at the Bibliothèque Nationale. On this occasion the statutes of the new Union were decreed, and on the last day Homolle presented the project for the *Corpus* of ancient vases, along with the other French projects.[8] An unfortunate omission was thus corrected; archaeology, which did not appear on the list of

---

[4] Darboux (1901).   [5] AIA (1901).

[6] Senart, Héron de Villefosse, Homolle, Croiset, Haussoulier, Prou, and Fournier were members of this committee, which held eight meetings from October to 10 Jan. 1919, when Fournier signed the general account; Institut de France, Archives of the Académie des Inscriptions et Belles-Lettres E 440 (meetings).

[7] UAI (1919: 2); cf. Lecointe and de Guchtenaere (1919).

[8] UAI (1919a: 9).

sciences provided for in article II of the first resolutions, was now added. The aim of the new association was as follows: 'international co-operation in the progress of study through collective research and publications, in the sciences cultivated by the scientific Academies and Institutions represented within the UAI: philology, archaeology, and history; the moral, political, and social sciences.'[9]

POTTIER'S PROJECT FOR VASES

The *Corpus* was one of the first projects examined and initiated by the members of the UAI, along with supplementary provisions for the corpora of Greek and Latin inscriptions and an archaeological map of the Roman Empire. It may be said that this was the first great enterprise of the new union; after being under consideration since 18 October 1919, the *Corpus* was accepted in principle by the executive committee of the UAI at the first annual session in Brussels in May 1920. A commission made up of Théophile Homolle, Frederick Kenyon, Michel Rostovtzeff, and Gaetano de Sanctis was appointed to make detailed plans for 'a work whose magnitude has been a constant source of alarm to cautious spirits, but which is of precisely the sort that a Union such as ours must organize and produce.'[10] The general editorship of the *CVA* was entrusted to Edmond Pottier, who undertook to provide a specimen of the published text and some plates in the near future, along with a system for making corrections in response to the committee's observations (in fact, Pottier added footnotes to his initial text).

A year later a special archaeological commission was set up to ratify the methods that were finally decided upon. It included the representatives of six nations (England, Belgium, Denmark, France, Holland, and Italy), and half of its members were academics and museum curators: Christian Blinckenberg (University of Copenhagen), Jean Capart (Musée du Cinquantenaire), Fernand Mayence (University of Louvain), Pottier, Frederik Poulsen (Ny Carlsberg Glyptotek, Copenhagen), Gaetano de Sanctis (University of Turin), Arthur Smith (British Museum), and Wilhem Vollgraff (University of Utrecht). The resolutions of the archaeological commission were unanimously adopted at the plenary meeting of the UAI delegates. After just under two years of preparation, each country represented on the archaeological commission on vases undertook to publish its public and private collections through their respective academies. These enjoyed a large degree of autonomy; the general editor's only task was to ensure, in consultation with the national editors, that various aspects of the publication, such as its external

---

[9] UAI (1923: 3–4).   [10] *CVA* (1921: 23).

appearance, and the way in which the plates were prepared and the text was written, were in keeping with the general directives laid down by the commission, 'in such a way as to achieve the allover unity of appearance and method that is indispensable to this collective work'.[11]

The organization of the *Corpus* was of course based on Pottier's plan. We can only gain a limited idea of the decisions taken by the various commissions that may have influenced the project. The only obvious mention of this is in the pamphlet published by the UAI in 1921 on the organization of the *Corpus Vasorum Antiquorum* (1919–21); this includes Pottier's statement, along with the corrections and an estimate of expenses and receipts, and a number of other documents, such as a list of the museum curators and university archaeologists invited to take part in an examination of the project in Brussels in May 1920, and an appendix giving details of a classification project proposed in competition to Pottier's by Blinckenberg, which was rejected by the special archaeological commission in 1921. It is interesting, however, if only because Blinckenberg placed even more emphasis than Pottier did on the East and on prehistory. The broad categories on which his classification was based were as follows: I. Egypt.—II. Elam and Persia.—III. Chaldaea and Mesopotamia.—IV. Assyria. V. Asia Minor. VI. Syria (Phoenicia, Palestine).— VII. Cyprus.—VIII. Greece. IX. Sicily. X. Italy and the Roman Empire.[12]

Organization and aims of the CVA

'What the last century did for inscriptions, this one must do for the science of painted pottery.'[13] By opening his 'Plan for a Corpus of ancient vases' with this declaration, Pottier was placing himself firmly in the footsteps of the epigraphists and philologists of the nineteenth century. He was well aware that a corpus of pottery would be even more difficult to achieve than a corpus of epigraphy, since in this case the objects needed to be illustrated. Yet it was the desire to give archaeologists easy access to reproductions of vases that justified his very existence, however difficult it might be to achieve.

One of the basic principles of the *CVA* was that vases should be published under the museums where they were conserved. Pottier had realized from the outset that this was the most practical method. In our remarks about the *Catalogue des vases antiques du Louvre*, and in particular about the Albums of vases, we have already indicated that an enterprise such as the *CVA* was a little like a large-scale version of a museum catalogue, as Pottier himself seemed to suggest in this statement: 'Nowadays most of the great museums publish descriptive catalogues accompanied by numerous illustrations; this is the best way of gradually building up that *Corpus Rerum* whose much-desired

---

[11] *CVA* (1921: 23).   [12] Ibid. (30–2).   [13] Ibid. 6 = Pottier (1937: 575).

completion will, along with the *Corpus Inscriptionum*, be the great achievement of modern archaeological science.'[14] This is even more true today, since
at first sight there is nothing to distinguish the *CVA* from a particularly rich
collection of catalogues offering an abundance of meticulous descriptions
and illustrations. It should be noted, however, that in Pottier's view it was not
the aim of the *CVA* to replace the museum catalogue: 'The *Corpus* does not
set out to replace the scientific catalogues of museums, with their detailed
descriptions and explanatory commentaries; its aim is to give official status
to every vase, of whatever type, so that it is known and available to every
researcher. Each type of work is different; they complement each other, but
they are not one and the same.'[15] In practical terms what was different about
the *CVA* was the shortness of its descriptions (a maximum of about ten lines
on each piece), and the modest size of its reproductions (these were overall
views measuring six to nine centimetres, except for the most outstanding
painted vases).

There were of course other differences of a less practical nature, and to
understand these we need to define the theoretical foundations of the *Corpus*.
In this sense, what distinguished it above all from previous publications was
the fact that it was so exhaustive and systematic. Certainly these earlier works,
which Pottier listed at the beginning of the project, were useful research
tools, but nonetheless as a whole they were 'of uneven value and lacking in a
homogeneous plan'.[16] The *Corpus* aimed to remedy these faults by adopting
from the outset a single viewpoint and a uniform appearance. The most striking aspect of the project, as has been said, was its extremely ambitious nature.
It aimed to cover not only all vases from the Mediterranean basin, 'whatever
their clay, method of production and shape, whether they be plain or decorated with ornaments and figures, incised, painted, or modelled in relief', but
also the products of more outlying regions.[17]

The following list of regions adopted by the archaeological commission will give an idea of the geographical area involved: I. The East. II.
The islands of the eastern Mediterranean. III. Greece. IV. Italy and Sicily;
Malta, Corsica and Sardinia. V. Spain and Portugal, North Africa. VI. Gaul,
Germania, Danube Valley. VII. Brittany, Scandinavia. VIII. Poland, Russia, and
neighbouring countries.[18] As a wise precaution they decided in principle
to start with classical vases (Greek, Italian, and Roman), and Eastern vases,
including those of prehistoric Greece and Italy, before moving on at a
later stage to the secondary categories, such as undecorated vases, those of
prehistoric Europe, etc.

---

[14] Pottier (1897: i, preface).   [15] *CVA* (1921: 13) = Pottier (1937: 583).
[16] *CVA* (1921: 7) = Pottier (1937: 576).   [17] Homolle (1923: 6–7).   [18] *CVA* (1921: 27–8).

It was Pottier who wanted so many different regions to be included, and we may wonder why he made such a plan, and why he included all the vases from the Near and Middle East as a priority along with those from the Mediterranean basin. He gave the reason for this in a statement which may be viewed as one of the essential foundations of the *Corpus*:

Are we to make a geographical cut-off point, by leaving aside the East (Elam, Turkestan, Chaldaea and Assyria, Asia Minor, Syria, Palestine and Egypt)? This would make the task a great deal simpler, but it would seem to me regrettable, since it is becoming more and more apparent that the pottery of Asia is connected with that of Ionia and the eastern islands of the Mediterranean; that the study of pre-Hellenism is closely linked with Eastern questions; that Crete and Cyprus cannot be separated from Asia on the one hand, and continental Greece on the other; that on the contrary, by bringing together Asia, Africa, and Europe, the *Corpus Vasorum Antiquorum* would contribute new scientific ideas on this subject which would be of very great interest.[19]

In other words, the *Corpus* must enable archaeologists to compare the forms and styles of pottery, so that they could study their distribution, identify the influences that may have passed from one region to another, and ultimately from one continent to another, and thus gain a better understanding of the cultural links between East and West. The scope of the project was in sharp contrast to the standard ideas of the time concerning ancient archaeology and art history, and especially of the history of artists. The science of art, as Pottier saw it, should follow the example of comparative ethnography and take as its basis the study of the art of primitive peoples; it would thus become possible to identify general laws, in other words the great aesthetic principles underlying the first attempts at artistic achievement.[20] Once these were established, attempts could be made to describe the models taken from life (animal, vegetable, and human) on which they were based, and to study their distribution, in order to find out whether it could be demonstrated that there was a relationship of cause and effect between art and a given civilization. Thus it was possible, for example, to imagine ascertaining whether the move from hunting to agriculture in very ancient societies was invariably accompanied by new techniques in the production of pottery. The *Corpus* could prove to be a particularly useful instrument in drawing these parallels, since it would enable comparisons between vases to be made with ease and, most important, make the possibility of comparing them available to all archaeologists, and to all historians, for whose use the *CVA* was in fact primarily intended. Pottier was always anxious that archaeology, and thus the study of pottery, should follow the lead of history:'Every archaeologist should first and

[19] *CVA* (1921: 10) = Pottier (1937: 579).   [20] Pottier (1907 = 1937: 33–50).

foremost be a historian.'[21] To his way of thinking, this type of history ought to be open to the great questions posed by anthropology as it was perceived at the time: questions concerning the origin of peoples, the evolution of races, and the relationship between East and West.

One of the weaknesses in Pottier's approach was perhaps that he regarded as settled something which in fact was still very much a problem. After all, what type of links between vases and a society in general could be established with the full weight of archaeological proof? What analytical tools should be selected in order to compare different geographical areas? By what criteria could the characteristics they shared be defined? Every attempt at comparison ought to begin with an endeavour to provide some answers to these questions. There can be little doubt that it was this fault in Pottier's method, along with the enormity of the task he was taking on before a single result had been achieved, that led to his successors' decision to revise the *CVA*'s objectives. The organizers of the Lyons colloquium were particularly concerned about the size of the project: 'The desire to include *all* ancient vases in the *Corpus* would make it an outrageously over-ambitious enterprise.'[22]

Criticisms and reactions

The first fascicle of the *CVA*, devoted to a series of vases in the Louvre and written of course by Pottier, was published at the end of 1922. Despite the difficulties arising from the experimental nature of the enterprise and its methodological principles and implications, the *CVA* came out very regularly, especially in the case of the Louvre fascicles, which were to serve as a kind of model for the publication of other museums' volumes (in ten years Pottier, with admirable regularity, wrote eight fascicles of the *CVA*).[23] He made it a point of honour to answer the criticisms and objections which this instrument was bound to provoke given that it was intended to become a standard work for archaeologists, and to justify the principal aspects of its organization.

In an article in the *Revue archéologique* of 1924, the founder, organizer, and general editor of the *CVA* replied without delay to the criticisms that had been made of the general organization of the *Corpus*,[24] notably by Gordon Childe, Georg Karo, and John Beazley. Childe's review was favourable on the whole; he expressed only one or two reservations, in particular questioning the exhaustive nature of the work, in other words the fundamental usefulness of publishing every example. Pottier retorted, in accordance with the

---

[21] Pottier (1908: 12).   [22] *CVA* (1957: 10).
[23] Pottier ([1922]; 1923; 1925; 1926; 1928a; 1929; 1932; 1933).
[24] Pottier (1924).

decisions of the 1920 commission, that a *Corpus* 'must by definition not leave out a single piece'.[25] Furthermore, Childe did not conceal his astonishment at the exclusion of Germany from a union which claimed to be resolutely international, and declared himself in favour of the expansion of the *CVA* to include Germany, given the services it had rendered to archaeological science and the importance of its collections. Since this was not Pottier's responsibility alone, he could do no more than refer to the provisions of article 10 of the UAI, which stated the conditions for new membership (a majority of three-quarters of all votes in the UAI), but he admitted that the wish expressed was 'legitimate'.[26]

It was clear, on the other hand, that he was rather shocked by the presumptuousness of some German scholars, such as Georg Karo, 'an archaeologist of high repute, and in times gone by very much the friend of our country who has collaborated on several French publications' (in particular he had collaborated with Pottier on the writing of an article on 'Pyelos' for the *Dictionnaire des antiquités grecques et romaines*). Karo had stressed the futility of 'the combined efforts of our enemies' compared with what German science could produce through the work of one single researcher, Ernst Pfuhl, whose important work, *Malerei und Zeichnung der Griechen*, had just been published a few months earlier.[27] This was a ground-breaking work, and Pottier too regarded it as 'one of the best books on Greek pottery ever published'.[28] Pfuhl's book certainly represented an impressive synthesis of a century of research into major painting and vase-painting in ancient Greece; it was no accident that Beazley translated into English the one-volume abridged edition of the work, which was published in 1924 under the title *Meisterwerke griechischer Zeichnung und Malerei*. Nevertheless, to contrast 'the fruits of the combined efforts of our enemies' with 'the task accomplished by a single German researcher who, alone and almost without assistance, sacrificing his entire personality, as much in pursuit of an ideal as of financial gain, has created and truly penetrated his subject matter', was to present things in a way which Pottier found rather offensive; it should be said that during the war he had suffered the loss of his only son Jean, who was killed in action at the age of 24 on 21 December 1915.[29] Nonetheless Karo's invective expressed a feeling of bitterness that was quite widespread among German and Austrian intellectuals, as was also seen in a symbolic gesture made by Leopold Conze, the son of the archaeologist Alexander Conze (who died before the war began, on 19 July 1914); in protest against the

---

[25] Childe (1924); cf. Pottier (1924: 286–7).   [26] Pottier (1924: 287).

[27] Karo (1923); Pottier (1924: 288–9); Pfuhl (1923).

[28] Pottier (1924: 288).   [29] Karo (1923: col. 903); Pottier (1924: 289).

demands for reparation he sent his father's foreign membership card back to the Institut de France.[30]

John Beazley was one of the academics invited to take part in a scrutiny of the *Corpus* project in May 1920 in Brussels, or to give their opinion by post if they were unable to attend in person. To our knowledge he did not take part in these deliberations, but he certainly was not hostile to the project. The two volumes of the *CVA* which Beazley wrote (the second in collaboration with Humfry Payne and Eleonor Price) on the Ashmolean Museum collections, in addition to the sixty-two reviews he gave the publication later, covering sixty-nine of its fascicles, are evidence of his keen interest in this scientific enterprise.[31] This exceptionally high number of reviews (on average nearly two a year) probably indicates that he was very eager to have the volumes of the *Corpus* in his possession, since they were a useful complement to his own photographic archives.

It is therefore not surprising that most of his remarks had to do with the methods by which vases were reproduced, since it was this aspect of the work that was most useful to him. His chief reservation concerned the tendency to publish vases with modern restorations, given that it was often difficult 'even for an expert, to tell from the reproduction alone where old ends and new begins'.[32] The implication was that in future vases should be cleaned as a matter of course before they were photographed and published.[33] This rather logical advice was on the whole quite closely adhered to. Another aspect of the method of publication that Beazley criticized was the silhouetting of vases.[34] Pottier was a great advocate of this process, which involved outlining the contour of vases so that they stood out better against a white background: 'The main advantage of silhouetting is that it adds to the artistic quality and unity of the plates, and makes the objects stand out more clearly.'[35] Compilers were not obliged to use this process, however; so long as they respected certain fundamental norms, they were entirely free to do as they pleased. The first collaborator on the *CVA* not to use silhouetting was Arthur Smith, the author of the first British Museum volume; it seemed that there was not much enthusiasm for the process in Britain.[36] It was gradually abandoned by scientific publications as being associated with an aesthetic approach that was more in vogue in the second half of the nineteenth century. One of the recommendations made to authors in 1956 was that 'except where it is completely unavoidable' the technique should be dropped completely.[37]

[30] Letter from L. Conze to the Académie des Sciences (Lübeck, 11 Feb. 1920); Institut de France, Archives of the Académie des Inscriptions et Belles-Lettres (E 443).

[31] Beazley (1927); Beazley, Payne, and Price (1931).   [32] Beazley (1925a).

[33] Beazley (1927a).   [34] Beazley (1923: 199; 1927a).

[35] Pottier (1923a: 89).   [36] Smith (1925).   [37] *CVA* (1957: 12).

What Pottier was particularly anxious to combat, however, since it struck at 'the very foundations' of the *CVA*, was any criticizm of the appropriateness of publishing a mixture of Eastern and Greek pottery in the same work. Beazley stated that 'the connexion between proto-Elamitic vases and Greek civilisation is comparatively slight', and recommended that the two series be published separately.[38] As planned, Pottier had given a range of samples of various series in the first three Louvre fascicles, and had given special prominence at the beginning of each volume to the pottery of Susa, representing the first and second periods of the proto-Elamite style (fourth and third millennia), and also to local pottery outside Susa, from the Moussian and Bender-Bouchir regions.[39] These vases had belonged to the Louvre collections since the Morgan Mission to Persia, a wide-ranging scientific programme which gave rise to the publication of several archaeological memoirs.[40] Pottier, who collaborated on one of these, thought particularly highly of the finesse and simplicity of these very early vases, especially those of the first period, 'which, as everyone agrees, can be regarded as the masterpieces of Asiatic pottery'. In fact, he became a specialist in the pottery of this period,[41] and the *CVA* was of course the ideal vehicle for raising awareness of its scientific and artistic importance.

In a more general sense it should not be forgotten that since 1910 Pottier had been at the head of the Department of Oriental Antiquities and Ancient Pottery at the Louvre. This administrative and scientific responsibility meant that he needed to put more and more into Eastern studies, so that he could write catalogues of the *Antiquités de la Susiane* and *Antiquités assyriennes*, and also a work on Hittite art.[42] In this respect it was the weight of the institution that determined the direction of his research, yet it would be wrong to think that there was no more to it than that; we find evidence of Pottier's deep interest in the East very early on in his writings, for example in the article from 1890 already quoted, in which he attempted to examine the connection between the art of pottery in Greece and Japan. 'Let us not forget,' he declared, 'that the cradle of Greece is in Ionia, that its art has its roots deep in the soil of Central Asia, and that even today its climate and customs make it an eastern country much more than a European one.'[43]

Pottier made many more statements of a similar kind, but this one example will perhaps be sufficient to illustrate the point, since a deeper examination of his interest in the East would take us further than we need to go here. It would also involve studying the views of Salomon Reinach, who in a long

[38] Beazley (1923: 199).
[39] Pottier ([1922]: pls. 1–12; 1923: pls. 1–8; 1925: pls. 1–14).   [40] See Chevalier (1997).
[41] Mecquenem, Morgan, and Pottier (1912); Pottier (1937: 99–112, 113–27, 128–43; quotation 119).
[42] Pézard and Pottier (1913); Pottier (1917a; 1926a–31).   [43] Pottier (1890 = 1937: 17).

article on 'Le Mirage oriental' adopted a decidedly different stance from that of his friend and colleague, and analysing at greater length the scientific and institutional consequences of combining ancient pottery with the Department of Oriental Antiquities at the Louvre.[44] Such an account would give us a better idea of the gulf that separated Pottier and Beazley on this point, but since this topic has already been covered in some considerable detail, it would seem more appropriate to conclude by examining another striking aspect of the *Corpus*: the possibility that it allowed for regrouping the series among themselves.

ON THE IMPORTANCE OF QUOTING
THE *CVA* CORRECTLY

One notable feature of the *Corpus* was the elaborate numbering system by which the vases were classified. In the top left-hand corner of each plate there was a Roman numeral indicating the main group (broad geographical area), an upper-case letter identifying the stylistic group, and a lower-case letter denoting a sub-group within the series. Only the first two of these were regarded as fixed and immutable; the third could vary from one museum and collection to another. At the Louvre, for example, III I *c* denoted a series of vases of Greek origin, in the Attic style, belonging to the group of vases in the severe style, and dating from the first half of the fifth century BC.[45]

Pottier knew that the volumes of supplements that are inevitable in any corpus complicated the task of researchers enormously, since the latter had to handle a large number of fascicles in order to find information relating to the same series of objects. To remedy this problem he devised a very ingenious system; in fact it was too ingenious, and what started out as a brilliant idea did not in the end achieve the desired results.

To recapitulate, Pottier wanted there to be a rational system for numbering vases, so that they could be divided into broad groups, within which there would be sub-groups. It would then be important to ensure that the text corresponded to the plates, which would not be bound together (a crucial detail) but inserted into a wallet to which new documents could be added, thus making it possible eventually to put together the various series of objects belonging to one category or one museum.

For the system to work it was also essential that when cross-references were made to the *CVA* in specialist works they gave only the classification numbers, and did not mention the number of the fascicle in the museum or country series, since the eventual aim was to regroup the series among themselves.

---

[44] Reinach (1893).   [45] Pottier ([1922]: p. vi).

It is no exaggeration to say that the plan worked like a dream. Even Beazley stuck faithfully to this principle in his Lists, mentioning only the classification numbers. Since then, however, the system has been abandoned,[46] and as a result the absence of fascicle numbers is quite a hindrance to finding a vase in the *Corpus*, especially for non-specialists, this despite the fact that the work was intended for wider use, notably by historians. It is true that this problem mainly affects the sections published between 1920 and 1950; after that it became clear that at least one of the other numbers ought to be quoted, preferably that of the fascicle in the museum series.[47] The fact that initially the rule was in general adhered to suggests that there was no doubt in anyone's mind about the feasibility of these later regroupings, which indeed were by no means unachievable.

The plan to regroup the fascicles relating to one museum or one series was occasionally carried through. The library of the Ashmolean Museum possesses one example of this; it belonged to Beazley himself, and contains the two fascicles of the museum written by him and his collaborators. The Louis-Gernet Centre in Paris also possesses two examples, and these deserve more than a passing mention, since they belonged to Pottier himself. The two boxed volumes, published by Champion, contain the text and plates of the *CVA* relating to the Louvre. They were bought a few years ago by François Lissarrague from the publisher and bookseller Picard in Paris, and they contain the ex-libris of Pierre Wuillemier, a professor at the University of Lyons, and also the stamp of the Salomon Reinach library which was set up in Lyons after Reinach's death in 1932. Since Wuillemier was Pottier's great-nephew, it can be assumed that the books came into his possession after Pottier's death in 1934, but that does not explain the presence of the Salomon Reinach library mark. Whatever the reason for that, it is important to note that these volumes contain a large number of annotations handwritten by Pottier himself, which indicates that he used them as work tools, and in particular for updating his bibliographical references. We discover, for instance, that he had scrupulously recorded Beazley's attributions in his own copies of the *CVA*. Thus he was very much aware of the English archaeologist's work as far as the attributions in *Attische Vasenmaler des rotfigurigen Stils* were concerned.

This discovery provides a good note on which to conclude, since it shows the influence that Beazley's biographical approach did eventually have on the *CVA*. And although it was Pottier who gave the vital inspiration for the project in the first place, the method of classification used today in the fascicles of the *CVA* is no doubt more in keeping with Beazley's recommenda-

---

[46] Moignard (1989) shows the abandonment of the idea of grouping different fascicles together.
[47] *CVA* (1957: 14).

tions than with his. We can see this in the following example. After the Lyons colloquium in 1956, which Beazley was unable to attend, he sent a note containing his comments, notably on the discussion as to whether to continue with the plan to publish Eastern and prehistoric pottery: 'I agree with those who suggest that the *Corpus* should be limited (as it is in fact at present) to Greek, Italian and Roman pottery, and that in general Eastern and prehistoric European pottery should be excluded. The mass of Eastern and prehistoric pottery is so enormous that the enterprise is in danger of being engulfed by it.'[48]

Should we regret the abandonment of the original project? From a practical point of view, it seems that it ran into insurmountable difficulties; the answer would thus be no. On the theoretical level, the answer will depend on whether the question is asked of a Hellenist or an Orientalist. It was of course because Pottier was both of these that he conceived the idea for the project. Since then the conditions of science have evolved, however, and it is no longer so easy to conduct comparative studies on the grand scale. In particular these conditions have led to increased specialization within the field of pottery, of which Beazley's work is an excellent example.

[48] *CVA* (1957: 30).

Epilogue

That you did combine them I saw by the character of the smile which
passed over your lips.

Edgar Allan Poe, *The Murders in the rue Morgue*

At the end of a long historiographical study, what food for thought can we
draw from the comparison between Beazley and Pottier? The reader already
has some idea of this, since it was indicated at an earlier point that the discussion of Carlo Ginzburg's 'clue paradigm' would be carried over to this conclusion. What is this theory? Ginzburg claims that the last quarter of the
nineteenth century saw the emergence of a new explanatory model in the
field of human sciences. This was based on the interpretation of apparently
trivial or anodyne details, individual elements viewed in their own right as
symptoms, clues, or signs, and giving access to a type of knowledge which had
eluded traditional methods of research. This semiotic paradigm could be seen
in operation in Morelli's works on painting, Freud's research into psychoanalysis, the investigations carried out by Conan Doyle's hero Sherlock
Holmes, and indeed in Bertillon's experiments in judicial anthropometry.
Ginzburg's analysis was coupled with another one of equal importance,
which involved placing the first model in a historical context, from prehistoric times when men hunted animals by interpreting their tracks, and con-
trasting it with the Galilean paradigm of exact sciences.[1] It is not my intention
to make any further comment on this analysis; I merely wish to make two or
three remarks which will cast a slightly different light on the comparison that
has formed the basis for this work.

   The full import of Ginzburg's article cannot be understood unless it is seen
against the background of the preoccupations of micro-history, a school of
thought which came into being after 1970. It was centred around the journal
Quaderni storici, and Ginzburg's article was in fact its most convincing mani-
festo. Jacques Revel observed that the result of Ginzburg's approach was to
give the micro-historians' venture 'a garment which was both a little too large
and a little too loose', but he maintained a keen interest in the discipline, and
the current head of the École des Hautes Études en Sciences Sociales has

[1] Ginzburg (1989).

recently co-ordinated a vast research project on the theme of 'Micro-history and the micro-social', which is an attempt to adapt the problematics of micro-history to the model of social sciences.[2]

Micro-history and the social sciences; very much the same contrast as our own, albeit in a slightly different form. In neither case is the conflict a neat one between two clearly definable polar opposites. What all the authors cited by Ginzburg to illustrate his model did have in common, however, was the accent they placed on individuality and a sense of detail. In art history there had always been an emphasis on personal identity, for the obvious reason that the store of material on which artists drew was not just an open field, but was limited to those works that were essential to the development of artistic forms, all of which had a name. It was in the importance that it also attached to detail that the discipline made real advances, which generally came under the common denominator of style.

We are familiar with Aby Warburg's motto: 'God dwells in minutiae' (*Der liebe Gott steckt im Detail*). His radically new attempt to create a historical psychology of human expression, which started as early as his thesis on the representation of garments and flowing hair in the Florentine painters of the fifteenth century, initially came within the more well-worn framework of stylistic studies, even if its intention was to break out of it.[3] Warburg's thesis focused specifically on the two famous mythological paintings by Sandro Botticelli, *The Birth of Venus* and the *Primavera*. On the subject of Botticelli and Lorenzo di Credi, Heinrich Wölfflin remarked in his mature work, *Kunstgeschichtliche Grundbegriffe*, that 'in the drawing of a mere nostril, we have to recognise the essential character of a style'.[4] He said the same of Hobbema and Ruysdael, claiming that one could tell the identity of the painter from a fragment of a branch, by looking for features that were intrinsic to the feeling of form. At the same time, however, we know that Wölfflin wanted to go beyond the history of artists and move on to a history of style in a broader sense, with the main emphasis on school, country, and race.[5] It has to be said, however, that his idea of a *Kunstgeschichte ohne Namen*, a history of art without artists' names, never really led anywhere; on the contrary, one need only glance at the contents page of *Die Klassische Kunst* (1899) to realize that his work was based entirely on the great names of traditional artists such as Leonardo, Raphael, and Michelangelo. For a justification for this one might perhaps look to one of Wölfflin's early works, *Renaissance und Barock*, in which he wrote: 'He [the historian of style] is concerned only with the great, the truly style-creating geniuses.'[6] This is not far from Morelli's

---

[2] Revel (1989: p. xiv); Revel (ed.) (1996: 8).   [3] Warburg (1999); see Agamben (1998).
[4] Wölfflin (1950: 2).   [5] Ibid. (6).   [6] Wölfflin (1964: 17).

statement that on principle the rules for the identification of paintings apply 'only to those artists who are worthy of that name, in other words those who have their own style, their own mode of conception and expression; only they deserve to be taken into consideration, not the mass of imitators, who count for nothing.'[7]

As we know, Beazley had a different conception of style which was more in keeping with what one might expect from an archaeological approach to vase-painting.[8] Perhaps the best way to move beyond the standard contrast between art history and archaeology, and between individual and collective history, is to shift the emphasis of the problem and approach it from an epistemological point of view. That is in fact what Ginzburg did in his article, and what explains its importance. We also have in mind Jean-Pierre Vernant's work on the mutations in the intellectual world in ancient Greece, the results of which he presented for the first time in *Les Origines de la pensée grecque*. Twenty-five years later, in an article on 'Raison et déraison chez les Grecs', he remarked that there was not just one form of Greek rationality, but various different forms, which could coexist at any given time. There was the rationality of the physicists and the Eleatics, of Parmenides and the Pythagoreans, of the sophists and philosophers of the fourth century BC: 'they actually competed, defined themselves and developed through polemical exchange, but they could not all be applied successfully to the same areas of reality.'[9] To return to Ginzburg, his long article was first published in 1979 in a collection of essays, *Crisi della ragione*. My impression is that in order to promote his method he was inclined to over-systematize the contrast between rationalism and irrationalism. I find, however, that his analysis of the emergence of a new epistemological model at the end of the nineteenth century is entirely convincing. This model is still in use today, through an ever more meticulous observation of facts, of reality. But the fact that it is still in use does not in any sense mean that it has entirely supplanted other modes of reasoning drawn from the past. Even so, there is no doubt that this model has much to offer to any definition of what exactly is meant by reason today.

[7] Lermolieff (1891: 5); cf. Damisch (1970).
[8] See Robertson (1987: 25).   [9] Vernant (1987 = 1995: 302).

Bibliography

ACTON, H. (1948), *Memoirs of an Aesthete* (London: Methuen).

AGAMBEN, G. (1998), 'Aby Warburg et la science sans nom', in id., *Image et mémoire* (Paris: Hoëbeke), 9–43.

AGOSTI, G., *et al.* (1993), *Giovanni Morelli e la cultura dei conoscitori*, proceedings of the international conference held in Bergamo (4–7 June 1987), 3 vols. (Bergamo: Lubrina).

AIA (1899), Minutes of the conference held in Wiesbaden (9–10 October 1899) with a view to founding an Association Internationale des Académies.

AIA (1901), First general meeting held in Paris (16–20 April 1901) under the direction of the Académie des Sciences and the Institut de France.

ALEXANDRE, C. (1841), *Dictionnaire grec-français* (Paris: Hachette).

ALLAN, G. A. T. (1924), *Christ's Hospital Exhibitioners to the Universities of Oxford and Cambridge (1566–1923)* (London: Council of Almoners of Christ's Hospital).

ANDERSON, J. (1987), 'Giovanni Morelli et sa définition de la *scienza dell'arte*', *Revue de l'art*, 75: 49–55.

——(ed.) (1999), *Collecting Connoisseurship and the Art Market in Risorgimento Italy: Giovanni Morelli's Letters to Giovanni Melli and Pietro Zavaritt, 1866–1872* (Venice: Istituto Veneto di Scienze, Lettere ed Arti).

ANDRÉN, A. (1986), *Deeds and Misdeeds in Classical Art and Antiquities* (Goterna: Kungälv).

ASHMOLE, B. (1970), 'Sir John Beazley (1885–1970)', *Proceedings of the British Academy*, 56: 443–61; =D. C. Kurtz (ed.) (1985), *Beazley and Oxford* (Oxford: Oxford University Committe for Archaeology), 57–71.

BALDIN, G. (n.d. [1983]), *Lorenzo Pécheux (1729–1821)*, catalogue of the exhibition at the via Roma in Turin, no. 11 (Mar.–June 1983) (Turin: Piazza).

BAROLSKY, P. (1984), 'Walter Pater and Bernard Berenson', *New Criterion*, April: 47–57.

BEARD, M. (1986), 'Signed against Unsigned', *TLS*, 12 September.

BEAZLEY, J. D. (1907), *Herodotus at the Zoo* (Gaisford Prize for Greek Prose) (Oxford: Blackwell).

——(1908), 'Three New Vases in the Ashmolean Museum', *JHS* 28: 313–18; pls. xxx–xxxii.

——(1910), 'Kleophrades', *JHS* 30: 38–68; pls. i–ix.

——(1911), 'The Master of the Berlin Amphora', *JHS* 31: 276–95; pls. viii–xvii.

——(1911a), 'Three Poems', *English Review*, April: 5–6.

——(1912), 'The Master of the Troilos-hydria in the British Museum', *JHS* 32: 171–3; pls. ii–iii.

——(1912a), 'The Master of the Boston Pan-krater', *JHS* 32: 354–69; pls. vi–ix.

——(1912b), 'The Master of the Villa Giulia Calyx-krater', *MDAI(R)* 27: 286–97.

BEAZLEY, J. D. (1912*c*), 'The Master of the Eucharides-Stamnos in Copenhagen', *BSA* 18 (1911–12): 217–33; pls. x–xv.

—— (1913), 'The Ballad of my Friend', in *Oxford Poetry (1910–1913)* (Oxford: Blackwell), 3–4.

—— (1913*a*), 'The Master of the Dutuit Oinochoe', *JHS* 33: 106–10; pls. viii–xii.

—— (1913*b*), 'The Master of the Stroganoff Nikoxenos Vase', *BSA* 18 (1912–13): 229–47; pls. xvi–xix.

—— (1914), 'The Master of the Achilles Amphora in the Vatican', *JHS* 34: 179–226; pls. xiii–xvi.

—— (1916), 'Two Vases in Harrow', *JHS* 36: 123–33; pls. vi–vii.

—— (1916*a*), 'Fragment of a Vase at Oxford and the Painter of the Tyszkiewicz Crater in Boston', *AJA* 20: 144–53.

—— (1917), review of J. C. Hoppin, *Euthymides and his Fellows*, in *JHS* 37: 233–7.

—— (1918), *Attic Red-figured Vases in American Museums* (Cambridge, Mass.: Harvard University Press).

—— (1920), *The Lewes House Collection of Ancient Gems* (Oxford: Clarendon Press).

—— (1922), 'Citharoedus', *JHS* 42: 70–98; pls. ii–v.

—— (1923), review of E. Pottier, *CVA. France 1, Louvre 1*, in *JHS* 43: 198–9.

—— (1925), *Attische Vasenmaler des rotfigurigen Stils* (Tübingen: Mohr).

—— (1925*a*), review of E. Pottier, *CVA. France 2 et 4, Louvre 2 et 3*; M. Flot, *France 3, Musée de Compiègne*; C. Blinkenberg, K. Friis Johansen, *Danemark 1, Copenhague, Musée National 1*; A. H. Smith, *Great Britain 1, British Museum 1*, in *JHS* 45: 285–6.

—— (1927), *CVA. Great Britain 3, Oxford, Ashmolean Museum 1* (Oxford: Clarendon Press).

—— (1927*a*), review of E. Pottier, *CVA. France 5, Louvre 4*, in *JHS* 47: 147.

—— (1928), review of E. Pottier, *CVA. France 8, Louvre 5*, in *JHS* 48: 270–1.

—— (1929), *Attic Black-figure: A Sketch* (London: Milford).

—— (1929*a*), 'Mr. E. P. Warren', *The Times*, 7 January.

—— (1929*b*), 'Edward Perry Warren', *Oxford Magazine*, 24 January.

—— (1930), review of E. Pottier, *CVA. France 9, Louvre 6*, in *JHS* 50: 161–2.

—— (1931*a*), review of H. B. Walters, *CVA. Great Britain 8, British Museum 6*, in *JHS* 51: 121–3.

—— (1933), *Campana Fragments in Florence* (Oxford: Oxford University Press).

—— (1941), 'Warren as Collector', in O. Burdett and E. H. Goddard, *Edward Perry Warren: The Biography of a Connoisseur* (London: Christophers), 331–63.

—— (1942), *Attic Red-figure Vase-painters* (Oxford: Clarendon Press).

—— (1943), 'The Training of Archaeologists: University Training', abridgement of the speech delivered at the Conference on the future of archaeology, published in *University of London, Institute of Archaeology, Occasional Paper 5*: 42–4.

—— (1946), *Potter and Painter in Ancient Athens* (London: Cumberlege).

—— (1956), *Attic Black-figure Vase-painters* (Oxford: Clarendon Press).

—— (1961), 'An Amphora by the Berlin Painter', *AK* 4: 49–67.

—— (1963), *Attic Red-figure Vase-painters²*, 3 vols. (Oxford: Clarendon Press).

——(1964), *The Berlin Painter* (Melbourne: Melbourne University Press).

——(1971), *Paralipomena: Additions to* Attic Black-figure Vase-painters *and to* Attic Red-figure Vase-painters[2] (Oxford: Oxford University Press).

——(1989), *Greek Vases, Lectures by J. D. Beazley*, ed. D. C. Kurtz (Oxford: Clarendon Press).

——and CASKEY, L. D. (1931–63), *Attic Vase Paintings in the Museum of Fine Arts, Boston*, 3 vols. (Boston, Mass. and London: Museum of Fine Arts; Oxford University Press).

——and MERLIN, A. (1936), 'Une nouvelle amphore du "Peintre de Berlin" (Musée du Louvre)', *MMAI* 35: 49–72; pl. iv.

——PAYNE, H. G. G., and PRICE, E. R. (1931), *CVA. Great Britain 9, Oxford Ashmolean Museum 2* (Oxford: Clarendon Press).

BENDA, J. (1918), *Essai sur l'esthétique de la présente société française* (Paris: Émile-Paul).

BÉRARD, C. (1990), 'Le satyre casseur', *Métis*, V/1–2: 75–87.

BERENSON, B. (1894), *The Venetian Painters of the Renaissance*, with an index to their works (New York and London: Putman).

——(1895), *Lorenzo Lotto: An Essay in Constructive Art Criticism* (London and New York: Putman).

——(1895a), *Venetian Painting, Chiefly before Titian, at the Exhibition of Venetian Art, the New Gallery* (privately printed).

——(1896), *The Florentine Painters of the Renaissance*, with an index to their works (New York and London: Putman).

——(1897), *The Central Italian Painters of the Renaissance* (New York and London: Putman).

——(1899), 'Amico di Sandro', *GBA* 41/I: 459–71; 41/II: 21–36.

——(1901–16), *The Study and Criticism of Italian Art*, 3 vols. (First Series, 1901; Second Series, 1902; Third Series, 1916) (London: Bell).

——(1903), *The Drawings of the Florentine Painters*, classified, criticized, and studied as documents in the history and appreciation of Tuscan art, with a copious catalogue raisonné, 2 vols. (London: Murray).

——(1907), *The North Italian Painters of the Renaissance* (New York and London: Putman).

——(1949), *Sketch for a Self-portrait* (London: Constable).

BERGE, L. (1975), 'Beazley's Myson: the Definition of an Artistic Personality in Attic Vase-Painting', thesis (D.Phil.), University of Oxford.

BERLIN, I. (1991), 'Sir Isaiah Berlin, esprit hardi', interview with Sir I. Berlin by F. du Sorbier, in F. du Sorbier (ed.), *Oxford (1919–1939), un creuset intellectuel ou les métamorphoses d'une génération* (Paris: Autrement), 57–69.

BEST MAN (1906), *The Best Man*, Eights' Week (Oxford).

BIRCH, S., and NEWTON, C. T. (1851–70), *Catalogue of the Greek and Etruscan Vases in the British Museum*, 2 vols. (London: Nicol-Woodfall and Kinder).

BOARDMAN, J. (1981), 'Epiktetos II R.I.P.' *Archäologischer Anzeiger*, 1981: 329–32.

——(1985), '100 Years of Classical Archaeology in Oxford', in D. C. Kurtz (ed.), *Beazley and Oxford* (Oxford: Oxford University Committee for Archaeology), 43–55.

BOROWITZ, H., and BOROWITZ, A. (1991), *Pawnshops and Palaces: The Fall and Rise of the Campana Art Museum* (Washington, DC: Smithsonian Institution).

BOTHMER, D. VON (1970), 'Sir John Beazley', *Oxford Magazine*, 12 June: 299–302.

——(1985), *The Amasis Painter and his World: Vase-painting in Sixth-century B. C. Athens* (Malibu, Calif.: J. Paul Getty Museum).

——(1987), 'Greek Vase-Painting: Two Hundred Years of Connoisseurship', in *Papers on the Amasis Painter and his World* (Malibu, Calif.: J. Paul Getty Museum), 184–204.

BÖTTIGER, C. A. (1797–1800), *Griechische Vasengemälde, mit archäologischen und artistischen Erläuterungen der Originalkupfer,* 3 vols. (Weimar and Magdeburg: Industrie-Comptoirs & Keil).

BOUILLET, M. N. (1842), *Dictionnaire universel d'histoire et de géographie* (Paris: Hachette).

BOURGET, P. (1907), 'Charles de Spoelberch de Lovenjoul', *Le Figaro*, 7 July.

——(1910), *La Dame qui avait perdu son peintre* (Paris: Plon).

BOWRA, C. M. (1966), *Memories (1898–1939)* (London: Weidenfeld).

BROWN, D. A. (1979), *Berenson and the Connoisseurship of Italian Painting: A Handbook to the Exhibition,* catalogue of the exhibition at the National Gallery of Art in Washington, DC (26 Jan.–13 May) (Washington: National Gallery of Art).

BRUNN, H. (1853–9), *Geschichte der griechischen Künstler,* 2 vols. (Brunswick and Stuttgart: Schwetschke-Ebner & Seubert).

BURDETT, O., and GODDARD, E. H. (1941), *Edward Perry Warren: The Biography of a Connoisseur* (London: Christophers).

BURN, L. (1987), *The Meidias Painter* (Oxford: Clarendon Press).

——(ed.) (1997), 'Sir William Hamilton, Collector and Connoisseur', *Journal of the History of Collections*, 9/2, special issue.

BUSTARRET, C. (1991), 'Les Premières Photographies archéologiques: Victor Place et les fouilles de Ninive', *Histoire de l'Art*, 13 and 14: 7–21.

CAGNAT, R. (1935), 'Notice sur la vie et les travaux de M. Edmond Pottier', *Institut de France, publications diverses de l'année 1935*, 105, no. 28 ter.

CALHOUN, C. (1987), 'An Acorn in the Forest', *Bowdoin Magazine*, September: 2–12.

CARBONELL, C.-O. (1976), *Histoire et historiens, une mutation idéologique des historiens français (1865–1885)* (Toulouse: Privat).

CASANOVA, N. (1995), *Sainte-Beuve* (Paris: Mercure de France).

CASKEY, L. D. (1925), *Museum of Fine Arts, Boston. Catalogue of Greek and Roman Sculpture* (Cambridge, Mass.: Harvard University Press).

CASTELNUOVO, E. (1989), 'Attribution (Histoire de l'art)', *Encyclopaedia universalis France*, 3: 411–15.

CAYLUS, A.-C. DE THUBIÈRES, COMTE DE (1752–67), *Recueil d'antiquités égyptiennes, étrusques, grecques, romaines et gauloises,* 7 vols. (Paris: Desaint & Saillant).

CHABERT, S. (1906), *Histoire sommaire des études d'épigraphie grecque* (Paris: Leroux).

CHANEY, E., and RITCHIE, N. (eds.) (1984), *Oxford, China and Italy*, writings in honour of Sir Harold Acton on his eightieth birthday (London: Thames & Hudson).

CHASTEL, A. (1980), *L'Histoire de l'art: Fins et moyens* (Paris: Flammarion).

CHEVALIER, N. (1997), *Musée du Louvre, département des Antiquités orientales. Une mission en Perse, 1897–1912* (Paris: Réunion des musés nationaux).

CHILDE, G. (1924), review of E. Pottier, *CVA. France, Musée du Louvre 1 & 2*, in *Man*, 33 March: 43–4.

CLARK, A. M. (1985), *Pompeo Batoni: A Complete Catalogue of his Works* (Oxford: Phaidon Press).

CLARK, K. (1974), *Another Part of the Wood: A Self-portrait* (London: Murray).

——(1981), 'The Work of Bernard Berenson', in id., *Moments of Vision and Other Essays* (New York: Harper & Row), 108–29.

CONNOR, P. (1989), 'Cast-collecting in the Nineteenth Century: Scholarship, Aesthetics, Connoisseurship', in G. W. Clarke and J. C. Eade (eds.), *Rediscovering Hellenism: The Hellenic Inheritance and the English Imagination* (Cambridge: Cambridge University Press), 187–235.

CONRY, Y. (1974), *L'Introduction du darwinisme en France au XIXe siècle* (Paris: Vrin).

CROWE, J. A., and CAVALCASELLE, G. B. (1864–6), *New History of Painting in Italy from the Second to the Sixteenth Century*, drawn up from fresh materials and recent researches in the archives of Italy; as well as from personal inspection of the works of art scattered throughout Europe, 3 vols. (London: Murray).

CVA (1921), *Organisation du* Corpus Vasorum Antiquorum *(1919–21)* (Paris: Champion).

CVA (1957), *Colloque international sur le* Corpus Vasorum Antiquorum, report written by C. Dugas, with the assistance of H. Metzger. Lyons, 3–5 July 1956, Centre national de la recherche scientifique.

DAMISCH, H. (1970), 'La Partie et le tout', *Revue d'esthétique*, 23: 168–88.

DARBOUX, G. (1901), 'L'Association internationale des Académies', *Journal des savants*: 5–23.

DAREMBERG, C., SAGLIO, E., and POTTIER, E. (1877–1919), *Dictionnaire des antiquités grecques et romaines*, based on texts and objects, containing explanations of terms relating to customs, institutions, religion, the arts, science, dress, furniture, warfare, life at sea, occupations, currency, weights and measures etc., etc., and in general to the public and private life of the ancients. The work was founded by C. Daremberg and compiled by a group of writers, archaeologists and academics, under the editorship of E. Saglio, with the assistance of E. Pottier and G. Lafaye. It contains more than 7,000 illustrations in the antique style, drawn by P. Sellier, J. Evrard etc. 5 vols., each in two parts (Paris: Hachette): (1877) Vol. 1, pt. 1 (A–B); (1887) vol. 1, pt. 2 (C); (1892) vol. 2, pt. 1 (D–E); (1896) vol. 2, pt. 2 (F–G); (1900) vol. 3, pt. 1 (H–K); (1904) vol. 3, pt. 2 (L–M); (1907) vol. 4, pt. 1 (N–Q); (1911) vol. 4, pt. 2 (R–S); (1917)

vol. 5, pt. 1 (T–Z); (1919) vol. 5, pt. 2 (tables, with the collaboration of J. Normand).

DEMPSTER, T. (1723–4) [1726], *De Etruria Regali libri VII, nunc primum editi curante Thoma Coke, Regiae Celsitudini Cosmi III Magni Ducis Etruriae*, 2 vols. (Florence: apud Joannem Cajetanum Tartinium, & Sanctem Franchium).

[D'HANCARVILLE, P.] (1766–7 [1767–76]), *Collection of Etruscan, Greek, and Roman Antiquities*, from the cabinet of the Honble. Wm. Hamilton, Her Majesty's Envoy Extraordinary and plenipotentiary at the court in Naples, 4 vols. (Naples: Morelli).

DIGEON, C. (1959), *La Crise allemande de la pensée française (1870–1914)* (Paris: Presses Universitaires de France), reprinted 1992.

DOWNES, K. (1988), 'Dreams of the Past and Forms for the Future', *TLS* 23–9 December.

DUCATI, P. (1909), 'I vasi dipinti nelle stile del ceramista Midia: contributo alla storia della ceramica antica', *Atti della R. Accademia dei Lincei, Memorie della Classe di scienze morali, storiche e filologiche*, 5th ser., 14: 95–173; pls. I–IV.

DUCHÊNE, H. (ed.) (1994), *Émile Bersot, Ernest Renan, Salomon Reinach. Notre École Normale* (Paris: Les Belles Lettres).

DUMONT, A. (1870), *Essai sur la chronologie des archontes athéniens postérieurs à la CXXIIᵉ Olympiade et sur la succession des magistrats éphébiques*, doctoral thesis submitted to the Faculté des Lettres in Paris (Paris: Firmin-Didot).

DUMONT, A. (1874), 'Les Études d'érudition en France et en Allemagne', *Revue des deux-mondes*, 15 October: 767–88.

[EASTLAKE, E.] (1891), 'Giovanni Morelli: The Patriot and Critic', *Quarterly Review*, 173, October: 235–52.

ÉFA (1996), 150th anniversary of the École française d'Athènes (1846–1996), special issue, *Bulletin de correspondance hellénique*, 120–1.

ELLIOTT, I. (ed.) (1934), *The Balliol College Register (1833–1933)* (Oxford: Oxford University Press).

EMILIANI, A. (1978), *Leggi, bandi e provvedimenti per la tutela dei beni artistici e culturali negli antichi stati italiani (1571–1860)* (Bologna: Alfa).

ERFFA, H. VON, and STALEY, A. (1986), *The Paintings of Benjamin West* (New Haven and London: Yale University Press).

ETIENNE, R., and ETIENNE, F. (1990), *La Grèce antique: Archéologie d'une découverte* (Paris: Gallimard); = (1992), *The Search for Ancient Greece*, trans. from the French (London: Thames & Hudson).

FINER, A., and SAVAGE, G. (eds.) (1965), *The Selected Letters of Josiah Wedgwood* (London: Cory, Adams & Mackay).

FINLEY, M. I. (1975), *The Use and Abuse of History* (London: Chatto & Windus).

FLECKER, J. E. (1910), *The Grecians: A Dialogue on Education* (London: Dent).

——(1916), *The Collected Poems of James Elroy Flecker*, ed. with an intro. by J. C. Squire (London: Secker).

——(1922), *Hassan: The Story of Hassan of Baghdad and how he came to make the Golden Journey to Samarkand*, a play in five acts, with an intro. by J. C. Squire (London: Heinemann).

——(1926), *The Letters of J. E. Flecker to Frank Savery* (London: The Beaumont Press).

——(1930), *Some Letters from Abroad of James Elroy Flecker*, with a few reminiscences by Hellé Flecker, and an intro. by J. C. Squire (London: Heinemann).

FOTHERGILL, B. (1969), *Sir William Hamilton, Envoy Extraordinary* (London: Faber & Faber).

FRANCE, A. (1897), *Le Mannequin d'osier* (Paris: Calmann-Lévy).

FREUD, S. (1985), 'Le Moïse de Michel-Ange' (1914), in id., *L'Inquiétante Étrangeté et autres essais*, trans. from the German by B. Féron (Paris: Gallimard), 83–125.

FRÖHNER, W. (1865), *Ministère de la Maison de l'Empereur, Musée impérial du Louvre, Département des antiques et de la sculpture moderne. Les Inscriptions grecques*, interpreted by W. Fröhner (Paris: impr. de Mourges).

——(1869), *Ministère de la Maison de l'Empereur et des Beaux-Arts. Notice de la sculpture antique du Musée impérial du Louvre*, vol. 1 (Paris: impr. de Mourgues).

FRONTISI-DUCROUX, F., and LISSARRAGUE, F. (1990), 'Vingt ans de vases grecs: tendances actuelles des études en iconographie grecque (1970–1990)', *Métis*, V/1–2: 205–24.

FUCHS, W. (1988), 'Friedrich Hauser (1859–1917)', in R. Lullies and W. Schiering (eds.), *Archäologenbildnisse* (Mainz: von Zabern), 132–3.

FUMAROLI, M. (1993), 'Un gentilhomme universel: Anne-Claude de Thubières, comte de Caylus (1694–1765)', *Annuaire du Collège de France* (1992–93), 93rd year: 563–81.

FURTWÄNGLER, A. (1885), *Beschreibung der Vasensammlung im Antiquarium*, 2 vols. (Berlin: Spemann).

——(1893), *Meisterwerke der griechischen Plastik: Kunstgeschichtliche Untersuchungen* (Leipzig and Berlin: Giesecke & Devrient); =(1895), *Masterpieces of Greek Sculpture: A Series of Essays on the History of Art*, trans. from the German by E. Sellers (London: Heinemann).

——(1894), review of P. Hartwig, *Die griechischen Meisterschalen der Blütezeit des strengen rotfigurigen Stils*, in *Berliner philologische Wochenschrift*, 20 January: cols. 105–14; 27 January: cols. 141–7.

——REICHHOLD, K., *et al.* (1904–32), *Griechische Vasenmalerei, Auswahl hervorragender Vasenbilder*, 3 vols. (Munich: Bruckmann): (1904) vol. 1, text and plates 1–60; (1909) vol. 2, text and plates 61–120; (1932) vol. 3, text and plates 121–80.

FURTWÄNGLER, A. E. (1990), 'Adolf Furtwängler (30 June 1853–11 Oct 1907)', in W. W. Briggs and W. M. Calder III (eds.), *Classical Scholarship: A Biographical Encyclopedia* (New York and London: Garland), 84–92.

GARDNER, P. (1889), *Classical Archaeology at Oxford* (Oxford, printed for private circulation).

——(1926), *New Chapters in Greek Art* (Oxford: Clarendon Press).

——(1933), *Autobiographica* (Oxford: Blackwell).

GARNETT, D. (ed.) (1938), *The Letters of T. E. Lawrence* (London: Cape).

GERHARD, E. (1831), 'Rapporto intorno i vasi volcenti', *Annali dell'Instituto di corrispondenza archeologica*, 3: 5–218.

——(1840), *Notice sur le vase de Midias au Musée Britannique* (Berlin: Impr. de l'Académie royale des Sciences).

——(1840*a*–58), *Auserlesene griechische Vasenbilder, hauptsächlich etruskischen Fundorts,* 4 vols. (Berlin: Reimer): (1840*a*) vol. 1, *Götterbilder,* pls. 1–78; (1843) vol. 2, *Heroenbilder,* pls. 79–150; (1847) vol. 3, *Heroenbilder,* pls. 151–240; (1858) vol. 4, *Griechisches Alltagsleben,* pls. 241–350.

GIBSON-WOOD, C. (1988), *Studies in the Theory of Connoisseurship from Vasari to Morelli* (London and New York: Garland).

GINZBURG, C. (1989), 'Clues: Roots of an Evidential Paradigm', in id., *Clues, Myths, and the Historical Method,* trans. from the Italian by J. and A. C. Tedeschi (Baltimore and London: Johns Hopkins University Press), 96–125; =(1979), 'Spie. Radici di un paradigma indiziario', in A. Gargani (ed.), *Crisi della ragione: Nuovi modelli nel rapporto tra sapere e attività umane* (Turin: Einaudi), 56–106.

GOLDRING, D. (1922), *James Elroy Flecker: An Appreciation with some Biographical Notes* (London: Chapman & Hall).

GOMBRICH, E. H. (1960), *Art and Illusion: A Study in the Psychology of Pictorial Representation* (London and New York: Phaidon Press; Pantheon Books).

——(1970), *Aby Warburg: An Intellectual Biography,* with a memoir on the history of the library by F. Saxl (London: Phaidon Press).

——(1984), *Tributes: Interpreters of our Cultural Tradition* (Oxford: Phaidon Press).

GORI, A. F. (1737[–43]), *Museum Etruscum, exhibens insignia veterum Etruscorum monumenta aereis tabulis cc. nunc primum edita et illustrata observationibus Antonii Francisci Gorii,* 3 vols. (Florence: In aedibus auctoris . . . excudit Caietanus Albizinius).

GOUREVITCH, D. (1990), 'La Mission médico-historique de Daremberg et de Renan à Rome (oct. 1849–juillet 1850): le problème du rapport', *Bulletin de la Société des antiquaires de France*: 232–42.

——(1993), 'Un épisode de l'histoire du *Dictionnaire des Antiquités* connu sous le nom de 'Daremberg et Saglio': la publication du *Dictionnaire des antiquités chrétiennes de l'abbé Marigny*', text of a speech given at the colloquium held in Bourg-en-Bresse (25–27 Sept. 1992); *Caesorodunum,* 27: 79–95.

GOVI, C. M. (1992), 'Le "style étrusque"', in *Les Étrusques et l'Europe,* catalogue of the exhibition at the Grand Palais in Paris (15 Sept.–14 Dec.) (Paris: Réunion des musées nationaux), 300–9.

GRAND PALAIS (1988), *Le Japonisme,* catalogue of the exhibition in the Galeries Nationales at the Grand Palais (17 May–15 Aug.) (Paris: Réunion des musées nationaux).

GREIFENHAGEN, A. (1938), *CVA. Deutschland 1, Bonn, Akademisches Kunstmuseum 1* (Munich: Beck).

——(1939), 'Griechische Vasen auf Bildnissen der Zeit Winckelmanns und des Klassizismus', *Nachrichten von der Gesellschaft der Wissenschaften zu Göttingen, philologisch-historische Klasse,* iii/7: 199–230; pls. i–xi.

GRIENER, P. (1992), *Le antichità etrusche, greche e romane (1766–1776) di Pierre Hugues* d'Hancarville, *La pubblicazione delle ceramiche antiche della prima collezione Hamilton* ([Rome]: Edizioni dell'Elefante).

GRUNDY, G. B. (1900), *The Recognition of Archaeology as a Study in Oxford* (Oxford: printed for private publication).

——(1945), *Fifty-five Years at Oxford: An Unconventional Autobiography* (London: Methuen).

HAMILTON, W. (1791–5), *Collection of Engravings from Ancient Vases mostly of Pure Greek Workmanship discovered in Sepulchres in the Kingdom of the Two Sicilies, but chiefly in the Neighbourhood of Naples during the Course of the Years 1789 and 1790*, now in the possession of Sir Wm. Hamilton, Her Majesty's Envoy Extraordinary and plenipotentiary in Naples, with remarks on each vase by the collector, 4 vols. (Naples: Tischbein).

HART-DAVIS, R. (ed.) (1962), *The Letters of Oscar Wilde* (London: Hart-Davis).

HARTSWICK, K. J. (1983), 'The Athena Lemnia Reconsidered', *AJA* 87: 335–46.

HARTWIG, P. (1893), *Die griechischen Meisterschalen der Blütezeit des strengen rotfigurigen Stiles* (Stuttgart and Berlin: Spemann).

——(1909), *Hans von Marées Fresken in Neapel* (Berlin: Cassirer).

HASKELL, F. (1976), *Rediscoveries in Art: Some Aspects of Taste, Fashion and Collecting in England and France* (London: Phaidon Press).

——(1980), 'Mecenatismo e collezionismo nella Napoli dei Borbone durante il XVIII secolo', in *Civiltà del'700 a Napoli* (1734–1799), catalogue of the exhibition in Naples (Dec. 1979–Oct. 1980), vol. 1 (Florence: Centro Di), 29–33.

——(1984), 'The Baron d'Hancarville: An Adventurer and Art Historian in Eighteenth-century Europe', in E. Chaney and N. Ritchie (eds.), *Oxford, China and Italy* (London: Thames & Hudson), 177–91.

——(1987), *The Painful Birth of the Art Book* (London: Thames & Hudson).

——(1987a), 'Compromises of a Connoisseur', *TLS*, 5 June.

——(1993), *History and its Images: Art and the Interpretation of the Past* (New Haven and London: Yale University Press).

HELLMANN, M.-C. (1992), 'Wilhelm Froehner, un collectionneur pas comme les autres (1834–1925)', in A.-F. Laurens and K. Pomian (eds.), *L'Anticomanie* (Paris: École des hautes études en sciences sociales), 251–64.

HEYDEMANN, H. (1866), *Iliupersis auf einer Trinkschale des Brygos* (Berlin: Enslin).

——(1872), *Die Vasensammlungen des Museo nazionale zu Neapel* (Berlin: Reimer).

HODGSON, G. (1925), *The Life of James Elroy Flecker*, from letters and material provided by his mother (Oxford: Blackwell).

HOFFMANN, H. (1979), 'In the Wake of Beazley: Prolegomena to an Anthropological Study of Greek Vase-painting', *Hephaistos*, 1: 61–70.

HOMOLLE, T. (1923), 'Un recueil universel des vases antiques d'argile: le *Corpus Vasorum Antiquorum*', *Revue de l'art ancien et moderne*, 43: 3–12.

HOPPIN, J. C. (1896), *Euthymides: A Study in Attic Vase-painting* (Leipzig: Harrassowitz).

——(1917), *Euthymides and his Fellows* (Cambridge, Mass.: Harvard University Press).

——(1919), *A Handbook of Attic Red-figured Vases*, signed by or attributed to the various Masters of the sixth and fifth centuries BC, 2 vols. (Cambridge, Mass.: Harvard University Press).

——(1924), *A Handbook of Greek Black-figured Vases*, with a chapter on the red-figured southern Italian vases (Paris: Champion).

HUNTER-BLAIR, O. (1908), 'Oxford as it is', *Catholic University Bulletin*, 14 October: 627–40.

ISLER-KERÉNYI, C. (1980), 'Beazley e la ceramologia', *Quaderni ticinesi di numismatica e antichità classiche*, 9: 7–23.

JAHN, O. (1854), *Beschreibung der Vasensammlung König Ludwigs in der Pinakothek zu München* (Munich: Lindauer).

JENKINS, I. (1988), 'Adam Buck and the Vogue for Greek Vases', *Burlington Magazine*, 130: 448–57.

JENKINS, I. (1992), 'La vente des vases Durand (Paris 1836) et leur réception en Grande-Bretagne', in A.-F. Laurens and K. Pomian (eds.), *L'Anticomanie* (Paris: École des hautes études en sciences sociales), 269–78.

——and SLOAN, K. (1996), *Vases and Volcanoes: Sir William Hamilton and his Collection* (London: British Museum Press).

JENKYNS, R. (1980), *The Victorians and Ancient Greece* (Oxford: Blackwell).

JOHNSON, H. A. (1990), 'Books belonging to Wedgwood and Bentley the 10th of Augt 1770', *Ars Ceramica*, 7: 13–23.

JONES, J. (1988), *Balliol College: A History (1263–1939)* (Oxford: Oxford University Press).

JONES, L. E. (1956), *An Edwardian Youth* (London: Macmillan).

JUNIUS, F. (1694), *De Pictura Veterum Libri Tres* (Rotterdam: Leers).

KARO, G. (1923), review of E. Pfuhl, *Malerei und Zeichnung der Griechen*, in *Philologische Wochenschrift*, September: cols. 901–4.

KLEIN, W. (1886), *Euphronios: Eine Studie zur Geschichte der griechischen Malerei*[2] (Vienna: Gerold).

——(1887), *Die griechischen Vasen mit Meistersignaturen*[2] (Vienna: Gerold).

KUNZE-GÖTTE, E. (1992), *Der Kleophrades-Maler unter Malern schwarzfiguriger Amphoren* (Mainz: von Zabern).

KURTZ, D. C. (1983), *The Berlin Painter*, with drawings by J. D. Beazley (Oxford: Clarendon Press).

——(1985), 'Beazley and the Connoisseurship of Greek Vases', *J. P. Getty Museum, Occasional Papers on Antiquities*, 3: 237–50.

——(ed.) (1985), *Beazley and Oxford*, lectures delivered at Wolfson College, Oxford on 28 June 1985 (Oxford: Oxford University Committee for Archaeology).

LAFAYE, G. (1917), 'L'Achèvement d'une œuvre française', *RA* 5: 271–81.

LALOUETTE, J. (1997), *La Libre Pensée en France (1848–1940)* (Paris: Albin Michel).

LANTIER, R., and PICARD, C. (1934), 'Edmond Pottier (1855–1934)', *RA* 4/II: pp. iv–xvii.

LANZI, L. (1806), *De' vasi antichi dipinti volgarmente chiamati etruschi* (Florence: Fantosini).

LAURENS, A.-F., and POMIAN, K. (eds.) (1992), *L'Anticomanie: La Collection d'antiquités aux 18ᵉ et 19ᵉ siècles* (Paris: École des hautes études en sciences sociales).

LAWRENCE, T. E. (1937), *An Essay on Flecker* (London: Corvinus Press).

LEBÈGUE, R. (1966), 'Discours à l'occasion de la mort de M. Charles Picard', *Institut de France, publications diverses de l'année 1966*, 136, no. 1.

LECOINTE, G., and GUCHTENAERE, H. DE (1919), 'Les relations intellectuelles internationales d'après guerre', *Académie royale de Belgique, Bulletins de la classe des lettres et des sciences morales et politiques*: 37–47.

LEE, R. W. (1967), Ut Pictura Poesis: *The Humanistic Theory of Painting* (New York: Norton).

LEIGHTON, R., and CASTELINO, C. (1990), 'Thomas Dempster and Ancient Etruria: A Review of the Autobiography and *De Etruria Regali*', *Papers of the British School at Rome*, 58: 337–52.

LENNON, M. (1993), 'Morelli and the Layard Collection: Influence as Intellectual Exchange', in G. Agosti *et al.*, *Giovanni Morelli e la cultura dei conoscitori*, vol. 1 (Bergamo: Lubrina), 241–52.

LERMOLIEFF, I. (1874), 'Die Galerien Roms, ein kritischer Versuch von Iwan Lermolieff. I. Die Galerie Borghese, Aus dem Russischen übersetzt von Dr Johannes Schwarze', *Zeitschrift für bildende Kunst*, 9: 1–11.

——(1880), *Die Werke italienischer Meister in den Galerien von München, Dresden und Berlin, ein kritischer Versuch*, aus dem Russischen übersetzt von Dr Johannes Schwarze (Leipzig: Seemann).

——(1890–3), *Kunstkritische Studien über italienische Malerei*, 3 vols. (Leipzig: Brockhaus): (1890) vol. 1, *Die Galerien Borghese und Doria Panfili in Rom*; (1891) vol. 2, *Die Galerien zu München und Dresden*; (1893) vol. 3, *Die Galerien zu Berlin*, ed. by G. Frizzoni.

LEROI-GOURHAN, A. (1964–5), *Le Geste et la parole*, 2 vols. (Paris: Albin Michel): vol. 1, *Technique et langage*; vol. 2, *La mémoire et les rythmes*.

LESSING, G.-E. (1874), *Laocöon* (1766), trans. with pref. and notes by Sir R. Phillimore (London: Macmillan).

LETRONNE, J.-A. (1883), 'Observations philologiques et archéologiques sur les noms des vases grecs', in *Œuvres choisies*. Pt. 3, *Archéologie et philologie*, vol. 1 (Paris: Leroux), 334–432.

LEVI, D. (1931), *CVA. Italia 8, Firenze 1*, n.d. (Milan and Rome: Bestetti & Tumminelli).

LICHTENAU, COUNTESS OF (1809), *Mémoires de la comtesse de Lichtenau*, written by herself in 1808, followed by a correspondence from her portfolio relating to her memoirs, trans. from the German, 2 vols. (London: Colburn).

LITTRÉ, E. (1863–77), *Dictionnaire de la langue française*, 5 vols. (Paris: Hachette).

LOUVRE (1990), *Euphronios, Peintre à Athènes au VIᵉ siècle avant J.-C.*, catalogue of the exhibition at the Musée du Louvre in Paris (18 Sept.–31 Dec.) (Paris: Réunion des musées nationaux).

LOUVRE (1994), *Égyptomania, l'Égypte dans l'art occidental (1730–1930)*, catalogue of the exhibition at the Musée du Louvre in Paris (20 Jan.–18 Apr.) (Paris: Réunion des musées nationaux).

LUCIAN (1925), 'Essay in Portraiture', trans. A. M. Harmon, vol. 4 (London and New York: Heinemann-Putman, Loeb Classical Library), 255–95.

LULLIES, R., and SCHIERING, W. (eds.) (1988), *Archäologenbildnisse, Porträts und Kurzbiographien von klassischen Archäologen* (Mainz: von Zabern).

LUYNES, H. D' ALBERT, DUC DE (1840), *Description de quelques vases peints étrusques, italiotes, siciliens et grecs* (Paris: Firmin-Didot).

LYONS, C. L. (1992), 'The *Museo Mastrilli* and the Culture of Collecting in Naples (1700–1755)', *Journal of the History of Collections*, 4/1: 1–26.

MACKENZIE, W. A. (1911), *Rowton House Rhymes* (Edinburgh and London: Blackwood).

McCOMB, A. K. (ed.) (1965), *The Selected Letters of Bernard Berenson* (London: Hutchinson).

MARCHAND, S. L. (1994), 'Archaeology and Cultural Politics in Germany (1800–1965), The Rise and Fall of Philhellenism', D.Phil., Princeton University.

——(1996), *Down from Olympus: Archaeology and Philhellenism in Germany (1750–1970)* (Princeton: Princeton University Press).

MARIANO, N. (1965), *The Berenson Archive: An Inventory of Correspondence* (Florence: Harvard University Press).

MARROU, H.-I. (1954), *De la connaissance historique* (Paris: Seuil).

MECQUENEM, R. DE, MORGAN, J. DE, and POTTIER, E. (1912), *Céramique peinte de Suse & petits monuments de l'époque archaïque*, 'Recherches archéologiques', 5th ser. (Paris: Leroux), Reports on delegation to Persia, 13.

MERLIN, A. (1934), 'L'œuvre d'Edmond Pottier au Musée et à l'École du Louvre', *Bulletin des musées de France*, 10: 190–203.

METZGER, H. (1987), 'Beazley et l'image', *AK* 30/2: 109–18; pls. 15–16.

MICHAELIS, A. (1874), 'Attischer Schulunterricht auf einer Schale des Duris', *Archäologische Zeitung*, 31: 1–14; pl. I.

——(1879), *Geschichte des Deutschen Archäologischen Instituts (1829–1879)* (Berlin: Asher).

——(1906), *Die archäologischen Entdeckungen des neunzehnten Jahrhunderts* (Leipzig: Seemann); =(1908), *A Century of Archaeological Discoveries*, trans. from the German by B. Kahnweiler, with a pref. by P. Gardner (London: Murray).

MIDDLETON MURRY, J. (1953), 'Endowed with Ancestors', *The Christ's Hospital Book* (London: Council of Almoners of Christ's Hospital), 270–3.

MILLIN, A. L. (1808–10), *Peintures de vases antiques vulgairement appelées étrusques*, taken from various collections and engraved by A. Clener, with illustrations by A. L. Millin, published by M. Dubois Maisonneuve, 2 vols. (Paris: Didot).

MISTLER, J. (1964), *La Librairie Hachette de 1826 à nos jours* (Paris: Hachette).

MOIGNARD, E. (1989), *CVA. Great Britain 16, The National Museums of Scotland, Edinburgh* (Oxford: Oxford University Press).

MOMIGLIANO, A. (1983), *Problèmes d'historiographie ancienne et moderne*, trans. from the Eng. and the Italian by A. Tachet, E. Cohen, L. Evrard, and A. Malamoud (Paris: Gallimard).

MOMIGLIANO, N. (1999), *Duncan Mackenzie: A Cautious Canny Highlander and the Palace of Minos at Knossos* (London: University of London, Institute of Classical Studies).

MONTARGIS, F. (1887), 'Rapport au ministre de l'Instruction publique sur l'organisation de l'enseignement de l'art dans les universités allemandes', *Journal Officiel*, 37, 7 February: 625–30.

MOREL, J. [Mme E. Pottier] (1905), *La Dette* (Paris: Calmann-Lévy).

MORELLI, G. (1883), *Italian Masters in German Galleries, A Critical Essay on the Italian Pictures in the Galleries of Munich, Dresden and Berlin*, Eng. trans. by L. M. Richter (London: Bell).

—— (1892–3), *Italian Painters, Critical Studies of their Works*: vol. 1, *The Borghese and Doria-Pamfili Galleries in Rome*; vol. 2, *The Galleries of Munich and Dresden*. Eng. trans. by C. J. Ffoulkes, with an intro. by A. H. Layard (London: Murray).

—— (1994), *De la peinture italienne: Les fondements de la théorie de l'attribution en peinture: À propos de la collection des galeries Borghèse et Doria-Pamphili*, ed. by J. Anderson, trans. from the Italian by N. Blamoutier (Paris: Lagune).

MORRISON, A. (ed.) (1893–4), *The Collection of Autographs, Letters and Historical Documents, second series. The Hamilton & Nelson Papers*, 2 vols.: (1893) vol. 1 (1756–1797); (1894) vol. 2 (1798–1815) (printed for private circulation).

NADALINI, G. (1993), 'De Rome au Louvre: les avatars du Musée Campana en 1857 et 1862', *Histoire de l'art*, 21 and 22: 47–58.

NICOLE, G. (1908), *Meidias et le style fleuri dans la céramique attique* (Geneva: Librairie de l'Institut genevois).

NISARD, C. (1877), *Correspondance inédite du comte de Caylus avec le P. Paciaudi, théatin (1757–1765), suivie de celles de l'abbé Barthélémy et de P. Mariette avec le même*, 2 vols. (Paris: Impr. nationale).

OFFNER, R. (1972), 'An Outline of a Theory of Method' (1927), in id., *Studies in Florentine Painters* (New York: Junius Press), 127–36.

OHLY, D. (1975), 'Vorwort', in M. Ohly-Dumm, *Attische Vasenbilder der Antikensammlungen in München nach Zeichnungen von Karl Reichhold* (Munich: Beck), 5–7.

PAGE, D. L. (ed.) (1970), *Select Papyri*. III: *Literary Papyri Poetry*[s], ed. with translations and notes by D. L. Page (Cambridge, Mass., and London: Harvard University Press; Heinemann).

PALAGIA, O. (1987), 'Ἐρύθημα . . . ἀντὶ κράνους, In Defence of Furtwängler's Athena Lemnia', *AJA* 91: 81–4.

PANOFKA, T. (1829), *Recherches sur les véritables noms des vases grecs et sur leur différens usages d'après les auteurs et les monumens anciens* (Paris: Debure).

PANOFSKY, E. (1975), 'Der Begriff des Kunstwollens' (1920), in id., *La Perspective comme forme symbolique et autres essais*, translation ed. by G. Ballangé (Paris: Les Éditions de Minuit), 197–221.

PAU, R. (1993), 'Le origini scientifiche del metodo morelliano', in G. Agosti et al., *Giovanni Morelli e la cultura dei conoscitori*, vol. 2 (Bergamo: Lubrina), 301–19.

PAUSANIAS (1918), *Description of Greece*, trans. by W. H. S. Jones, vol. 1 (London and New York: Heinemann-Putman, Loeb Classical Library).

PÉZARD, M., and POTTIER, E. (1913), *Musée du Louvre, Les Antiquités de la Susiane (mission J. de Morgan)* (Paris: Leroux).

PFUHL, E. (1923), *Malerei und Zeichnung der Griechen*, 3 vols. (Munich: Bruckmann).

——(1924), *Meisterwerke griechischer Zeichnung und Malerei*; =(1926), *Masterpieces of Greek Drawing and Painting*, trans. from the German by J. D. Beazley (London: Chatto & Windus).

PHILLIPS, C. (1890), 'Signor Morelli's New Book, *Die Galerien Borghese und Doria-Panfili in Rom*. Von Ivan Lermolieff (Leipzig)', *The Academy*, 3 May.

POLLAK, L. (1994), *Römische Memorien, Künstler, Kunstliebhaber und Gelehrte (1893–1943)*, ed. by M. Merkel Guldan (Rome: 'L'Erma' di Bretschneider).

POMIAN, K. (1992), 'Les Deux Pôles de la curiosité antiquaire', in A.-F. Laurens and K. Pomian (eds.), *L'Anticomanie* (Paris: École des hautes études en sciences sociales), 59–68.

POPE-HENNESSY, J. (1987), *The Robert Lehman Collection*. Vol. 1: *Italian Paintings* (New York: The Metropolitan Museum).

POTTIER, E. (1872), 'Charles V à ses conseillers', first prize for French Speech, *Concours généraux* (Paris: Delalain), 54–9.

——(1883), *Étude sur les lécythes blancs attiques à représentations funéraires* (Paris: Thorin).

——(1883a), *Quam ob causam Graeci in sepulcris figlina sigilla deposuerint* (Paris: Thorin).

——(1884), *De la place que doit occuper l'archéologie dans l'enseignement de l'art*, inaugural lecture on Archaeology and History of Art at the École des Beaux-Arts (Paris: Impr. Schiller).

——(1890), ' Grèce et Japon', *GBA* 4/II: 105–32.

——(1894), 'A quoi sert un musée de vases antiques', *Revue de Paris*, 1 June: 194–224.

——(1896–1906), *Musée national du Louvre. Catalogue des vases antiques de terre cuite, Études sur l'histoire de la peinture et du dessin dans l'antiquité*, 3 vols. (Paris: Motteroz): (1896) vol. 1, *Les Origines*; (1899) vol. 2, *L'École ionienne*; (1906) vol. 3, *L'École attique*.

——(1897–1928), *Vases antiques du Louvre*, photoengravings and drawings by J. Devillard, 3 vols. (Paris: Hachette): (1897) vol. 1, Rooms A–E: *Les Origines, les styles primitifs, écoles rhodienne et corinthienne*; (1901) vol. 2, Rooms E–G: *Le Style archaïque à figures noires et à figures rouges, écoles ionienne et attique*; (1922) vol. 3, Room G: *Le style attique à figures rouges*; (1928) Rooms A–G: *Index analytique des trois fascicules*.

——(1902), 'Etudes de céramique grecque: A propos de deux publications récentes', *GBA* 27/I: 19–36; 221–38.

——(1902*a*), 'Le Palais de Minos', *Revue de Paris*, 15 February: 827–50; 1 March: 169–99.

——(1905), *Douris et les peintres de vases grecs, Étude critique*, n.d. (Paris: Laurens).

——(1906), 'Études de céramique grecque', *GBA* 36/II: 441–55.

——(1907), 'Les Origines populaires de l'art', *GBA* 38/II: 441–55.

——(1908), *Le Problème de l'art dorien* (Paris: Leroux).

——(1909), 'Ouvrages sur l'archéologie préhistorique', *Bulletin des bibliothèques populaires*: 2–4.

——(1910), *Diphilos et les modeleurs de terres cuites grecques. Étude critique*, n.d. (Paris: Laurens).

——(1911), 'Le jubilé de M. Léon Heuzey', *Revue de Paris*, 15 November: 277–94.

——(1917), 'Études de céramique grecque: Le Peintre de vases Euthymidès', *GBA* 13: 433–46.

——(1917*a*), *Musée du Louvre, Les antiquités assyriennes* (Paris: Braun).

——(1918), *La Pensée libre: Entretien pour ceux qui ne croient pas* (Paris: Union pour la Vérité).

——(1922), *CVA. France [1], Louvre 1*, n.d. (Paris: Champion).

——(1922*a*), 'Léon Heuzey, conservateur au Musée du Louvre (souvenirs d'un collaborateur)', *RA* 15/I: 324–31.

——(1923), *CVA. France 2, Louvre 2* (Paris: Champion).

——(1923*a*), 'Rapport sur le Corpus des vases antiques', *Bulletin de la Classe des Lettres de l'Académie royale de Bruxelles*: 85–94.

——(1924), 'A propos du *Corpus Vasorum Antiquorum*', *RA* 19/I: 280–94.

——(1925), *CVA. France 4, Louvre 3* (Paris: Champion).

——(1926), *CVA. France 5, Louvre 4* (Paris: Champion).

——(1926*a*–31), *L'Art hittite*, 2 fascs. (Paris: Geuthner).

——(1928), 'Deux silènes démolissant un tertre funéraire (vase Vagnonville et cratère du Louvre)', *MMAI* 29:149–92.

——(1928*a*), *CVA. France 8, Louvre 5* (Paris: Champion).

——(1929), *CVA. France 9, Louvre 6* (Paris: Champion).

——(1932), *CVA. France 11, Louvre 7* (Paris: Champion).

——(1933), *CVA. France 12, Louvre 8* (Paris: Champion).

——(1937), *Recueil Edmond Pottier: Études d'art et d'archéologie* (Paris: de Boccard).

PREVITALI, G. (1978), 'A propos de Morelli', *Revue de l'art*, 4: 27–31.

PROTZMANN, H. (1984), 'Antiquarische Nachlese zu den Statuen der sogenannten Lemnia Furtwänglers in Dresden', *Jahrbuch der Staatlichen Kunstsammlungen Dresden*, 16: 7–22.

PROUST, M. (1954), *Contre Sainte-Beuve* (Paris: Gallimard).

——(1971), *Contre Sainte-Beuve*, preceded by *Pastiches et mélanges*, followed by *Essais et articles*, Pléiade edn., ed. P. Clarac, with the collaboration of Y. Sandres (Paris: Gallimard).

RADET, G. (1901), *L'Histoire et l'œuvre de l'École française d'Athènes* (Paris: Fontemoing).

RAMAGE, N. H. (1987), 'The Initial Letters in Sir William Hamilton's "Collection of Antiquities"', *Burlington Magazine*, 129, July: 446–56.

——(1989), 'Owed to a Grecian Urn: The Debt of Flaxman and Wedgwood to Hamilton', *Ars Ceramica*, 6: 8–12.

——(1990), 'Sir William Hamilton as Collector, Exporter, and Dealer: The Acquisition and Dispersal of his Collections', *AJA* 94: 469–80.

——(1991), 'Publication Dates of Sir Hamilton's Four Volumes', *Ars Ceramica*, 8: 35.

RAYET, O. (1887), 'Rapport sur la richesse et l'organisation comparées du Louvre, du Cabinet des Médailles, du Musée de Berlin, du British Museum et de l'Hermitage', *Journal Officiel*, parliamentary reports (Chambre des Députés), March–April: 641–7.

REHM, W. (ed.) (1952–7), *Johann Joachim Winckelmann, Briefe*, ed. by W. Rehm in collaboration with H. Diepolder, 4 vols. (Berlin: de Gruyter).

REICHHOLD, K. (1919), *Skizzenbuch griechischer Meister: Ein Einblick in das griechische Kunststudium auf Grund der Vasenbilder* (Munich: Bruckmann).

REILLY, R. (1989), *Wedgwood*, 2 vols. (London and New York: Macmillan; Stockton Press).

REINACH, S. (1891), *Peintures de vases antiques recueillies par Millin (1808) et Millingen (1813)*, published and with commentary by S. Reinach, no. 2 in the series 'Bibliothèque des monuments figurés grecs et romains' (Paris: Firmin-Didot).

——(1893), 'Le Mirage oriental', *L'Anthropologie*, 4: 539–78; 699–732.

——(1895), review of B. Berenson, *Lorenzo Lotto*, in *Revue critique d'histoire et de la littérature*, 39: 271–6.

——(1907), 'Adolphe Furtwaengler', *Chronique des arts*: 309–11.

——(1911), 'Edmond Saglio', *RA* II: 456–8.

REITLINGER, G. (1961–70), *The Economics of Taste*, 3 vols. (London: Barrie & Rockliff): (1961) vol. 1, *The Rise and Fall of Picture Prices (1760–1960)*; (1963) vol. 2, *The Rise and Fall of Objets d'Art since 1750*; (1970) vol. 3, *The Art Market in the 1960s*.

REVEL, J. (1989), 'L'Histoire au ras du sol', in G. Levi, *Le Pouvoir au village, Histoire d'un exorciste dans le Piémont du XVIIᵉ siècle*, trans. from the Italian by M. Aymard (Paris: Gallimard), pp. i–xxxiii.

——(ed.) (1996), *Jeux d'échelles, La micro-analyse à l'expérience* (Paris: Seuil-Gallimard).

REYNAUD, N. (1978), 'Les Maîtres à noms de convention', *Revue de l'art*, 42: 41–52.

REYNOLDS, J. (1988), *Discourses on Art* (1769–90), ed. by R. R. Wark (New Haven and London: Yale University Press).

RICH, A. (1849), *The Illustrated Companion to the Latin Dictionary, and Greek Lexicon*, Forming a glossary of all the words representing visible objects connected with the arts, manufactures, and every-day life of the Greeks and Romans, with representations of nearly two thousand objects from the antique (London: Longman, Brown, Green, and Longmans).

RICHTER, G., and RICHTER, I. (eds.) (1960), *Italienische Malerei der Renaissance im*

Briefwechsel von Giovanni Morelli und Jean Paul Richter (1876–1891) (Baden-Baden: Grimm).

RICHTER, G. M. A. (1936), 'The Kleophrades Painter', *AJA* 40: 100–15.

ROBERTSON, M. (1971), 'John Davidson Beazley', *Gnomon*: 429–32.

——(1976), 'Beazley and After', *Münchner Jahrbuch der bildenden Kunst*, 27: 29–46.

——(1985), Beazley and Attic Vase Painting', in D. C. Kurtz (ed.), *Beazley and Oxford* (Oxford: Oxford University Committee for Archaeology), 19–30.

——(1987), 'The State of Attic Vase-painting in the Mid-Sixth Century', in *Papers on the Amasis Painter and his World* (Malibu, Calif.: J. Paul Getty Museum), 13–28.

——(1989), 'Beazley's Use of Terms', in *Beazley Addenda², Additional References to ABV, ARV²* & *Paralipomena*, comp. by T. H. Carpenter, with T. Mannack and M. Mendonça (Oxford: Oxford University Press), pp. xii–xx.

——(1992), *The Art of Vase-painting in Classical Athens* (Cambridge: Cambridge University Press).

ROCHEBLAVE, S. (1889), *Essai sur le comte de Caylus, l'homme, l'artiste, l'antiquaire* (Paris: Hachette).

ROCHETTE, R. (1832), *Lettre à M. Schorn sur quelques noms d'artistes omis ou insérés à tort dans le catalogue de Mr le Dr Sillig* (Paris: printed for private publication).

——(1845), *Lettre à M. Schorn, Supplément au catalogue des artistes de l'antiquité grecque et romaine*, 2nd edn., revised and expanded (Paris: Impr. de Crapelet).

ROWE, A. L. (1984), 'The Good-Natured Man', in E. Chaney and N. Ritchie (eds.), *Oxford, China and Italy* (London: Thames & Hudson), 63–5.

SAERENS, C. (1995), '*Die Athener schreiben keine Lyrik*. Essai de mise au point', in A. Verbanck and D. Viviers (eds.), *Culture et cité: L'avènement d'Athènes à l'époque archaïque*, proceedings of the international colloquium held at the Université libre de Bruxelles (25–27 April) by the Institut des hautes études de Belgique and the Fondation archéologique at the U.L.B. (Brussels: de Boccard), 27–43.

SAINTE-BEUVE, C.-A. (1865), *Nouveaux Lundis*, vol. 3 (Paris: Lévy).

SAISSELIN, R. G. (1985), *Bricabracomania: The Bourgeois and the Bibelot* (London: Thames & Hudson).

——(1992), *The Enlightenment against the Baroque: Economics and Aesthetics in the Eighteenth Century* (Berkeley: University of California Press).

SALVINI, R. (1988), *Pure visibilité et formalisme dans la critique d'art au début du XXᵉ siècle* (Paris: Klincksieck).

SAMUELS, E. (1979), *Bernard Berenson: The Making of a Connoisseur* (Cambridge, Mass.: Harvard University Press).

——(1987), *Bernard Berenson: The Making of a Legend*, with the collaboration of J. Newcomer Samuels (Cambridge, Mass.: Harvard University Press).

SCHAPIRO, M. (1961), 'Mr. Berenson's Values', *Encounter*, 88, January: 57–65.

SCHIERING, W. (1988), 'Wilhelm Klein (1850–1924)', in R. Lullies and W. Schiering (eds.), *Archäologenbildnisse* (Mainz: von Zabern), 98–9.

SCHNAPP, A. (1985), 'Des vases, des images et de quelques-uns de leurs usages sociaux', *Dialoghi di archeologia*, 1: 69–75.

——(1993), *La Conquête du passé, aux origines de l'archéologie* (Paris: Carré); = (1996), *The Discovery of the Past: The Origins of Archaeology* (London: British Museum Press).

SCIOLLA, G. C. (1993), 'Il metodo morelliano e la "Scuola di Vienna" (1880–1915): una traccia di ricerca', in G. Agosti *et al.*, *Giovanni Morelli e la cultura dei conoscitori*, vol. 2 (Bergamo: Lubrina), 371–87.

SÉRIEYS, A. (ed.) (1802), *Lettres de Paciaudi au comte de Caylus* (Paris: Tardieu).

SHERWOOD, J. (1973), *No Golden Journey: A Biography of James Elroy Flecker* (London: Heinemann).

SILLIG, J. (1827), *Catalogus artificum, sive architecti, statuarii, sculptores, pictores, caelatores et sculptores, Graecorum et Romanorum, litterarum ordine dispositi a Julio Sillig* (Dresden: Arnold); =(1836), *Dictionary of the Artists of Antiquity, Architects, Carvers, Engravers, Modellers, Painters, Sculptors, Statuaries, and Workers in Bronze, Gold, Ivory, and Silver, with Three Chronological Tables*, trans. from the Latin original by the Revd H. W. Williams (London: Black & Armstrong).

SIMAR, T. (1922), *Étude critique sur la formation de la doctrine des races au XVIIIe siècle et son expansion au XIXe siècle* (Brussels: Lamertin).

SIMPSON, C. (1987), *The Partnership: The Secret Association of Bernard Berenson and Joseph Duveen* (London: Bodley Head).

SIRINELLI, J.-F. (1994), 'Une institution peu à peu sacralisée sous la IIIe République', in J.-F. Sirinelli (ed.), *École normale supérieure, Le Livre du centenaire* (Paris: Presses Universitaires de France), 115–35.

SIX, J. (1888), 'Kleophrades Sohn des Amasis', *Mitteilungen des Deutschen archäologischen Instituts, römische Abteilung*, 3: 233–4.

SMITH, A. H. (1925), *CVA. Great Britain 1, British Museum (Department of Greek and Roman Antiquities) 1* (London: British Museum).

SOX, D. (1991), *Bachelors of Art: Edward Perry Warren & the Lewes House Brotherhood* (London: Fourth Estate).

SPARKES, B. A. (1991), *Greek Art* (Oxford: Oxford University Press).

STALLWORTHY, J. (1995), *Louis MacNeice* (London and Boston: Faber & Faber).

STENDHAL (1826), *Voyages en Italie, Rome, Naples et Florence*; =(1973), Pléiade edn., ed. with an intro. and notes by V. del Litto (Paris: Gallimard).

STEPHANI, L. (1869), *Die Vasensammlung der Kaiserlichen Ermitage*, 2 vols. (St Petersburg: Buchdruckerei der Kaiserlichen Akademie der Wissenschaften).

STERNE, L. (1768), *A Sentimental Journey through France and Italy, By Mr Yorick*; = (1984), with *The Journal to Eliza* and *A Political Romance*, ed. with an intro. by I. Jack (Oxford and New York: Oxford University Press).

TADIÉ, J.-Y. (1996), *Marcel Proust, Biographie* (Paris: Gallimard).

TAINE, H. (1865), *Philosophie de l'art, Nature et production de l'œuvre d'art*, lectures delivered at the École des Beaux-Arts (Paris: Baillière).

——(1866), *Philosophie de l'art en Italie*, lectures delivered at the École des Beaux-Arts (Paris: Baillière).

——(1867), *De l'Idéal dans l'art*, lectures delivered at the École des Beaux-Arts (Paris: Baillière).

—— (1869), *Philosophie de l'art en Grèce*, lectures delivered at the École des Beaux-Arts (Paris: Baillière).

—— (1869*a*), *Philosophie de l'art dans les Pays-Bas*, lectures delivered at the École des Beaux-Arts (Paris: Baillière).

—— (1894), *Derniers essais de critique et d'histoire* (Paris: Hachette).

TREVES, M. (1941), '*Maniera*: The History of a Word', *Marsyas*, 1: 69–88.

UAI (1919), report on the preliminary conference (held in Paris on 15 and 17 May) of the Union Académique Internationale, a body set up for publication and research; statutes proposed by the committee of delegates, in *Institut de France, publications diverses de l'année 1919*, 89, no. 274.

UAI (1919*a*), report on the Union's second international conference (held in Paris on 15–18 October) (Paris: Impr. de l'Institut).

UAI (1923), *Union Académique Internationale, Statuts*, as agreed on 18 April (Gembloux: Impr. Duculot).

URLICHS, L. (1875), *Der Vasenmaler Brygos* (Würzburg).

VATICAN (1842), *Monumenti del Museo Etrusco Vaticano*, acquistati dalla munificenza di Gregorio XVI, Pontifice massimo e per di lui ordine disegnati e publicati, 2 vols. (Rome).

VENTURI, L. (1936), *History of Art Criticism*, trans. from the Italian by C. Marriott (New York: Dutton); =(1938), *Histoire de la critique d'art*, Fr. trans. from the Italian by J. Bertrand (Brussels: Éditions de la Connaissance).

VERNANT, J.-P. (1962), *Les Origines de la pensée grecque* (Paris: Presses Universitaires de France); =(1982), *The Origins of Greek Thought*, trans. from the French (London: Methuen).

—— (1987), 'Raison et déraison chez les Grecs', *Raison présente*, 84: 119–33; (1995), reprinted in R. di Donato (ed.), *Passé et Présent, Contributions à une psychologie historique*, vol. 1 (Rome: Edizioni di storia e letteratura), 295–310.

VICKERS, M. (1985), 'Artful Crafts: The Influence of Metalwork on Athenian Painted Pottery', *JHS* 105: 108–28.

—— and GILL, D. (1994), *Artful Crafts: Ancient Greek Silverware and Pottery* (Oxford: Clarendon Press).

VIDAL-NAQUET, P. (1985), 'Finley, les Anciens et les Modernes', in M. I. Finley, *L'Invention de la politique, Démocratie et politique en Grèce et dans la Rome républicaine*, trans. from the English by J. Carlier (Paris: Flammarion), 5–15.

VILLARD, F. (1978), 'Les Peintres de vases grecs', *Revue de l'art*, 42: 15–20.

WALTERS, H. B., SMITH, C. H., and FORSDYKE, E. J. (1893–1925), *Catalogue of the Greek and Etruscan Vases in the British Museum*, 4 vols. in 5 (London): (1912) vol. 1, pt. 2, *Cypriote, Italian and Etruscan Pottery*; (1893) vol. 2, *Black-figured Vases*; (1896) vol. 3, *Vases of the Finest Period*; (1896) vol. 4, *Vases of the Latest Period*; (1925) vol. 1, pt. 1, *Prehistoric Aegean Pottery*.

WARBURG, A. (1999), 'Sandro Botticelli's "Birth of Venus" and "Spring"', in *The Renewal of Pagan Antiquity: Contributions to the Cultural History of the European Renaissance*, trans. D. Britt (Los Angeles: Getty Research Institute for the History of Art and the Humanities), 89–156; =(1932), 'Sandro Botticellis

"Geburt der Venus" und "Frühling"' (1893), in G. Bing (ed., in association with F. Rougemont), *Die Erneuerung der heidnischen Antike: Kulturwissenschaftliche Beiträge zur Geschichte der europäischen Renaissance*, vol. 1 (Leipzig: Teubner), 1–59.

WILLIAMS, D. (1993), *CVA. Great Britain 17, The British Museum 9* (London: British Museum Press).

WILSON, J. (1989), *Lawrence of Arabia: The Authorised Biography of T. E. Lawrence* (London: Heinemann).

WINCKELMANN, J. J. (1789), *Histoire de l'art chez les Anciens* (1764), Fr. trans. from the German by M. Huber, new, revised and corrected, 3 vols. (Paris: Barrois & Savoye).

WITTE, J. DE (1848), *Noms des fabricants et dessinateurs de vases peints* (Paris: Leleux).

WÖLFFLIN, H. (1950), *Principles of Art History: The Problem of the Development of Style in Later Art*, trans. M. D. Hottinger (New York: Dover); =(1915), *Kunstgeschichtliche Grundbegriffe: Das Problem der Stilentwicklung in der neueren Kunst* (Munich: Bruckmann).

——(1952), *Classic Art: An Introduction to the Italian Renaissance*, trans. by P. and L. Murray (London: Phaidon Press); =(1899), *Die klassische Kunst: Eine Einführung in die italienische Renaissance* (Munich: Bruckmann).

WÖLFFLIN, H. (1964), *Renaissance and Baroque*, trans. by K. Simon, with an intro. by P. Murray (London: Fontana Library); =(1888), *Renaissance und Barock: Eine Untersuchung über Wesen und Entstehung des Barockstils in Italien* (Munich: Bruckmann).

WOLTERS, P. (1925), 'Vorwort', in B. Graef and E. Langlotz, *Die antiken Vasen von der Akropolis zu Athen*, vol. 1 (Berlin: de Gruyter), pp. iii–iv.

YOUNG, H. (ed.) (1995), *The Genius of Wedgwood*, catalogue of the exhibition at the Victoria and Albert Museum in London (London: Victoria and Albert Museum).

ZERI, F. (1980), *Italian Paintings: A Catalogue of the Metropolitan Museum of Art: Sienese and Central Italian Schools* (New York: Metropolitan Museum).

Index

1. Portrait of Sir William Hamilton, K.B., 1777, from the Workshop of Reynolds. London, National Portrait Gallery, 680. By Courtesy of the National Portrait Gallery, London

2. Athenian red-figure hydria signed by Meidias, with Castor and Pollux abducting the daughters of Leucippos. Engraving from the second volume of d'Hancarville's publication of the Hamilton Collection

3. Portrait of Karl Wilhelm
Ferdinand, late Duke of Brunswick
and Lüneburg, 1796, by Pompeo
Batoni. Brunswick, Herzog Anton
Ulrich-Museum 676

4. British Manufactory: A Sketch, painting by Benjamin West, 1789–91. Cleveland, Cleveland
Museum of Art, Gift of the John Huntington Art and Polytechnic Trust, 1919. 1018

5. Athenian red-figure calyx-crater signed by Euphronios as painter, with Herakles and Antaios. Paris, Musée du Louvre G 103

6. Marble head of Athena in Bologna (Museo Archeologico) thought by some to be a copy of the Athena Pheidias made for the Lemnians

7. Graduation Class from the École Normale, 1874

8. Sketch of Edmond Pottier by Salomon Reinach, 1880. Saint-Germain-en-Laye, Musée des Antiquités nationales

9. The Campana Gallery of the Louvre after Pottier's rearrangement of the collection

10. Giovanni Morelli in his study in the University of Munich, around 1835 by an anonymous artist. Bergamo, Willi Zavaritt Collection

11. Photograph of Bernard Berenson visiting the Borghese Gallery in Rome, by David Seymour, 1955

12. Portait of John Beazley by
R.H. Wilenski, 1911. Oxford,
Beazley Archive

13. Painting of Saint-Ansan
by Simone Martini after 1333.
New York, Metropolitan
Museum of Art 1975.1.13

14. Athenian red-figure pelike attributed to the Eucharides Painter, with satyrs and (?)Hermes. Oxford, Ashmolean Museum 563

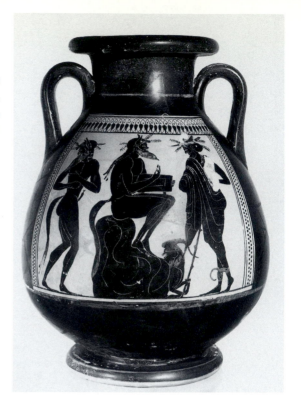

15. Athenian red-figure pelike attributed to the Kleophrades Painter, with a goddess. Berlin, Staatliche Museen 2170

16. Athenian red-figure cup signed by Epiktetos as painter, with a komos. London, British Museum E 38

17. Athenian red-figure amphora attributed to the Berlin Painter in New York (Metropolitan Museum of Art 56.272.38), with a judge. Drawing by Beazley (Oxford, Beazley Archive)